My Friend '

Growing Up and Travelling the World by Sea

By
Douglas Model

With love & thanks for your help editing it.

Douglas 2-6-21.

The names of some of the characters described have been changed to protect their privacy.

Every reasonable care has been taken to avoid copyright infringements, and any valid issues that may arise will be corrected in subsequent editions.

Copyright Douglas Model 2018

ISBN: 978-0-244-69749-5

No part of this book may be reproduced, stored in a retrieval system, or transmitted by any means without the written permission of the author.

The painting on the Front Cover is *Raleigh's Boyhood by Millais*, reproduced with permission of the Tate Gallery

For my wife Jillie, my best friend, companion and confidante

Acknowledgements

I am indebted to my friend and old shipmate Captain Philip Griffin and to my brother Richard for reading, correcting and offering helpful suggestions about the manuscript. Without their help and encouragement I would not have had the confidence to publish this book

The author aged 19, a cadet in Shaw Savill Shipping Company

Chapters

1. Call of the Sea..1
2. H.M.S. *Worcester*...8
3. Apprentice to the Sea......................................45
4. Life as a Sailor..53
5. All Manner of Men...81
6. A Royal Ship...100
7. An Officer at Last.. 120
8. The Smiling Bastard......................................142
9. A Life of Riley..158
10. Beginning of the End..................................182
11. End of an Era..206
12. Postscript...218

Photographs

1. The Author aged 19……………………...Inside front cover

2. HMS *Worcester* & the Clipper Sailing Ship *Cutty Sark*..9

3. Coming alongside……………………………….. 13

4. HMS *Worcester* Main Deck……………………...15

5. HMS *Worcester* Lower Deck…………………….16

6. HMS *Worcester* Scrubbing the Upper Deck…………17

7. Commander Gordon Steele, V.C, R.N………….... 19

8. Cartoon by Cadet Chris Field……………………. 27

9. Celebrating the Glorious First of June………………...31

10. King George VI & Queen Elizabeth………………...41

11. Receiving a prize from Lord Montgomery…………….43

12. m.v.* *Waipawa*………………………………….. 46

13. m.v. *Delphic*…………….............................81

14. s.s.* *Gothic*……………………………………....100

15. s.s. *Corinthic*………………………………….113

16. s.s. *New Australia*……………………………...122

17. s.s. *Ceramic*…………………………………...142

18. Bay Class Ship...158

19. The Second Mate..187

20. m.v. *Carnatic*..206

    m.v.=motor vessel, s.s.=steam ship

1

Call Of The Sea

"Tell that boy of yours not to go into the Royal Navy, and that he'll have a much better life in the Merchant Navy."

It is ten o'clock on an October morning and my father and a friend named Mr Glass are at the fourth hole of the Royal Berkshire Golf Course. It is the type of day my father likes most, overcast with a touch of autumn melancholy about it, as if in some way nature is mourning the passing of the summer. In the distance, some 300 yards along the fairway, the green of the trees has a distinctly blue hue. What more could a man ask, my father says to himself as he looks down at the grass at his feet, still covered in dew.

Having commented on my wish to enter the Royal Navy, Mr Glass watches as my father steps up to the tee and carefully places a ball on a wooden golf peg. My father is forty-one years old, and the Second World War in which he served as a policeman during the London Blitz, is behind him. He is a big man, over six feet two inches tall, and he has powerful arms and if he connects well with the ball he can drive it as far as any professional. He places the head of his club behind the ball, parts his legs, looks down at the ball and then looks up along the fairway in the direction in which he hopes the ball will travel. In quick succession he repeats these movements, looking down at the ball, along the fairway, then back at the ball. Finally he swings his club back over his shoulder. At the next moment there is a smart thwack as the head of the club strikes the ball and sends it on its way up into the overcast sky.

Beside him, Mr Glass mutters approvingly, "Nice shot, Joe!"

He makes his own shot, and then the two of them move off along the fairway, chatting companionably as they go. Mr Glass is a few years older than my father and is the Engineer Superintendent for the whole of the Shell oil tanker fleet in Europe.

"As I just said, Joe," Mr Glass says. "My advice is for that boy of yours to go into the Merchant Navy." Then as an afterthought, he adds, "Perhaps you might tell him that I'm going to Tilbury next week to spend a day on one of our tankers. If he wants, he can accompany me to see what life's like in the Merchant Navy."

The year is 1948. I am fifteen years old; Britain is exhausted from the effort of winning the Second World War and is suffering severe austerity, but still has a formidable navy and the largest empire the world has ever seen.

*

A week later I was sitting opposite Mr Glass on a train bound from Fenchurch Street Station in London to the Port of Tilbury at the mouth of the River Thames. Mr Glass was a big egg-shaped man and after a few pleasantries during which he asked me about my intention to go to sea, he buried himself behind the pink pages of the *Financial Times*. As I watched I could not help but be fascinated by the movements of the bottom of the paper, which was resting on his abdomen, and was moving rhythmically in and out in time with his breathing.

By contrast with him I was a shy spotty fifteen-year old lad, dressed in a school blazer, as I did not possess a suit. By then I was already over six feet tall, a thin, not very attractive gawky streak of a lad with what I believed were Semitic features that I hated to see in a mirror. Why, I thought, can't I look like my friend Bob Walker, who has Aryan blue eyes and blond hair, or like the Head Boy of the school we attend, Jonathan Rushcutter, whose name is *so* English and who is so assured and such a *splendid fellow* in the best English sense of the words. By comparison, I was so shy and concerned about my identity and who I was that when visitors came to my home I usually retreated and went up to the room I shared with my brothers and sat on the window box facing the main road on which we lived and comforted myself by looking out of the window and quietly playing my recorder.

Apart from the fact that I was bothered by the usual teenage doubts, one of the main reasons I was so troubled was that my parents were of different religions and I did not know whether or not I was a Jew or merely partly Jewish. In today's multicultural secular world that might not matter as much as it did in 1948 when everyone was aware of their religion and the important part it played in their lives. Only three years earlier the world had become aware that during the war Hitler had exterminated more than six million Jews. Anti-Semitism was still rife in Britain and most golf clubs and private schools had 'Jewish quotas' that kept Jews out. At all levels of British society it was not uncommon to hear people say, 'Hitler did one good job, he got rid of the Jews.'

*

For as long as I can remember I had wanted to do only one thing when I grew up – to go to sea and become an officer in the Royal Navy. When other boys gave up the idea of becoming a cowboy or a train driver, I continued to dream of being a sailor. Goodness knows where the idea came from; my family had no connection with the sea. Perhaps it originated with my Jewish grandfather, who apart from being very religious, was an intrepid adventurer, and in 1878, at the age of twelve, stowed away on a ship bound for America where his father had gone on a business trip. A few years later, in 1886, only a year after he married, Grandpa shipped out to South Africa and joined the gold rush, but was called back by Grandma before he had a chance to discover any gold. Four years later, in 1890 he and Grandma immigrated to Australia, but returned after two years as they had not been successful and Grandma missed her parents and wider family. While they were in Australia my Aunty Rose was born.

To me the sea represented a life of adventure and the chance to travel and to live the life of a man. At that time, just after the Second World War, the age of the jet airliner was still fifteen years away and there was very little travel by air. Only a few privileged people had travelled outside England and most of them had been only as far as France, Italy or Spain.

My passion for the sea is best conveyed by the famous 1870 painting by Millais of Sir Walter Raleigh as a boy, reproduced on the Front Cover of this book. A copy of the picture hung on a wall in the hall of the house belonging to the grandparents of a friend of mine, and whenever I saw it I felt a pulse of excitement and curiosity race through me. In the painting Sir Walter is shown as a pink-cheeked boy sitting on a wall by the sea with his arms clasped about his knees, looking up with wonder in his eyes as he listens to an old seadog who is sitting with his arm raised and pointing across the sea to distant lands beyond the horizon.

I was – and still am – fascinated by stories of distant lands, sailing ships, Cape Horn and tropical islands, and I wanted to experience them for myself. But there were certain problems with the idea. First it would be necessary to pass the competitive entrance examination to get into the Royal Navy College at Dartmouth. Then there was the fact that I was half-Jewish. What in their wisdom would their Lordships at the Admiralty say about that? There were probably very few, if any Jewish or half-Jewish officers in the Royal Navy. In addition there was also the by no means small problem of a private income. In those days it was said that in order to pay their mess bills, officers in any of the three armed services needed a private income to supplement their pay, and that was something I did not have. Nonetheless, despite these obstacles, I sent for the prospectus for Dartmouth and attempted to read a couple of books about, as I perceived it, the almost unobtainable life of an officer in the Royal Navy.

*

As the industrial slums of east London slipped past the windows of the train I realised I was both excited at the prospect of visiting a real ship and at the same time apprehensive. My knowledge of the Merchant Navy was practically non-existent. I knew nothing of its great contributions to the British war effort and the fact that it had suffered a higher casualty rate than any of the three fighting services. I thought it consisted of little more than a few fishing vessels and some dredgers. It never occurred to me that the Queen Elizabeth, the Queen Mary and the other great Cunarders, and the ships of companies like P & O belonged to the Merchant Navy. As a result I was pleasantly surprised when I saw the huge ship to which Mr Glass was taking me. Its enormous white superstructure towered so high above the dock that it seemed as if it might topple over onto us as we ascended the gangway suspended from its side.

On board we climbed several gangways leading up to the captain's cabin, which was behind the bridge. I stood awkwardly listening and feeling out of place as Mr Glass introduced me to the captain, a short squat man in naval uniform with four gold stripes on his sleeves. He looked at my chest as he spoke to me, avoiding my eyes, as if he did not wish to engage properly with me. "It's not a bad life. I've had forty years of it and it's served me well," he said in a gruff northern voice. Then apparently not knowing what more to say, he passed me to the chief officer from whom I learnt that the ship had come from the Persian Gulf laden with thousands of tons of crude oil. For a while I stood awkwardly drinking coffee and trying to understand what Mr Glass was saying to the chief engineer about the ship's engines, then I was taken to a cadet who had been assigned to show me round the ship.

Our first stop was the bridge. The superstructure of the ship was at its stern and the bridge was on top of it. As I looked out from the bridge windows, I could see the deck some twenty feet below running forward to the bow more than three hundred-and-fifty feet away. In the centre of the deck was a narrow catwalk with handrails on either side of it. Running parallel on either side of the catwalk was a row of raised manholes, each of which led down into an oil tank.

My companion showed me the compass, the radar and the steering wheel and told me about his work that included helping with the loading and discharge of the cargo when the ship was in port and with the navigation of the ship when it was at sea. It sounded interesting, although from his unruly blond hair and the scruffy worn appearance of his uniform I could not help wondering what I might be letting myself in for if I joined the Merchant Navy.

The cadet, whose name was William, told me that by going to a pre-sea training school for two years I could earn a year's remission from the four year apprenticeship that was required to become an officer in the Merchant Navy, and later, as we inspected the meteorology equipment on the exposed flying bridge above the main part of the bridge I learned that my guide had been to a training ship or school named HMS *Worcester* and that there were three other similar schools, the training ship HMS *Conway* anchored in the Menai Straits in North Wales and the shore establishments *Pangbourne* and *Southampton*.

At lunchtime I was taken to the officers' mess and sat at the captain's table with Mr Glass and was served by a steward in a smart white jacket. The lunch consisted of a four course meal that included roast lamb and roast potatoes followed by apple tart and ice-cream that in its turn was followed by cheese and biscuits served with coffee in tiny posh cups of a type I had never seen before. It was a formula likely to appeal to many boys in austerity Britain, where food was still rationed, and later on the way home I decided to take Mr Glass' advice and join the Merchant Navy. But first, in order to prepare myself as well as possible, I decided that I would like to go to HMS *Worcester* for two years if my father could afford it. However, at almost two hundred pounds a year, I wasn't sure what he would say, as the fees at John Lyon School, the small day public school I attended in Harrow, were £8.12.6 per term when I started in 1944 and twelve guineas at the time about which I am writing. Some parents considered the increase outrageous and threatened to take their sons away, although none did so in practice. To my surprise my father was encouraging, although he stipulated one condition, namely that I had to pass the School Certificate Examination before he would allow me to leave John Lyon School. At the time I did not appreciate the wisdom of his advice or how useful having the School Certificate would be at a later date, but it stimulated me enough to work hard and pass the exam sufficiently well to matriculate and, if I wished, to go to university.

On my last day at John Lyon School I went round the school and said goodbye to my friends and the masters. Britain was very class-bound in those days, and the masters at John Lyon School had no doubt of their superior position in society as university-educated men and the importance of the job they were doing. Although most of them lived in ordinary semi-detached houses of the two-up, two-down or perhaps four-up, three-down type, they appeared to be very sure of themselves. In keeping with their picture of themselves, they wore mortarboards and gowns and held their heads high as they wafted around the school between classes. In much the same way, I suspect that their wives dressed up in their best and wore gloves and a hat and carried a handbag when they went to the West End of London. Boys who were interested in the navy were expected to go to Dartmouth, not into some weird occupation like the Merchant Navy. No one expressed this more clearly on the day I left than the English master, Mr Cowan, a kindly fat balding middle-aged man who smoked incessantly and smelt of tobacco. Why wasn't I going into the sixth form, he asked? I had not been one of his favourite pupils and when I told him that I was going into the Merchant Navy he frowned and looking away, said, "What on earth is a boy from a school like this going in for a career like that?"

2

HMS *Worcester*

It is five to seven in the morning on the cadet training ship HMS *Worcester* – a ship that is rigged with masts and yardarms and looks like a ship-of-the-line of Nelson's time. A corpulent elderly man in an old-fashioned high-lapelled petty officer's naval uniform is walking between rows of hammocks in which a hundred boys are still asleep. On his head he is wearing an old fashioned narrow-topped peaked cap of the type seen in photographs of the Victorian Navy. Above his upper lip is a most un-navy-like nicotine stained walrus moustache. Jack Reid, or 'Jackie' as he is known to the cadets, is seventy years old if he is a day and is loved like a rather fierce uncle by the boys. On the deck below, another less popular petty officer is walking between similar rows of sleeping boys.

"Wakie, wakie! Rise and shine! Wakie, wakie! It's seven o'clock!" Jackie rasps in a thick smoker's voice. He gives the hammock nearest to him a friendly poke with the ebony stick he is carrying. "That boy there! Come on, get up and get out of your sack!"

In their hammocks, which are packed so tightly together that they almost touch, the boys stir and enjoy the near orgasmic pleasure of a final stretch in their narrow cribs. Another day on HMS *Worcester* is about to begin…

*

Worcester III and the clipper ship Cutty Sark at Greenhithe, Kent. Reproduced with permission of the artist, Roger Morris

Before I could go to the *Worcester* I had to have a uniform. This was an officer's blue naval uniform with gold tags on the lapels to indicate that I was a cadet. It was supplied by S W Silver & Co, the official tailor to the *Worcester*. Silver's has gone now, but in its day it was one of London's leading tailors, making livery for occasions such as the Opening of Parliament and for people such as Winston Churchill.

The official advice from the *Worcester* was to get used to the uniform by going out in it a few times before the term began. But first I had to get into it, which meant getting into a shirt with a separate detached stiff white collar and double cuffs secured by cuff links.

Most people born after 1960 have probably never seen a detached stiff collar, but before that time shirts for formal wear did not come with attached collars. Instead, the wearer had to attach a separate stiffly starched collar to the body of the shirt by a stud at the front and a stud at the back. Many shirts came with two collars enabling the shirt to be worn for anything between two to seven days without appearing to be dirty. In principle it should have been easy to attach the collar to the shirt, but in practice it was extremely difficult for someone who had never done it before, as skills take time to acquire. The back of the collar had to be attached first. The only way I could align the hole at the back of the collar with the stud I had already placed in the back of the shirt was by bending forwards so that my neck and back were horizontal rather than vertical. In that position I was able to balance the collar on the back of my neck while I struggled to attach it to the shirt. For half-an-hour I fought with it, but the round flange on the stud would not go through the almost closed slit in the collar, and in the end, in a fury of despair, sweating, I stood up and almost crying, considered tearing the damned thing apart. I had failed before I had started. In desperation I went downstairs and asked my father to help me and stood watching like a horse being shod as he attached the collar to the shirt.

Getting the cufflinks through the narrow holes in the cuffs at the bottom of the shirtsleeves was not much easier, as there was nothing firm against which to push them, and the holes in the cuffs kept sliding away from my fingers as I tried to insert the link.

At last, when I was finally dressed, I went with my parents by Underground train to see a play in London's West End. But I was not happy with the way I looked, and felt that everyone in the carriage was staring at me, and that I was being singled out. I don't belong in this circus outfit, I thought wretchedly, trying to avoid people's eyes; I'm a clown, a fraud. I'm not a sailor. I'm a landlubber; I know nothing about the navy, ships or life at sea.

A few days later, feeling barely more confident, I took a train from Charing Cross Station in London to Greenhithe in Kent, a village towards the mouth of the Thames, where the *Worcester* was moored. Sitting opposite me in the carriage were two other cadets who were joining the Ship for the first time. By chance both lived in Harrow, a town near my home in Wembley. Baddock had been a pupil at Westminster Choir School. Sweatenham had been at the same school as me, although he had been in a different class and I hardly knew him. We had our first intimation of things to come as the train was about to leave the station. A cadet, whose name we soon learned was Lasky, jumped into our carriage as the train was beginning to move along the platform. No sooner had he got his breath back than he proceeded to terrorise us with stories of the punishments he had received during his first term on the Ship.

"I was beaten a hundred-and-ten times during my first term. It's a dreadful place and I'm not sure that I want to go back. But I'm a second termer now and it should be better," he said.

He spat the words out and looked at us with pained blue eyes, seeking both our approval and admiration. If he was to be believed he had been beaten more than once a day, which was a frightening prospect, and as the train began to trundle through the industrial belt along the north coast of Kent, I looked out of the window and wondered what I had let myself in for.

Lasky was the only Jew I met at sea. He was short, no more than five feet six inches tall, but unlike most Jews, he was so muscular and broad shouldered that he appeared to be almost square. His neck was as thick as the trunk of a small tree and his legs were short and powerful and as a result he looked like a small bull. Sadly, the power of his brain was inversely proportional to the strength of his body. In fact he was one of the dumbest people I have ever met. On one occasion when we were in class, the headmaster, Mr Bickmore, who we called Old Beaky on account of his long aquiline nose, looked at Lasky over the top of his half glasses and said in a clipped Oxford accent, "Lasky, if $A = B$ and $B = C$, what else does A also equal?"

It was a cruel question to ask a boy with very little brain in front of a class of twenty-five brighter boys and the rest of us squirmed in our desks with embarrassment for Lasky as the seconds ticked by and the furrows in his brow became deeper and deeper and a look of confusion shone out of his pale Jewish blue eyes. When the headmaster was satisfied that he had shown up Lasky for the fool that he was, he told him to sit down and summarily dismissed him.

Subsequently Lasky just about survived the *Worcester*, but three years later when he was almost at the end of his apprenticeship, he deserted ship in Haifa and settled in the newly created state of Israel. For an *Old Worcester* there was no greater disgrace than deserting ship, and his name, surrounded by a rectangle drawn in thick black ink, was posted on a notice board on the Ship for all to see and he was struck off the list of boys who had been there.

*

It was cold and blustery by the time we arrived at Greenhithe. Ragged clouds scudded low across a wintery sky and spots of rain stung my face and I shivered in my great coat as I walked along the only street in the village of Greenhithe. The scene might have come straight out of Dickens. Everywhere was covered in a thick grey layer of cement dust that had been spewed out by the cement works a couple of hundred yards astern of the *Worcester*. Today Greenhithe is an attractive little riverside village of pubs, cottages and a few larger houses, but when I first saw it on that cold winter's day, the windows of the cottages and houses, their roofs, the pavements, the platforms of the railway station and even the grass were covered in dust the colour of battleship grey. But it had not always been like that. Before the advent of the cement works, in earlier times the village had been a pleasant little port from which several famous expeditions had set forth, including Sir John Franklin's ill-fated expedition to the Arctic in 1845 and Scott's expedition to the Antarctic in 1901.

At the end of the street we passed through large wrought iron gates and entered the grounds of Ingress Abbey, the estate belonging to the *Worcester*. Immediately on the right was a solitary building containing the college's indoor swimming pool, but it wasn't that that attracted my attention, it was the masts and black and white striped hull of a ship of a type known as a Wooden Wall lying at anchor just over a hundred yards from the end of a wooden causeway that ran out across the mud from the shore for a hundred yards like a tongue protruding from a lizard's mouth.

Moored immediately outside the *Worcester* was another sailing ship – the *Cutty Sark* – one of the most famous tea-clippers of the nineteenth century. The two ships represented a different world to anything I had ever seen, a world that harped backed to a past that was both exciting and forbidding. Here near the mouth of the River Thames was the world that was to be my home for the next two years.

Normally the Ship was reached by one of a number of boats rowed by cadets, but as it was the first day of term and cadets had not yet been assigned to the crews, we were taken on board in an open motor launch steered by a petty officer. As the launch gathered speed and its bow rose slightly and turned towards the Ship, fine drops of river water splashed on board and for the first time I smelt the never-to-be-forgotten smell of decaying vegetation and organic matter that is the smell of the River Thames. At the top of the gangway the officer-of-the-day told us to turn aft and salute the flag. My life on the *Worcester* had begun.

Coming alongside

*

The *Worcester*, or to give it its full name, the Incorporated Thames Nautical Training College, was unlike any other school in the world, except for HMS. *Conway* and one or two other training ships. In essence it was a vestige from the past, a dinosaur that lived-on from the Victorian age, an old Wooden Wall or ship-of-the-line, replete with masts and yardarms. However, in reality it was not as old as it looked, as it had been specially constructed as a school ship at the beginning of the twentieth century. From its decks, for many years hundreds of boys who wanted nothing more than to sail the seven seas, dreamed of the voyages they hoped to make and the far-off places they hoped to visit as they watched great liners and cargo ships come and go from all over the world as they plied their way up and down the river to and from the great port of London.

There had been three *Worcester* training ships. The first, known as *Worcester 1*, was a 1500-ton wooden frigate mounting fifty18-pound muzzle-loading cannons. *Worcester 1* had been built for the Royal Navy in 1843, and had been purchased by the school when it was founded in 1862 'to establish a school-ship on the Thames for the education of boys destined to become officers in the Merchant Service.' The second *Worcester*, known as *Worcester 11*, was a larger wooden ship-of-the-line mounting seventy-four guns that had been purchased by the school in 1877 when it became apparent that *Worcester 1* was too cramped and more space was needed. *Worcester 11* had served the school until the beginning of the Second World War when she had been abandoned because it was thought she was vulnerable to bombing. Throughout the war the college was housed in Foots Cray Place, a Palladian inspired eighteenth century building near Sidcup in the county of Kent. After the war the school moved to a specially constructed steel school ship named the *Exmouth* that had been built in 1905 for training boys destined to be ordinary seamen in both the Merchant and Royal Navies.

Throughout the war the *Exmouth* had been moored in Scapa Flow in the Orkney Islands off the north coast of Scotland and had served as the parent ship to a flotilla of minesweepers. With the cessation of hostilities she had been towed south, and after being refitted and renamed *Worcester 111*, had been moored about two hundred yards from the shore at Greenhithe.

The *Cutty Sark*, the ship moored outside the *Worcester*, had been built in 1869 to bring tea as fast as possible from China to Britain. Initially she had a glorious career, on one occasion sailing 363 nautical miles in 24 hours at an average speed of 15 knots (17 mph), but due to the advent of steamships, her later career had been somewhat chequered. Eventually, in 1938 she was given into the care of the *Worcester*, and today, after a devastating fire in 2007, is in dry dock in Greenwich, where she is looked upon as a national treasure and is visited by thousands of tourists each year.

Astern of the two ships, a hundred or so yards down the river, were a series of wharfs serving a paper mill and the cement works. On the opposite side of the river was a wild desolate shore along which the wind often howled.

*

There were four decks on the *Worcester*, the Upper Deck that was open to the sky and was used for parades and recreation; the Main Deck that was used for study and recreation away from the elements; and two lower decks that were used for sleeping. At the stern of the lower of the two sleeping decks was a series of classrooms.

The Main Deck showing the old fashioned desks that served as furniture

To imagine how we lived, picture the inside of an old wooden sailing ship dating back to the time of Trafalgar. The only difference was that *Worcester III* was made of steel and had a ceiling height or headroom of about seven feet.

It was a Spartan existence. The decks were long open draughty spaces that stretched from almost one end of the Ship to the other. Instead of gun ports in the ship's side there were sash windows that let in almost as much wind as gun ports would have done. There was practically no furniture. On the main deck, a few old brown benches served as seats, and on the sleeping decks the only things that might have been called furniture were rows of black sea chests placed apart at precise intervals.

Most of our belongings were kept in these chests, which were inspected once or twice a week to see that everything inside them was neatly folded and arranged in the proscribed manner. If they were not, the culprit was warned and on a second occasion was likely to receive three strokes of a stick across the backside.

There were no beds or bunks. Instead we slept in hammocks in which there was a tiny pillow and a mattress about a foot wide. Surprisingly, sleeping in a hammock was remarkably comfortable, although until you got used to it, getting in and out of it and turning over was difficult.

The Lower Deck where we slept. Note the sea chests arranged in rows and the uniforms hanging from bars on the left

Each morning the hammocks were taken down and stored in a special area known as a hammock store, and each night were brought out and slung from specially placed horizontal steel bars.

The cadets cleaned the Ship. For this we were divided into teams, and each morning dusted and swept the area of the ship in which we slept. On Saturday mornings we put on sea-boots and lined up across the deck with brooms. Then singing the latest pop songs such as *You May Not Be An Angel, Slow Boat to China* and *Ghost Riders In The Sky*, we advanced in unison and in line along the deck, scrubbing and moving up and down each piece of planking twelve times.

Scrubbing the Upper Deck on a Saturday morning

The boys also painted the Ship. When our studies and exams were over at the end of the summer term we put on our oldest clothes and, with a friend, were lowered over the Ship's side on a small platform to spend a few days painting. There was a certain amount of danger to this, as if we fell into the river we were likely to be swept away by the fast flowing tide and never heard of again. That had happened on one or two occasions in the past, and going over the side as we did would not be allowed today due to Health & Safety Regulations. But we did not think about it. We were young and were possessed by the invincibility of youth, and did not worry about the dangers of drowning. Instead, we enjoyed being cut off from the world, free to chat or allow our thoughts to roam as they pleased with just the river rushing by below us and the side of the Ship towering above us.

Apart from painting the Ship, we also 'coaled' her once a year. This involved shovelling coal into the ship's bunkers from a barge that was moored alongside for a couple of days. Although it was filthy work we enjoyed the physical challenge it presented, even though by the end of each day we were black with coal dust and looked more like coal miners than aspiring young ship's officers.

*

There were two types of staff on the *Worcester*, officers who taught us about ships and seamanship, and schoolmasters who taught academic subjects such as French and English and special subjects such as navigation and ship stability. The officers were assisted by Jack Reid and several other ex-navy petty officers, who taught practical subjects such as tying knots and splicing ropes.

The officer in overall charge was the Captain Superintendent, a retired naval officer named Commander Gordon Steele VC, RN.

Commander Steele was a handsome kindly man, who himself had been a cadet on the *Worcester* from 1907-1909. In 1920 he had won the VC during an attack by motor torpedo boats on the Bolshevik naval base of Kronstadt in the Baltic. He had been a lieutenant in the Royal Navy at the time, and when the captain was killed, had taken command of the boat and subsequently had succeeded in torpedoing and sinking a Russian battleship and a battle cruiser. To us cadets he was a remote character who lived in a suite of rooms at the after end of the Ship. We did not see him very often, and perhaps because of that, somewhat disrespectfully referred to him as 'Diddy'. "Have you seen Diddy?" we would ask if we suspected he was around, or, on his approach, "Watch out, here comes Diddy!"

On his approach all the cadets in the vicinity would freeze to attention. This was not as absurd as it might sound and owes its origin to naval history. On a crowded ship the best way of not bringing down wrath upon oneself as a result of bumping into the Old Man, as the captain was known, was by standing to attention until he passed.

Commander Gordon Steele, VC, RN.

*

I was tolerated but was not very popular for much of the first five terms I was on the *Worcester*. In part this was because without being consciously aware of it, I dealt with my new life and the insecurities and threats I felt on account of my background, by adopting a cold efficient exterior that hid my inner feelings from everyone around me including myself. I was a goody-goody, an automaton, a serious narrow-minded fellow who looked neither to left nor right and did not allow himself much fun. I came from an academic school and was a prig and a paragon of virtue. I was also usually top of my class and as a consequence was known as 'Brain,' which was not meant as a compliment. The Merchant Navy did not attract many academic boys, such as those at the top of the 'A' stream at John Lyon School. Instead, the spread of academic ability among the boys on the *Worcester* was much greater, although many *Old Worcesters* subsequently went on to have successful and even distinguished careers in different walks of life. I think this was because they had other qualities that are necessary for a successful career, such as good luck, good judgement, flexibility and drive, some or all of which are sometimes missing from people who are merely academic. The most famous Old Worcester was Admiral Togo of the Imperial Japanese Navy. In 1905 he was the commander of the Japanese fleet on the occasion it destroyed the Russian Baltic Fleet at the Battle of Tsushima. In 1906 King Edward VII made him a member of the British Order of Merit.

I was not helped on the *Worcester* by *The Jewish Thing*. After I had been on the Ship for a few weeks I was nicknamed 'Neb', standing for Nebuchadnezzar, King of the Jews. I got used to it and it did not bother me after a while, but I never got used to the anti-Semitism that I sensed was lurking beneath the surface of everyday life on the *Worcester*. One day one of the masters announced to the class with a smirk that I had come top once again. In response a boy named Clarke, with whom I normally got on quite well, shouted, "What do you expect, Sir? It's easy for Model. He's a Jew!" He was joking rather than being seriously anti-Semitic, but I did not like it and cringed like a whipped dog in my desk and blushed with shame and embarrassment. Attention had been drawn to a part of me about which I was confused and did not know how to acknowledge, and all I could think of was getting out of the class and escaping to somewhere where I could be on my own and comfort myself.

You may well ask why my parents had not talked about religion and had not told my brother Richard or me that we were half Jewish and half Catholic. The reason was that religion had caused a great deal of trouble in both their families. My mother's family were Jews from Poland who came to Britain in the 1860s and had run a string of fish shops and other types of shops in Essex and the East End of London, and my grandfather on my father's side was a Catholic from Germany, who probably came to England in the late 1870s to escape the consequences of having made a girl pregnant.

On two occasions my mother's family, which was normally very loving, was almost torn apart by religious strife. The first occasion was in 1912 when Grandpa Morris sent a son aged sixteen to Australia on a sailing ship because he had fallen in love with a Christian girl and refused to give her up. The boy was so upset that on the way to Australia he wrote to his mother saying that he hoped that the ship would sink and take him down with it. A similar thing happened in 1925, only on that occasion the son was in his twenties. Fortunately Grandpa had mellowed by the time my mother and father were old enough to think about marrying. No doubt Grandpa was encouraged by Grandma, who said she was not going to lose another child as a result of his strict Orthodox religion and that she would divorce him if he sent my mother to Australia. To make matters easier for Grandpa, my father said that he was willing to be circumcised and nominally become a Jew, although secretly in his heart he always remained a Catholic.

Before my parents married they decided that because of the difficulties religion had caused in both their families they would not discuss religion with any children they might have, but instead would bring them up to believe in God, but without any particular faith. They meant well, but I think they made a mistake, as religion was still so important at that time that people identified themselves by their faith and were suspicious of people of other faiths. Most Protestants disliked Catholics, most Catholics disliked Protestants and both hated Jews. No wonder then that I was sensitive about my identity and felt threatened. Was I a member of a despised race that warranted extermination, and if so, what had I done to deserve being so despised? I knew that my aunts and uncles on my mother's side were Jewish, but I was not sure if that meant that I was, and I was not sure how to react when people said that I looked like a Jew.

Although I was not very popular on the *Worcester*, I did have friends. There were almost two hundred boys on the Ship. Boys joined the Ship between the ages of thirteen and sixteen. The shortest course was two years, but you had to be sixteen before you could begin an apprenticeship at sea, so boys who started at the age of thirteen usually spent three years on the Ship. Barry Browning was from Swindon and like me was almost sixteen when he joined the Ship. In those days every region of England had its own dialect. Sadly, since the advent of television and expansion of the media, that has changed and the richness of dialects is less pronounced today than it was when we were on the *Worcester*. Barry spoke with a broad Wiltshire brogue and as a result was known on the Ship as

Brurrh, partly because of the way he spoke and partly because he had buckteeth, a snub nose and looked like *Brere Rabbit*. He shared the same interests as me and within a short time we were firm friends. One of the oldest traditions on the *Worcester* was *slewing*, that is, walking arm in arm round and round the upper deck in order to get fresh air and exercise. Barry and I slewed for hours in all sorts of weather, talking about our parents, our brothers and our unfolding futures and careers at sea, and we still keep in contact to this day. Barry had a restless nature, and although he planned to stay at sea, about eighteen months after leaving the *Worcester* he found that he did not like the confined life on a ship, and so he packed it up and emigrated to Canada where he was first a navigator in the Royal Canadian Air Force, then a student and bursar of a university and finally a lawyer.

I also had other friends. Chris Dally had an independent spirit that might have put him on a collision course with the strict discipline on the *Worcester*, but it did not and he fitted in well and did well on the Ship. Chris and I became friends for life. Unfortunately, after leaving the *Worcester* he was afflicted by polio on two occasions and was left with a limp that obliged him to give up his dream of becoming the captain of a large ship. Instead, he changed departments and worked as an assistant purser on passenger ships before coming ashore and having a successful career, first in the oil business in the Far East, then as a artist.

Other friends on the *Worcester* included several foreign boys from widely dispersed countries. One of the most popular was a diminutive Burmese named Win. Win had copper-coloured skin and slanting Chinese eyes. He also had a ready laugh and a great heart despite his tiny 5' 2" height, and when he mounted the rostrum on the annual Speech Day to collect a prize he was given the biggest ovation of the day. Padmanabun came from India and was very black and had flashing black eyes and a large hooknose like an eagle's beak. Like Win, he had a great sense of humour and to all intents and purposes was as English as any of the English boys on the Ship. One day he told me with flashing eyes and a wicked grin that his sperm was "as white as an Englishman's". The Toupazada brothers were from Egypt. They kept their distance from the rest of us and were not as friendly as Win or Padmanabun, although as they slung their hammocks next to mine, I became quite friendly with them. Fathey Bey was an Egyptian aristocrat with curly black hair, coal black eyes and surprisingly pink cheeks set in a swarthy coffee coloured skin. Fathey carried a knife and one day during an argument with another cadet, drew it and said in a thick guttural voice, "I have killed men for less than that!" He suspected that I was a Jew, and initially was suspicious of me, as Egypt and Israel were deadly enemies at the time. But we became friendly and sat together at mealtimes at one of the long mess tables in the dining room and shared the various little food luxuries our parents sent us to help eke out the diabolical diet that was served on the *Worcester*. Niarkos was a Greek and came from a family that owned a shipping company of the same name, and today is in charge of it. Toupalopolos was another Greek, a small young man with appealing large brown eyes and a face pock-marked by acne. 'Wog' Westbrook was a white Kenyan who excelled at sport, and before I left the *Worcester* there was even an American cadet with whom I became quite friendly. One day I asked him why he had come to the *Worcester*, to which he replied, "Because running ships is second nature to the British, and they do it with such superb aplomb. People in America respect that and believe that a British naval officer's word is his bond."

Not all the boys on the *Worcester* were from such exotic backgrounds. Curd was the son of a local postman, a working class lad who had won a scholarship to the Ship. He was intelligent and I liked him a lot, but like me, he was not very popular. Physically he was a big overweight lad with elephant-like ears and thick rubbery lips, on account of which he was known somewhat unkindly as Slobber Lips, a title he bore with considerable humour. At the time of the 1951 General Election he declared that he was a socialist and said that if he had been old enough to vote he would have voted Labour. I was developing a liking for the underdog and I sympathised with him, but no one else did. It was as if they had a traitor in their midst. To a man they were Tory and as blue as it was possible to be, and the Second Officer, Mr Donner, said to Curd, "Curd, I don't know what the world's coming to when a *Worcester* cadet says he'd vote socialist."

*

On Sunday mornings we assembled in our best uniforms for Church Parade on the Upper Deck if the weather was good, or on the Main deck if it was raining. Everyone, including the captain, the officers and the masters were there, although Lasky, the Jewish cadet, and the Roman Catholics were excused. I attended the service, partly because it was the least likely option to draw attention to myself, and partly because my experience of morning prayers at John Lyon School had given me a smattering of knowledge about Anglicanism. Not surprisingly, on the *Worcester* the boys' favourite hymn was *For Those in Peril on the Sea*, and we sang it as if our lives depended on it. At one time while I was on the Ship the captain tried to have the hymn omitted, but the boys protested and in the end the captain gave way and accepted that it was part of the ritual of life on the *Worcester*.

Spiritually, the boys were ministered to by an Anglican priest. For most of my time on the Ship he was a rather sad man. The Reverend Day was far too kind and passive to be the spiritual guide to almost two hundred boisterous cadets, and we gave him hell, poor man, and asked him about such things as the temptations of the flesh and masturbation and wet dreams. In reply he would look at us with sad cadaverous eyes, and with a ghost of a smile on his long forlorn-looking grey face, would say, "Well, I don't know... But really, Our Lord was against the sins of the flesh..." It was always *Our Lord*. *Our Lord* said this and *Our Lord* said that; but we did not care. All we wanted was to embarrass him.

As religion was so important in those days, after I had been on the Ship for about six months I decided I wanted to be confirmed into the Anglican Church like most of the other cadets. My motive was to be like the other boys rather than from religious conviction. But my father objected and forbade me, saying I was to wait until I was mature enough to think the matter through for myself and make an adult decision without any undue external influences. At the time I was disappointed, as it meant I would not be like the other boys but would remain different and an outsider. But as I respected and loved my father more than anyone else in the world it never occurred to me to disobey him. He was my pillar, my strength. It was from him that I had obtained my values. Although I was physically much more adventurous than him, morally I was, and still am, very like him. He gave me my conscience. He instilled in me a very clear sense of what is right and wrong, and I am still tortured if knowingly I do something I know to be wrong. Without actually mentioning the Ten Commandments or the Sermon on the Mount, he instilled their values in me. Thou shalt not kill, you shalt not steal, honour thy father and thy mother, love thy neighbour as thyself, do good to those which hate you... Although such values are not often enunciated today, in my opinion they are still as relevant as guidelines to life as they were on the day on which they were enunciated.

*

The stated aim of education on the *Worcester* was 'to make fine sailors'. Apart from teaching the formal subjects necessary to achieve this, it also aimed to inculcate a certain attitude into us. 'Before a boy can command he must learn to obey' read the opening paragraph of the prospectus of the *Worcester*. Today I expect that such a sentiment seems old fashioned, but writing in the nineteenth century an *Old Worcester* commented, "The first rule was 'obedience is the soul of service.'" Obedience on the Ship was achieved through discipline. If a senior cadet or a member of the staff said, "Jump!" you jumped or faced the consequences – which were usually three strokes across the backside with a stick fashioned from half a broomstick. In many ways the *Worcester* was like borstal – only in borstal you were probably less likely to be subjected to physical punishment.

As part of the discipline to which we were subjected, we were only occasionally allowed beyond the boundaries of the playing fields that the Ship owned, and during our first two terms we were allowed ashore for a walk only once a month. On those occasions we had to wear our best uniforms – including brown leather gloves – and had to keep to country lanes and avoid talking to people. Because it contained a pub and was home to a bevy of girls, we were forbidden to enter the village of Greenhithe, although some of the more senior boys dared to do so and formed liaisons with local girls. For me that was not a temptation, as I was frightened of all women except those aged older than about thirty-five.

Our parents were allowed to visit us on three Wednesday or Saturday afternoons each term, and almost without exception, after welcoming them, we would ask them to take us to a teashop in the nearby town of Gravesend, where because of the atrocious diet served on the *Worcester*, we stuffed ourselves with doughnuts and pastries while our doting parents looked on lovingly, wondering where their sons were putting all the food.

*

Generally, discipline and the traditions of the Ship were enforced by the boys, rather than by the officers and the masters. At designated times of the day we were not allowed to walk between one deck and another or different parts of the Ship, but had to run, or as it was known, *double*. Failure to do so elicited a warning on the first occasion. Thereafter it occasioned three strokes with a stick across the backside. Often the punishment was administered on the spot, but sometimes we were put on *The Cabin list*, which involved going to *The Cabin* or prefects' room after evening prayers to be given a formal beating by the Chief Cadet Captain or head-boy of the school. After a beating most boys laughed to show their contempt and to disguise their true feelings, but a few cried.

On the first occasion I was caught not doubling, the cadet-captain in charge of the deck shouted at me, "Hey, you there! You know the rules. You were not doubling. Bend over!"

I had been caught red-handed, and as there was nothing I could do about it, I bent over where I was standing beside a gangway. For a second or two I was aware of the stick swishing through the air above my backside, and experienced an unpleasant sensation bordering on fear. Then I felt a sting like an electric shock, as the stick struck my buttocks.

Two more blows followed. Then I stood up and doubled away.

It did not take me long to realise that the easiest way to avoid such punishments was to do as you were told. It was as simple as that, and during the two years I was on the Ship I was beaten only about six times. On each occasion I felt humiliated and white with anger at myself for being so stupid as to be caught committing some minor misdemeanour.

Cartoon by Cadet Chris Field

New-boys, as new cadets were known, were given three days to settle in and then subjected to a process of initiation. This involved such rituals as not speaking to a senior cadet until spoken to, and not putting one's hands in one's pockets no matter how cold it was on the Upper Deck. Fourth termers and more senior boys who wanted a minor job done were allowed to shout "New-boy!" and the last new-boy to arrive would be assigned the task. This happened to me on one occasion. Unfortunately I was the last to arrive when the call went out about two weeks after I had joined the Ship. Looking directly at me through a gap in the shoulders of the crowd of new-boys that had gathered round him, the cadet-captain who had shouted "New boy!" shouted at me, "Hey, you there! New Boy, come here! I want you to go up to the *heads* and warm a seat for me."

Fortunately, I knew what to do. Among the more unwelcome chores a new-boy might be required to perform was to go up to *the heads* or toilets and sit on a seat and warm it for a senior boy.

Undoubtedly the most difficult rite we were required to perform as a new boy was to get undressed from our best uniforms and into our pyjamas and hammock in thirty seconds. We were required to do this on three consecutive nights, and were encouraged by the thought of the beating that awaited us if we did not accomplish it. To help us we were allowed a fortnight in which to complete the task, starting with three minutes on the first night, then gradually working down each night until we were able to do it in thirty seconds. The test was carried out immediately after evening prayers that were said kneeling beside our sea chests with our hammocks suspended above our heads. To make it easier, without being seen, as I knelt by my sea chest I surreptitiously undid the gold buttons on my uniform jacket, loosened my tie and undid the studs holding the stiff white collar round my neck and untied my shoe laces in preparation for tearing off everything I was wearing as soon as prayers were over. When they were, I jumped up and in a panic undressed and got into my pyjamas. Then came the really difficult task of getting into my hammock. As soon as I placed a leg against the wretched thing I pushed it away and was left hopping on my other foot with the leg that should have been in the hammock pointing up at the deck-head above me. On the first two or three occasions that happened I fell onto the deck and saw my hammock swinging above my head, and had to dress and start all over again. Fortunately the prefect or cadet-captain in charge of the section in which I slept was a big soft-hearted rugby-playing fellow named Pete Holloway. So long as we tried, if we failed he merely gave us three symbolic taps across the backside with his stick. But not everyone was as lucky. Boys under several other cadet-captains received a proper beating each time they failed the test after the two-week run-in period.

There wasn't much *fagging*, i.e. waiting on senior cadets, on the *Worcester*. A few new-boys became *hammock hands* and folded and stowed away a cadet-captain's hammock in the morning and slung it again in the evening, but there were rewards for doing this. It kept them out of the cold on the upper deck for a while, and usually the cadet-captain they were looking after looked after them and protected them from the more extreme rigours of life on the Ship.

You may ask why we put up with such harsh discipline and punishments. There are several answers to this. Firstly, by obliging us to call upon our reserves, the harsh discipline helped us to measure ourselves and learn how we might react in an emergency or in response to the hard knocks and adversities of life. Many men like this form of learning. How else can one account for the fact that men volunteer for the French Foreign Legion, the S.A.S. and the American Marine Corps? We were volunteers and did not have to stay if we did not want to. During the two years that I was on the *Worcester* only one boy ran away. His name was Thomas, and he stowed away in a boat one night and rowed himself to the shore, and after beaching the boat on the mud, made his way through the mud to the railway station and home. But it was not held against him. After a couple of days he came back to the Ship and did very well and eventually became a cadet-captain.

The system of discipline on the *Worcester* also had its checks and balances, and with some exceptions was usually fair. We were not crushed; if anything, the officers and masters treated us with humour and indulged and cherished our personalities. Beatings did not make me feel I might want to leave the Ship, as the discipline provided me with easily identified boundaries within which I could live securely. This was particularly important at that stage of my life, as I was a confused teenager who did not know who he was at a time when, as I have said, religion and religious denomination were still very important in Britain. Against the background of the security that the *Worcester* provided I thrived and the two years I spent on the Ship are among the happiest of my life. I was young and full of idealism, and like many cadets, I had but one purpose – to go down to the sea in ships. London was still the greatest port in the world and from the decks of the Ship I could see the great ships of the world plying their way up and down the Thames on their way to and from places such as Australia, the Near East, the Far East and the Americas. What more could a boy who wanted to go to sea desire?

Another reason that the system of discipline and punishments on the *Worcester* was accepted was that to a large degree it was controlled by the senior cadets and to a certain extent depended upon the consent of the rest of us. A cadet who felt wrongly accused could appeal to the chief officer. I did that on one or two occasions. On the first occasion I was accused of not doubling by a cadet-captain who was at the far end of the deck and could hardly see what I was doing. The following morning I mustered in front of the chief officer on the main deck with one or two other boys and stepped forward and saluted when my name was called.

I towered over the chief officer, who was no more than 5 feet 4 inches or so in height. But there was no doubt about who was in charge or the fact that I was subordinate. Mr Richardson had been a cadet on the *Worcester* about thirty years previously and was the most respected member of the staff and a role model for the boys. He did not need to say a word; his mere presence was a guarantee of order. One look from his dark brown eyes and we were all as quiet as mice. Wherever he appeared we were immediately on our best behaviour, even though he was so small that when he was an officer in P & O, it was said he needed a stool to stand on in order to see over the dodger or front of the bridge. His head was huge and quite out of proportion to his tiny body, but from his closely shaved black jowls to his unflinching gaze we all knew we were dealing with a man. Without implying any hint of homosexuality, apart from being known as *Chief*, he was also known as *Poof* on account of his habit of puffing out his cheeks and blowing out his breath as he listened to the excuses we made when we were up on a charge in front of him.

"Well, boy, what are you here for?" he asked, as I stood bolt upright in front of him.

"Sir, Cadet-captain Bruce says I wasn't doubling, but he was at the far end of the deck and was too far away to see what I was doing," I said, looking straight to the front and over the Chief's head.

He whispered a question or two to the chief-cadet-captain who was standing to attention at his side, and when he had heard the answer, he fixed me with a penetrating stare that made me feel he was seeing right to the core of me, and then pursing his lips and blowing out his cheeks as I had anticipated, he said, "Poof, boy! I think I understand. This time I'll take your word for it, but don't let it happen again."

With that I was dismissed and after giving a smart salute, I turned right and marched quickly away. I had been believed and felt vindicated. Without contradicting what the cadet captain had said, Mr Richardson had given me the benefit of the doubt. But I wasn't so lucky the next time I appealed to him and had to accept three strokes of a stick across the backside.

Commemorating the victory at sea on the Glorious First of June 1794

Looking back, I am aware that the discipline on the *Worcester* was Victorian and would not be accepted today, but I cannot help but believe that it contained a principle from which modern society might benefit, and that is that we all, or nearly all, need a *little* fear of the consequences of not behaving optimally or acquitting ourselves to the best of our abilities.

Apart from being able to appeal against decisions regarding punishment, the discipline on the *Worcester* was self-regulating in other ways. A cadet-captain who was too free with the stick was known as a *Sadist* and soon got to know about it from the calls of "*Sadist!*" that were muttered behind his back or shouted out anonymously after lights-out at night. Sadists needed to beware. The knots supporting their hammocks were likely to be tampered-with and their hammocks were likely to crash to the deck when they tried to get into them. Similarly, on the last night of term Sadists who were leaving the *Worcester* were often pounced upon by their former victims and given a sound thrashing, safe in the knowledge that on the following morning we would all be leaving the Ship to return to our homes.

Not all the boys felt or in retrospect feel as I do about the *Worcester*. Sixty years after leaving the Ship I sat in a pub with a group of grey haired *Old Worcesters* after a Remembrance Day service at the Merchant Navy War Memorial on Tower Hill by the Tower of London, and asked them what they felt about their time on the Ship. Of the ten or eleven round the table, at least four said they had bad memories of it and resented the harsh life and the discipline to which they had been subjected.

The most serious punishment on the Ship was *the rope's end*, which was administered by a petty officer in the presence of the chief officer, and had nothing to do with the discipline meted out by the boys. However, it was administered only very occasionally. In essence it consisted of three strokes across the backside with a rope that was said to be about an inch or so in diameter and bound with cord. The rope's end was greatly feared and when it was to be administered its effect on the morale of the boys was like the effect of a hanging in prison. As the appointed hour of the punishment approached the atmosphere throughout the Ship became very tense, and at the precise moment of the beating we all stopped what we were doing for a second or two and thought of the poor chap who was receiving it. During my time on the Ship it was administered on only two occasions. A fourth termer called Nick Slack was caught smoking on the first day of term and was subsequently given the rope. He was an excellent chap and took it in his stride, but when the term ended ten weeks later, he still had three fading brown marks on the cheeks of his backside. However, the offence he had committed was not held against him and subsequently he went on to become chief-cadet-captain or head-boy of the Ship.

*

The main complaint on the *Worcester* was about the food, not the harsh discipline or the punishments. The cooks – chef is too complimentary a word to describe them – were hardly fit to prepare food for animals. When I joined the *Worcester* I was a finicky eater, but because there was no alternative to the atrocious food that was served, by the time I left I would eat almost anything. As one *Old Worcester* put it, 'you learned to eat as much as you could, and as often as you could, as you never knew whether the next meal would be edible.' At breakfast there was bacon floating in fat and fried eggs that were like rubber, and at lunch lumps of fat that were said to be meat, floating in watery cold brown gravy. On Fridays, a desert made of scraps of bread and milk baked so hard that it almost broke our teeth was plonked down in front of us and not unreasonably was known as 'Dynamite.'

One morning during my second summer on the Ship the porridge was so rotten that it contained maggots. Two independently-minded senior cadets named Hodges and Mason took a bowl of it to the chief officer, who poked it disparagingly with a spoon and muttered 'Poof!' then pronounced that there was nothing the matter with it.

To make the poor diet more tolerable, when we returned to the Ship from holiday we brought enough breakfast cereal, biscuits, jam and butter or margarine to last until our parents visited us and we were able to stock up again.

*

The Ship had a laundry that was housed in an old building on the *Worcester* estate and was run by a team of ladies from the village. Each week we were allowed to send one shirt, two collars, one or two sets of underwear, a pair of pyjamas and two pairs of socks to be washed. But although most of it was returned to its rightful owner, the machines were always breaking down or malfunctioning, and our shirts gradually became greyer and greyer, and it was not uncommon for a shirt or pyjama top to come back with one of its arms missing or its buttons ripped off.

The Ship also boasted a Sick Bay, but you had to be almost dead to get into it. It was overseen by a petty officer nicknamed Moh – standing for *Ministry Of Health*. Moh was a middle-aged man with a bent back that caused him to lean forwards. He looked disreputable and shuffled around with his cap on the back of his head and his hands in his trouser pockets. He was mad and we baited him mercilessly, but he had his revenge. His favourite medicine was a foul-tasting black laxative named Black Draught that he gave for almost every complaint. The mere thought of it would cause his previously dead dark eyes to light up and his podgy white face to crease into a smile, and tipping his head back and looking at us through his half-glasses, he would say, "Here, you, come here, you little devil, I know what you need ... Come, open your mouth and take this!"

*

The highlight of the week on the Ship was the Saturday night film. Everyone went to it, including Captain Steele. To accommodate the audience, the games room at the forward end of the lowest deck was converted into a cinema. We sat on rows of benches brought down from the mess-room on the deck above, and the captain and other staff sat on chairs in front of us. Films that we saw included *Scott of the Antarctic*, starring John Mills, and *Sanders of the River*, starring Paul Robeson. Both were about empire and imperialism and were very popular, even though by then the British Empire was already beginning its terminal decline.

On Wednesday evenings in the winter a dance-master came on board and gave dancing lessons to those who could afford them and wished to learn to dance. The dance-master was a pallid little gnome of a man, but under his direction I learned to waltz, foxtrot, tango and samba. My partner was a boy named Hobkirk, and one of us acted as a woman and danced backwards, the other as a man and danced forwards. The most popular tunes we danced to were the hits of the day, such as *A Slow Boat To China* and *You May Not Be An Angel*, but the music of Glenn Miller and Louis Armstrong was also very popular, as was jiving to *Twelfth Street Rag*.

Because of the close proximity in which we lived it is not unreasonable to wonder whether there were any homosexuality on the *Worcester*, particularly as we were isolated and cut off from female company. The answer is that there were definitely some affectionate exchanges between certain boys, but I have no knowledge of any actual homosexual penetration. Later, when I was on long voyages to Australia and New Zealand there were usually one or two stewards on the ships I served on who were overtly effeminate and *gay*, and with whom certain of the sailors 'slept', but I never knew an officer who was *gay*. On the *Worcester* the boys were young and emerging from the chrysalis-like state of childhood's neutral sexuality. At this in-between stage of their development, some of them went and stood beside the hammocks of other boys before lights out and goofed around and made suggestive remarks and perhaps touched one another a little. When I was a senior cadet, Hobkirk, the chap with whom I danced, came and stood by my hammock a couple of times and we goofed around, but we both felt uncomfortable about it and apart from a few giggles and saying such things as, "You're a very attractive fellow, you know", nothing came of it.

Two of the masters on the Ship were openly *gay* and invited certain boys to their cabins for tea, where I was told, they fooled around and acted suggestively. I was never invited, but as the boys went in twos or threes I doubt whether anything much really happened. One of two masters liked to creep up behind boys as they sat at their desks in class, and push his nose into their hair, presumably to smell their body odour. He had been a colonel in the army during the war. The other had been in the air force and had been wounded in the leg during the Battle of Britain, and took great delight – which I suspect was sexual – in caning boys with the walking stick he used to steady himself.

*

The classrooms on the *Worcester* were on the lower deck in the bottom of the Ship where the decks sloped up steeply towards the stern. *Worcester* French was a joke and was very different to the rigorous French that had forced into me at John Lyon School. On the other hand, maths and subjects such as navigation and ship stability were taught to a high standard, although I have a feeling that some boys did not really understand what they were being taught. I was lucky, and learned sufficient on the *Worcester* to carry me through all my exams as an officer in the Merchant Navy, right up to Master's Certificate, and when I finally got to sea, all I needed to learn was the practical application of what I had learned on the Ship.

Some of the individual teachers on the *Worcester* were excellent. English was taught by a Welshman named Mr Howells, or – as he was known on account of his huge belly – *Belly 'owells*. I related to Belly in a way that I had not related to Mr Cowan, the English master at John Lyon School, and for the first time in my life I found

English to be fun. Among the books we read with Belly were Sheridan's classic play *The Rivals*, and other books such as *The Autobiography of a Super Tramp* by WH Davies, and *The Gentleman of the Party* by A G Street. Today these works are largely forgotten, but at that time they were widely read. Belly had a soft lilting Welsh accent, and when he came into the class he would look at us through a pair of spectacles that were so large they made his face look like the face of an owl, and with his double chins wobbling, would say in a lilting Welsh voice, "Take out your *Rivals*" or "Take out your *Super Tramps*", and we would settle back and know that we were in for a good time.

I am indebted to Belly for opening my eyes to the world of books, although I suspect it also had something to do with the fact that I was growing up and was becoming more interested in the world around me.

Belly spent most evenings ashore in the village pub with another master named Mr Steven, and it was not difficult to imagine his big sloppy red lips opening to allow pint after pint of beer to slide down one way in exchange for rich belches, like farts, rising up the other way.

Steve, as Mr Steven was known, taught geography and current affairs, and was a desiccated old roué with a nose like an eagle's beak and a face like crumpled paper. He was well over sixty-five and had begun to lose weight in the way that many elderly people do, and his clothes hung on him making him look like a scarecrow. His teaching was not organised, but if he were to be believed, he had been everywhere and done everything. According to him, he had roamed through South America, had been a sheep farmer in Australia and had lived in the United States and travelled throughout Europe.

When I was a cadet-captain, I was in charge of the cutter or rowing boat in which Steve and Belly were rowed back to the Ship from their nightly excursions to the pub, and on one occasion as we were leaving the causeway Belly suddenly stood up in the stern of the boat and swaying and rocking it, looked up into the night sky, and in a drunken voice said in a rich lilting Welsh accent, "Look, Steve, the moon is rising backwards!"

Ship stability and ship construction were taught by a poor little man named Mr Tippen or as we called him to his face, Mr Tie-pin. If I remember correctly, his son had been drowned at sea during the war, and as a result he felt a calling to teach boys like us who were preparing for a career at sea. He was an excellent teacher, but was far too kind to keep order in a class of twenty-eight rumbustious boys, and as a consequence although we loved him, we made his life hell, poor man. His plight was not helped by his Cockney accent. "Mr Tie-pin, I say Mr Tie-pin, I didn' quite ge' that las' poin' yer made," some wag at the back of the class would say, mimicking a Cockney accent with the sole purpose of interrupting the lesson. Then for the third or fourth time poor Mr Tippen would repeat what he had already explained very clearly.

Among the things about Mr Tippen we made fun of was the old Morris Seven car he parked in the grounds of Ingress Abbey, the old manor house belonging to the *Worcester*. One day when we were ashore, out of sheer devilment a group of us lifted the car and deposited it at the top of the steps leading into the Abbey. As a result Mr Tippen could not drive home when he came ashore that evening. But we made up for our cruelty at the end of the following term. By then I was one of the most senior boys on the Ship, and near the end of the term I got permission for three of us to go ashore to the nearby town of Gravesend where we bought a silver cigarette case that I presented to Mr Tippen on behalf of the class. "'ere, Mr Tie-pin..." I began, mimicking his Cockney accent as I stood in front of the class. "On be'alf of all these 'ere boys I wou' like to presen' yer wiv this 'ere tokin of aur appreciation of all yer efforts on aur be'alf..."

When I had finished I stood waiting for his response, but none of us had anticipated that the poor man would be so overcome by emotion that he would break down and cry.

*

The greatest honour a cadet on the *Worcester* could have was to win the Queen's Gold Medal. This dated back to 1867 when Queen Victoria had endowed a gold medal to be awarded each year to the cadet thought most likely to make the best sailor. The masters and officers selected the names of five boys they considered fulfilled the criteria laid down by the Queen, and each cadet then voted for one of the five. Usually the five boys were in their sixth and final term on the Ship. In many respects the vote was a popularity contest. Although I was not popular among the boys, the masters liked me, and in my fifth term, much to my surprise, I was one of the five boys whose names were put forward for the vote. But because I was not popular all I got were two miserable votes. However, my poor showing was not unique. The following year a good chap named Tim Casey got just three votes.

Had the vote been in my last term it is possible that the outcome might have been different. At John Lyon School I had played soccer, and as a result, during my first few terms on the *Worcester* I did not understand rugby. Then suddenly the game clicked in my mind and within a few weeks of beginning my final term I was in the First XV. To be in the First XV was a great honour and just the stimulus needed to bring me out of my shell, and within a short while I was more confident and sure of myself, and began to assert myself. I was growing up and was beginning to do things my way. I became known as something of a character and on long journeys by coach to away matches, I led the singing of such songs as *It's a long way to Tipperary* and *Slow Boat to China*.

I underwent other changes. Because of the difficulties I had experienced over *the Jewish Thing* I had developed a natural sympathy for the underdog and when I was a cadet-captain I found it easy to identify with cadets who would normally have been beaten for committing an offence against the rules of the Ship. So instead of beating them or sending them to *the Cabin*, I tried psychology and talked to them and gave them a warning, at the same time making it clear that I was not a soft touch. Usually it worked and within a very short time I heard boys saying, "Old Neb's not such a bad chap after all. He didn't beat me when I was caught not doubling earlier today!" It was a way of working I adopted when I was an officer at sea. On one or two occasions it brought me into conflict with authority and the captains with whom I sailed, but in the main it served me well, and on one occasion helped me to quell a mutiny, as I talked to the sailors when I was on watch with them and they knew that I liked them and as a result they trusted me.

Although I felt more confident with my peers during my last term on the *Worcester*, I was still hopelessly shy with girls. I had had trouble with them ever since I had become more aware of myself at about the age of fourteen. I was so beset by lack of confidence that the more I tried the less confident I seemed to be when dealing with them. They might well have been creatures from another planet. In the presence of a girl I clammed up and was embarrassingly silent. The only girls I could deal with were in the world of my fantasies. In that world there were two types of girl, untouchable princesses who were on a pedestal and who I held in high esteem, and the other type who I could maul around in my mind and fantasise over sexually. I admired the first and desired the second. *The Jewish Thing* did not help. The doubts that many teenage boys have about sex and girls were magnified by it. The Nazi atrocities had affected me deeply. Perhaps I am a filthy Jew fit only for the gas chambers, I thought; who would want to go out with me?

Matters came to a head over the Summer Ball that was held on the Main Deck of the Ship. Parents and friends were invited; a six piece band was hired, the bulkheads surrounding the area of the deck on which the dance was to be held was bedecked with flags; bunting was hung everywhere, and by the day of the dance an atmosphere of anticipation had built up on the Ship. John Norrington, a boy who had followed me to the *Worcester* from John Lyon School, arranged for his parents to bring his twin sister to dance with me. Only he did not tell me about it until the morning of the dance. Shirley was a beautiful blonde, in every way an English Rose, a *princess* if ever there was one, and I should have been overjoyed to see her. But I wasn't. Instead I was terrified at the thought of having to talk and dance with her, and so immediately after lunch on the day of the dance I took off, and like a frightened animal, did a bunk and hid in one of the classrooms in the bottom of the Ship and stayed there surrounded by desks and the previous days' writing on the blackboard, until the dance was over and I was sure that Shirley was safely on her way back to London.

*

During my last term on the *Worcester* I was one of two cadets invited to form part of a guard of honour for the King and Queen.

The occasion was a visit by King George VI and Queen Elizabeth – later to become the Queen Mother – to HQS *Wellington*, the headquarters ship of the Honourable Company of Master Mariners, moored alongside the north side of the Thames Embankment in London, where it is still moored to this day.

It was a dull morning in December when we boarded the *Wellington*. The sky was overcast and a blanket of grey cloud hung over the city like a low grey ceiling. On the Embankment traffic roared by, indifferent to the post war austerity that gripped the country or the two lines of boys standing excitedly to attention on the rather cramped main deck of the ship with the upper deck only a foot or so above their heads. Nearly every nautical school in Britain that trained boys to be officers in the Merchant Navy was represented. Most wore naval uniforms of one sort or another, but in keeping with the outdoor traditions for which they were famed, the two representatives from Gordonstoun, the school that Prince Philip and later Prince Charles attended, were dressed in open-neck grey shirts, blue sweaters and short grey trousers.

The sense of excitement was almost palpable when finally their Majesties arrived and slowly began making their way along the ranks of the boys, talking at random to cadets as they went.

"And which college are you from?" the diminutive lady wearing a pale blue coat and hat, asked me with a smile and what I can only describe as great interest, particularly when one considers how many people she had to speak to each day.

I had been warned that if the King or the Queen spoke to me I was to reply either 'Your Majesty' or 'Ma'am', so because I felt more comfortable with 'Ma'am' and that it was less obsequious, I replied, "HMS *Worcester*, Ma'am," wondering at the last moment whether out of politeness I should look down at her and make eye contact or whether I should look straight ahead like a guardsman.

"And how long have you been there?" the Queen enquired.

"Almost two years, Ma'am."

"Well, I hope you have a very good career."

With that she was gone and a moment later was talking animatedly to another cadet somewhere further along the line.

A few days later photographs of the event arrived on the Ship and Captain Steele sent for me.

"Well, boy, where are you?" the captain asked, looking up at me from his desk and pointing to the two lines of photographs laid out in front of him.

From the other side of the desk the pictures looked upside down to me. In vain I searched for a photograph of myself; then I realised what had happened. Pointing to a photo in the bottom line, I said, "Sir, I am in this one, but you can't see me. I'm blotted out by the King. There I am, standing with the King in front of me."

Their Majesties King George VI & Queen Elizabeth, subsequently the Queen Mother, visiting HQS Wellington. The Queen is chatting to the author, who cannot be seen, as he is 'blotted out' by the King

The photograph I pointed to showed the King standing with his back to the camera, in front of a tall cadet, who as a result was hardly visible.

"Waw, boy!" the captain roared. "Don't worry about that! It's an honour to be blotted out by the King!"

*

The most important day in the *Worcester* calendar was Speech Day at the end of the summer term. Each July a steamer named the *Royal Sovereign* was chartered and decked out with flags in readiness for carrying several hundred guests – including our parents decked out in their Sunday best – down the river to Greenhithe and the *Worcester*. The passengers boarded the ship at the pier in front of the Tower of London and watched as Tower Bridge was raised to let them through. It was a grand occasion in anyone's terms, the type of day of which memories are made, and for years afterwards my mother referred to the two Speech Days when I was on the *Worcester* as two of the happiest days of her life.

Usually the weather was kind on the day, and after the steamer had passed through the bridge, an orchestra struck up and our parents tucked in to a lunch that included pieces of chicken and salmon, both of which are common now but were uncommon and considered great delicacies in those days of austerity.

The route down the Thames took the *Royal Sovereign* passed the Royal Docks where dozens of ships from all over the world were being loaded and unloaded, passed the gasworks at Barking and the eighteenth century Royal Naval College at Greenwich, passed the Ford factory at Dagenham, until at last the *Worcester* hove into sight, looking like a ship-of-the-line with her masts and some of her newly rigged yardarms in place and her black-and-white hull freshly painted. Alongside her, the *Cutty Sark*, a mass of ropes, masts and yardarms, completed the picture.

In anticipation of the great day, for the previous week we had been busy over the side of the Ship, slapping paint everywhere and generally making her shipshape-and-Bristol fashion. As the *Royal Sovereign* came alongside all two hundred cadets on the Ship rushed to the Ship's side in their best uniforms, and gave three cheers for their guests.

The prize-giving ceremony took place under a huge awning that had been spread over the upper deck. The cadets and their parents sat on rows of chairs that had been brought on board especially for the occasion. Invariably, a well-known dignitary gave out the prizes.

The author receiving a prize from Lord Montgomery, Speech Day 1950

During the two years I was on the Ship the dignitaries were Admiral of the Fleet, Lord Fraser of North Cape and Field-Marshall Lord Montgomery of El Alemein. As part of his speech Lord Fraser told a story about how small things can be important at times of great events. The Battle of the North Cape was fought off the north coast of Norway in complete darkness, due to the high latitude and the northern winter. The German battle cruiser *Scharnhorst* could not be seen but was located by British radar during the late morning. Several hours more passed before she was within range of the British guns, and by then it was time for afternoon tea. The admiral was therefore faced with a dilemma – should he order an attack on the German ship before tea or wait until after the sailors had had their afternoon refreshment? Thinking that they would probably fight better with something in their stomachs, he decided to have tea first and then attack the *Scharnhorst*. The strategy worked and the *Scharnhorst* was sunk, but not without drama. Some of the German sailors were such fanatical Nazis that they refused to be rescued, preferring instead to drown, giving the Nazi salute and shouting "Heil Hitler!" as they sank beneath the icy waves.

When my turn came to receive a prize, Lord Fraser handed me a copy of J.B. Priestley's, *The Good Companions* and, staring me straight in the eye, said, "Congratulations! And always make sure you are a good companion and a good shipmate."

After the prizes had been distributed we left the Ship to three rousing cheers and joined our parents for the journey back to London on the *Royal Sovereign*.

The greatest Speech Day of all was in 1962 when our present queen, Queen Elizabeth II, distributed the prizes on the occasion of the *Worcester's* centenary, but by then I had long since departed.

In December 1950 I left the *Worcester* to start an apprenticeship with a company named Shaw Savill and Albion that ran to Australia and New Zealand. Subsequently I have been asked why I did not choose Cunard, as in the public's mind Cunard is generally thought to be the most prestigious company in the British Merchant Navy. But although it may appear to be prestigious to the public, to a seafarer it is just another shipping company. There were also other reasons why I chose Shaw Savill. The entrance requirements to be a cadet in that company were among the most stringent in the Merchant Navy and that appealed to my competitive nature. Another reason was that I wanted to travel to a part of the world that was warm and to avoid the gale-ridden North Atlantic Ocean. I also wanted to take in as much of the world as I could, and to travel to places where English was spoken and it would be easy to communicate with the local people, and Shaw Savill fulfilled all those criteria.

3

Apprentice to the Sea

I was apprenticed to the sea in February 1951, just after my eighteenth birthday. It was the morning of my life and the Merchant Navy was my gateway to the world. My indentures said that I would *'faithfully obey the lawful commands, both of the said Company and their Assigns and of all officers of any vessel on board of which he may be serving under this Indenture, and that the said Apprentice will not absent himself from their service without leave.'* For this I was paid the princely sum of £90 a year or £1.73 per week during my first year. That may not sound like much in today's terms, but at the time the average national wage in Britain was about £7-8 a week, and all my board and lodgings were provided and there was little to spend money on while the ship was at sea. My £1.73 per week was therefore really pocket money. Once a ship was out of British territorial waters, cigarettes and alcohol were sold at duty-free rates. Fifty cigarettes cost two shillings-and-threepence or 12p in today's terms, a tin of beer cost eight pence or between 3-4p. Gin and whisky were available for the officers, but not for cadets or the crew. Gin cost five shillings or 25p a bottle, and whisky eight-and-sixpence or 42½p.

My first ship was the *Waipawa* – meaning *Steaming Water* in Maori.

It was a cold winter's day when I joined her in the London docks, and earlier that morning the sun had crept up red and angry over the ice bound city like a bloodshot eye after a night's heavy drinking.

My father drove me to the ship, partly I suspect to see me off, but also because he was still enough of a boy to wish to explore her.

m.v. Waipawa

The *Waipawa* was lying in the King George V dock, part of a large group of docks to the east of London. There were about thirty other ships in the dock, and at my first sight of her lying heavy and low alongside the quay, surrounded by cranes lifting cargo into her, I felt my wrists tighten and a shaft of excitement lift my state of consciousness and appreciation of the world around me. There she is, I thought, my new home, the magic carpet on which I am about to be conveyed to the farthest ends of the Earth – or to be more precise, to Australia and New Zealand. Simply to look at her, with her white superstructure and buff and black funnel poking up above the surrounding warehouses, conjured up thoughts in my mind of foreign travel and exotic faraway places.

The world at that time was still relatively undeveloped and globalization was still over thirty years away. With the exception of the Marshall Plan for rebuilding Europe after the devastation of the Second World War, there was little international finance, or for that matter, not much international travel or tourism. Each country was still itself, and for those like me who were lucky enough to travel at that time it was a last chance to see the world as it had been for a hundred years or more. The reduction to the American or Mid-Atlantic Way of Life had not yet occurred. There were no coasts lined with rows of international hotels, no Hiltons or Inns on the Park; no McDonald's or Burger Kings. Each country was still fairly isolated. Australia was still Australia; Fiji was still Fiji; and Japan was still traditional Japan. The twenty-five mile long coastal resort of Cancun in Mexico was still no more than a tiny fishing village. The Gold Coast in Australia was still a few hundred unvisited sand dunes beside the sea, and the Mediterranean coast of Spain was not three hundred miles of hotels, fish-and-chip shops and *English spoken here*. Instead, Spain was the way it had been for many decades, the Eternal Spain of mules, old lady's dressed in black, old white houses and the siesta.

As the car drew alongside the gangway I saw an officer sloping along the quay wearing a regulation greatcoat and cap and carrying a holdall, and thought how experienced he looked and what an old sea-dog he must be, only to learn when I got on board that he was Trevor Salmon, and that like me he was a cadet making his first voyage to sea.

I had been told to report to the chief officer's cabin, but it did not occur to either my father or me that the officers' accommodation was high up behind the bridge, and so it took us at least ten minutes to find it. First we went along the deck at the top of the gangway and entered a narrow passageway that lead into the crew's quarters, then down a ladder that led to the engine room before a member of the crew kindly put us right and pointed us up a gangway that led to the bridge.

I squirmed with embarrassment when my father asked the chief officer Michael Collins, who like all the officers was known by the prefix *Mister*, if he would look after me. But I need not have worried; the stout old chap with a pop-belly and rather fierce-looking blue eyes, standing in the doorway of the chief officer's cabin, understood my father's concern.

"Don't you worry, Sir," he said in a broad Irish brogue, his stomach protruding in front of him like an inflated balloon, "I'll look after him well I can assure you... Now tell me, Sonny, what's your name? Are you married or are you single?"

It was a good start and my father laughed and concluded that I was being left in good hands.

*

The last of the cargo was still being loaded. At that time Britain was still one of the greatest manufacturing nations in the world and hundreds of tons of steel had been loaded in the bottom of the ship to provide stability and prevent her rolling too far in the heavy seas we were likely to encounter. Above the steel, cars, bulldozers, refrigerators, textiles, cases of beer such as Guinness, barrels of whisky, Meccano-like pieces of bridges, and several generators for the hydroelectric scheme then being developed on the Snowy Mountain River in New South Wales had been loaded. Some of the cars were pre-packed in large wooden crates; others were uncrated and were swung aboard in slings slung under their wheels. Once in the hold, they were secured with ropes and wires to prevent them sliding about as the ship pitched and tossed.

Loading and discharging cargo was labour intensive at that time and very different from today. Containers had not yet been invented. Instead, cranes lifted the cargo in or out of the ship, and it was then manhandled by gangs of dockers. Each hold in the ship was serviced by a gang. In London, Shaw Savill employed its own gangs, and they worked what was known as piecework, meaning that the more cargo they shifted per hour, the more they earned. It was a double edged sword, as it induced them to work so hard that, although they could earn up to about £40 per week at a time when the average national wage was about £7-8, most of them were worn out by the age of about fifty, particularly as many of them smoked and drank a lot. By-and-large they were nice men, and realising that Trevor and I were making our first voyage, they took us under their wing and helped us understand what they were doing, and were kind to us each time the ships we were on docked in London.

The *Waipawa* sailed on the day after I joined her. By then I had learned quite a lot about her. She had been built in 1934 and, although she looked rather old-fashioned, was one of the stoutest vessels Shaw Savill ever owned. She was 530 feet long and 70 feet wide and when fully laden, drew 33 feet of water. She was powered by two large diesel engines that gave her a cruising speed of between 15-16 knots. At her forward end, she had an old fashioned perpendicular up-and-down bow that cut through the water like a knife. Her registered tonnage was twelve-and-a-half thousand tons. Food was still rationed in Britain at that time, and later on, on our way home from New Zealand, I calculated that she had such a large capacity that, in addition to several thousand tons of lamb, she was able to carry enough butter to supply every person in Britain with his or her ration for a week.

We left our moorings at 10 p.m. I had been assigned to the 12-4 watch, which meant I was to be on watch with the second officer, and like him was stationed at the stern each time we entered or left port.

As I picked my way along the semi-lit deck to the stern I was filled by a host of conflicting emotions. On one hand I was thrilled to be starting my travels and the career I had dreamed of for so long; on the other hand I was aware of the leap into the unknown I was about to make, and that for the next few months I would be at the mercy of a group of men I did not know. I was also worried by the fact that I was not sure what was expected of me or whether I would measure up to those expectations when I found out what they were. There was also the fact that it was almost midnight by the time we got out into the river, and I had already been working since nine that morning and was worried about lack of sleep, as I would have to remain up until four o'clock in the morning, and after that would have to get up and go on the bridge at 8.30 a.m. to relieve Trevor, the other cadet, so that he could go down to the dining room for his breakfast.

There were three routes to Australia. For ships heading to Sydney or other ports on the east coast of that continent, the most direct route was across the Atlantic Ocean and through the Panama Canal and then cross the Pacific Ocean, a total distance of about 13000 miles. For ships heading to Perth and the west coast of Australia, the most direct route was via the Mediterranean Sea, the Suez Canal and the Indian Ocean, although alternatively, if as we had, the ship had cargo for Capetown or Durban, it could go round the Cape of Good Hope at the tip of South Africa and across the bottom of the Indian Ocean.

At the stern my job was to assist the second officer, Mr Clarke-Lens, by answering the telephone and relaying messages from the captain and the pilot on the bridge. I was also required to watch out for any trouble that might be developing, such as ropes fouling the propellers or men in danger of being injured as the wires and ropes that held the ship alongside the quay were released and winched on board. One false move and a wire subjected to too much strain might snap and cut a man in two or amputate an arm or a leg.

Suddenly I was startled by the piercing sound of the telephone bell ringing at my elbow. In a panic I reached for it.

"Let go everything aft!" a shrill voice shouted down the phone.

"Let go everything aft!" I relayed to Mr Clarke-Lens, and watched as he repeated the order and the silhouettes of half a dozen men leapt forward in the half-light of the yellow glare cast by the lights on the dockside.

A moment later the ropes were splashing into the murky waters of the dock and the propellers were churning. We were on our way to Australia.

The feelings of doubt I had experienced earlier were not helped by the situation I found when I arrived on the bridge at just before one. All the lights in the wheelhouse had been extinguished and all I could see were the lights of instruments and the silhouettes of men moving about in the darkness. I knew enough to know that it would be a serious mistake to bump into the captain or the pilot, and so I groped around carefully trying to avoid everyone as I looked for Trevor. Then someone grabbed my sleeve and led me to a small table in a corner of the wheelhouse. It was Trevor. By the light of a torch he was keeping the official logbook, writing down the time the ship passed each headland and buoy as we made our way down the River Thames to the open sea. We were already almost at Erith when I took over and he went to his bunk. From the list of entries I could see that he had noted every buoy. By comparison with him, I was hopeless and soon realised I had missed several buoys and did not know where we were. All I could see beyond the ship was an indecipherable jumble of lights on the land, some of which were flashing. It was now almost two o'clock and I was feeling desperate. Oh God! I thought, as I tried to distinguish between the lights of navigational aids and the lights of streetlamps flashing as they passed behind buildings and trees as we made our way down the river. What on earth was the name of that buoy we have just passed on the port bow? *Lower Sea Reach* or *Mucking Buoy No.1*? As I concentrated, I heard the lonely moan of the buoy's gong sound an ominous warning.

After vacillating for a while I went into the chartroom at the back of the bridge, to see if I could find out where we were by looking at the chart.

"Don't spend too much time in there!" the second officer called out from the darkness of the wheelhouse. It was my first telling-off of the voyage.

For the next hour or so I struggled with the lights and the logbook, and received another telling-off before being told at a quarter-to-four to leave the bridge and call the chief and fourth officers for the 4-8 watch, and to make a pot of tea for them and another for the captain and the pilot. By then we were at the mouth of the river, and were off the coast of Kent and the southeast corner of England. On our starboard or right-hand bow the lights of Deal were to be seen twinkling in the cold black darkness of the early morning. A cold stiff south-westerly breeze had begun to blow. Suddenly I felt very lonely and insecure and far from home.

Calling Mr Collins was the same each night that I was on the 12-4 watch. As I stepped into his cabin and groped about in the darkness for the light switch, I was struck by the sweet odour of the man, and the fact that when finally I got the light on, Old Mick, as he was known, was lying on his back in his bunk, snoring rhythmically, and wearing only a pair of faded old long-Johns that reached down from his neck to his ankles. He looked defenceless and like a character from a Disney cartoon. His teeth were in a glass on a shelf beside him, and his mouth was open as if catching flies. His belly was almost hanging over the side of his bunk, and as he breathed, it moved in and out like a pair of bellows. Captivated by the scene, I could not help but notice his tiny penis showing through the fly of his garb like a tiny pink tongue or an offering on a plate.

"Mr Collins, Sir!" I called urgently, embarrassed and looking away. "Mr Collins! It's one bell, a quarter to four, Sir! Time to get up, Sir! I'm making some tea, and will be back in ten minutes to call you again."

At five-to-four I went back to check that he and the fourth officer, a man named Barry Tomlin were up, and when they appeared on the bridge a few minutes later I was told I was free to go below to sleep. By then it was well after four o'clock, and when eventually I got into my bunk I was far too tense and strung-up to relax, let alone sleep. For one thing I was distressed by the negative impression I seemed to have made compared with Trevor, and so I tossed and turned until half-past-seven when I heard Trevor get up and get dressed for the 8-12 watch. For another half-an-hour I tried to sleep; then finally at eight o'clock, feeling as if my insides had been kicked and I had been pulled through a shredder, I gave up and heaved myself out of my bunk and got dressed and prepared for my first day at sea.

The ship was well out into the Channel by the time I got onto the bridge to relieve Trevor for breakfast. The wind had increased to force 8 or 9, and was so strong that it had blown the sea flat and covered it in frothy white spume. The ship was driving straight into it, and it howled in the rigging and held the vessel upright in its grip, shaking it, and causing the deck to vibrate.

From behind the protection of the dodger, the fourth officer, who was relieving the third officer for breakfast, pointed out the salient landmarks to me. Far away, abaft the starboard beam, looking no thicker than a sliver of toothpaste spread along the horizon, I had my last glimpse of England, as the five hundred feet high white cliffs of Beachy Head slipped slowly beneath the horizon.

4

Life as a Sailor

Our path lay southwards towards the Equator and the Cape of Good Hope at the tip of South Africa. While we were still near land Trevor and I remained on the watches to which we had been assigned. This involved helping the officer-of-the-watch keep a lookout, and when we were more experienced, laying off courses on the chart or determining the direction of the sun or stars with an instrument known as an azimuth in order to calculate the correction to be applied to the ship's compasses.

Despite the novelty of my new life, as the ship made its way to our first port of call at Las Palmas in the Canary Islands, I began to realise that the life of a cadet/apprentice on the *Waipawa* was not without its problems. As a cadet-captain on the *Worcester* I had been an important person and had held an important position during my last two terms; but as an apprentice on the ocean-going *Waipawa* I was the lowest form of life on the ship and at everyone's beck and call.

My first brush with authority came when we were three days out and the captain was making his rounds. At home under the tutelage of my mother, and later, the discipline of the *Worcester*, I had learnt the meaning of the words *spruce* and *tidy* and knew what was meant by the word *dirty*, and that when Trevor and I had finished scrubbing our cabin and bathroom in preparation for the captain's rounds, they were among the cleanest on the ship. But that did not stop George Campbell, the captain, finding fault with them. For fear of upsetting the crew, he did not say anything about their quarters, even though the portholes in them had not been opened for days, and they were stuffy and smelt of tobacco and were not particularly clean or tidy. But when he and his entourage, consisting of the chief officer, the chief engineer, the chief steward and the bo'sun reached our cabin he picked on us with a relish. A dour little man of grey appearance and grey personality, he opened drawers and lifted the mattresses on our bunks to see if he could find any dust, and when he could not, he complained to the chief officer about the shine on the brass round our portholes and on the coaming of the door that lead into our cabin.

Afterwards Old Mick summoned us to the bridge.

"Now, see here, yous boys!" Old Mick said, as we stood to attention in front of him. "The captain isn't very pleased with yous. Yer's place was filthy this morning. Yer'd better scrub it out again and polish that brass, and I'll come by and inspect it later."

Apart from the weekly complaints we received about the state of our accommodation, we did not have much contact with the captain, but somehow the regularity of those complaints and the way I was treated by the officers, with the exception of Old Mick, came to epitomise much of my apprenticeship. It was as if they were saying, "Don't ask me why, but I had it tough, so now you'll have it tough; shut up and do as you're told!"

Another thing that made the beginning of my apprenticeship difficult was that try as I might, I could not get used to the 12-4 watch and sleeping for only three-and-a-half hours at a time. As a result I was always tired and felt as if my mind had been pulled inside out. It was not the same on the other watches. When I was on the 8-12 or the 4-8 watches I had at least seven hours uninterrupted sleep. Admittedly on the 4-8 watch I had to get up in time to be on the bridge at 4 a.m., but there were compensations for that. For one thing, there was the beauty of the dawn and later the sunrise, and in the evening, dusk and sunset. I was also able to learn how to use a sextant to take star sights at dawn and dusk – the two times of the day when it is dark enough to see the stars yet light enough to see the horizon, and to measure the angle between them.

*

Four days after leaving London we arrived at Las Palmas in the Canary Islands to take on oil. By now the grey wintery skies and windswept seas of the North Atlantic Ocean had given way to a dappled blue sea and blue skies studded with puffs of white cumulus cloud.

Waiting to greet us on the quay was a line of old taxis dating back to the 1930s that included Bugattis with enormous white leather seats, silver headlamps and bonnets that seemed to stretch on for ever, Rolls Royces with tucked-in backs and horizontal bars on the grilles at their fronts, and Daimler-Benz with wire wheels and white spats on their tyres. But sadly none of the crew, including us, were allowed ashore as we were there for only six hours and the captain was concerned that we would not be back by the time the ship was ready to sail. Instead we had to content ourselves with bartering with the horde of swarthy tobacco-smelling Spanish traders who swarmed on board the ship and spread their goods out on the decks as soon as the gangway was down. For the sum of £3 I bought a hand-woven lace tablecloth for my mother that she treasured for the rest of her life but rarely used, as like most of her treasured possessions, it remained in a drawer until the day she died. On the advice of the second officer, Mr Clarke-Lens, Trevor and I bartered for a case of Williams and Hubbard Dry Sac, which we got for £4, or just 33p a bottle

*

As the ship headed south from Las Palmas to Capetown, Trevor and I changed from watch-keeping to what was known as *day-work*. This meant that we no longer worked on the bridge or wore our cadet uniforms when working, but instead wore dungarees, or shorts when the weather turned hot, and worked from seven in the morning till five in the evening much like members of the crew, scrubbing decks, washing paintwork, painting the ship and sometimes splicing ropes and attempting to splice wires. It was work I enjoyed, as it gave me a feeling of caring for the ship and taught me the dignity of manual labour and working with one's hands. It also ensured a full night's sleep.

A few days after we started day-work, the ship crossed the equator and entered the Southern Hemisphere, but as the *Waipawa* did not carry passengers there was no Crossing-of-the-Line ceremony. Instead I spent an uncomfortable day and night, unable to lie flat on my back after exposing my lily-white English skin to the tropical sun for just half-an-hour. But it was a start, and within two or three months I was able to work on deck all day in the hottest sun wearing only a pair of shorts and plimsolls.

At times Trevor and I spent several whole days sitting or kneeling on a deck, chipping away at rust with a chipping hammer. It was menial work, but I did not mind it. With only the sky and the heavens for company, my mind was free to wander wherever it wanted. Psychologically, of course, the impact on us of this type of work was very different to the effect it had on the crew. For us it was merely a temporary phase in our careers designed to teach us how the crew worked, whereas for them it was the way they would work for the rest of their working lives.

The days I liked most on day-work were spent working with the lamptrimmer, as the petty officer who looked after the ship's ropes and other deck stores, was known. For days on end we sat with him in the sun on the covering of No 2 hold in front of the bridge, splicing the dozens of ropes that would later hold the derricks in place when cargo was being loaded and unloaded. At first, the rough sisal of the ropes inflamed the skin on our fingers and made them sore, but in much the same way as we quickly became used to the burning sun, the skin on our hands soon became thickened and hard and every finger as tough as a marlinspike, as the saying goes, or so I liked to think and tell friends ashore.

*

The memory of my first visit to Capetown is still with me. Nowhere in the world is the approach by sea more beautiful. I was on the bridge as we neared the land and from ten miles out I could see the flat top of Table Mountain, lying low on the horizon with a baguette of white cloud suspended above it. As we drew nearer, little white dots at the foot of the mountain gradually increased in size and number until it was clear that they were buildings, but even so, they looked no larger than toys. Then, when we were about two miles out, it became possible to make out windows and roofs and see trees and sense a bustle of activity in the city.

After the ship had docked I was hardly able to contain myself as, accompanied by Trevor, I began to explore my first foreign port. Here I am, I thought, aged eighteen, with my life in front of me, at the southernmost tip of Africa. Immediately ahead of me is a city of lights and magic and shops stuffed with goods of a type I have never seen. To the north, across six thousand miles of unbroken land, lie the pyramids and the great historical cities of Alexandria and Cairo.

We had left England in a freezing British winter in a country suffering post-war austerity. Food was still rationed and consumer goods scarce. Now, just two weeks later we were in a land of sunshine and plenty. To a young man who had never been out of England before, the contrast was almost too much and I was as incredulous as a small child at Christmas. In London the temperature had been below zero. In Capetown it was the height of the southern summer and the city was basking in sunshine and oozed wealth of a type I had not seen before.

Surprisingly, considering we were in Africa, apart from a few doormen and labourers digging the streets, most of the people we saw were White. Later I learned that this was because of Apartheid, and the fact that except for servants and manual workers, most of the Africans in the area were confined to townships outside the main city.

For an hour or so we wandered round, delighting in the shops and the white Dutch colonial architecture. Then because we had known only austerity and had never tasted pineapple, for 3d or 1¼p, we each bought a pineapple that seemed almost as large as a rugby football from one of the few African street traders we saw. He sliced them for us and we ate them as we walked back to the ship, laughing with delight as the juice ran down our chins and onto our shirts.

The following morning I had my first real experience of Apartheid. I had never seen anything like it before. A gang of black convicts were walking along a road adjacent to the quay, and each man in the gang was chained to the man next to him. All were dressed in only red cloaks and khaki shorts. Behind them was a white man carrying a rifle. From the slow way the gang shuffled along and the way they kept their heads bowed and their eyes fixed to the ground as they walked, it was clear that they were oppressed and had turned in on themselves and had given up all hope.

*

Two days later we sailed north to Durban, along a route that took us parallel with the famous coastal road known as *the Garden Route*.

In Durban I realized that trips ashore were often lonely, as apart from the occasion when Trevor and I went ashore together in Capetown, when one of us was off duty the other was required to remain on-board the ship to help supervise the loading and unloading of the cargo. In addition, rightly or wrongly, I sensed a hierarchy on the ship that would have made it difficult for me to go ashore with either an officer or a member of the crew. The realization of this was brought home to me one afternoon as I was whiling away a couple of hours on the waterfront, watching as row after row of huge rollers rose up from the sea. As they approached the shore they coursed forward like chariots advancing across a battlefield, to crash in a cloud of white spray onto mile after mile of almost deserted sandy beaches that later I learned were segregated along racial lines, with areas for Whites and areas for Blacks and areas for the mixed race people known as *Cape Coloureds.*

On another afternoon while the ship was in Durban I witnessed an almost unimaginable crime. I was on a double-decker bus, similar to a London bus, and was on my way from the port to the city, a distance of perhaps two or three miles. The conductor was European. The upstairs of the bus was reserved for Africans and the downstairs for Europeans. At a stop by the whaling station, a group of Africans workers dressed in rags got on and filed upstairs. Most of them found seats, but one did not and came down and sat on the long seat at the back of the lower deck of the bus. By then the vehicle was travelling at about twenty miles-an-hour. On seeing an African sitting in a seat reserved for Europeans, the white conductor grabbed him by the scruff of the neck, and shouting at him, dragged him onto the platform at the rear of the vehicle and threw him into the road without so much as looking to see how the poor fellow had fared.

Attracted by the shouting, I turned in my seat halfway along the lower deck and saw the whole incident, but was so shocked that for a moment I hardly knew what to do or to say. I had never seen anything like it before and was taken completely by surprise. How could anyone do such a thing to another human being? In a fury I wanted to shout at the conductor and tell him to stop the bus, but I was young and not very sure of myself, a foreigner in a foreign land without any knowledge of the local laws and customs. Many years later when I was working in Rhodesia, or Zimbabwe as it is known today, I got into trouble for opposing less violent forms of maltreating Africans, but on that occasion in Durban I felt impotent and could only hope that one of the other passengers would speak out and do something that might help to put matters right. But no one stirred. Instead, they pretended they had not seen a thing and merely stared straight ahead or looked out of the windows.

*

From Durban we sailed east across the bottom of the Indian Ocean to Fremantle in Western Australia. Normally on such a long ocean voyage the course chosen by the captain and the second officer would have been the shortest possible distance between the port we were leaving and the port we were making for. This would have involved travelling along a straight line known as *a great circle* that due to the curvature of the earth would have appeared as a curve or part of a circle rather than a straight line on most of the charts used by navigators.

A great circle would have taken us down towards the South Pole and would have exposed us to the danger of icebergs and other hazards of the Southern Ocean, and so a compromise was made and we went down as far as 40^0 South and then sailed due east along the fortieth parallel of latitude. On the way we passed relatively close to the desolate island of St Paul, which was uninhabited and so isolated that a permanent store of food was maintained on it in case any mariners were shipwrecked near it and needed food and supplies until hopefully they were rescued.

Despite going down to only forty south, the wind was cold and for days the sky was covered by a blanket of dull grey cloud that reached endlessly over the horizon both in front and behind the ship. Beneath us, huge great lazy rollers, twenty or thirty feet high, rolled in from the Antarctic, several thousands of miles away, and lifted the ship up like a toy and then rolled her slowly over onto her side, ready for the descent into the trough of the next great wave. If ever you were likely to be seasick, this was the time and place for it. At one moment the ship was on the crest of a roller, at the next she was sliding slowly down into the bottom of a great black chasm. With the passage of each wave the deck rotated and faced the opposite way.

At one moment the port side was facing up to the sky, at the next it was pointing down at the bottom of the ocean. In these conditions it was difficult to get about and rope lifelines were rigged along exposed decks and we held onto them as we walked about with a sailor's wide-based gait. When we climbed into our bunks we wedged ourselves between the mattress and the bulkhead and slept as best we could. In the dining room, wooden slats, known as *fiddles*, were erected round the edges of the tables, and the tablecloths were wetted to prevent cutlery and plates sliding off and crashing onto the deck.

Apart from our shipmates, our only companions were the great albatrosses that glided effortlessly across the sky, searching for any waste we discharged. At that time I did not pay much attention to them, and certainly did not appreciate the opportunity they presented for studying birds. Some had wingspans as much as eight feet, and when a bucket of slops was thrown over the side a dozen or so of them would glide down and fight over it in a mass of squawking beaks and wings.

At about this time the realisation dawned on me that I was not very happy with my new life. Trevor was a good companion, but we did not have much in common and I missed Barry Browning and the other two hundred cadets I had known on the *Worcester*. Trevor was affable, tidy and scrupulously honest and good at his work, but we were very different. He had the ability to always come up smiling, and as a consequence, unlike me, did not appear to be bothered by the foolish and often unnecessary orders we were sometimes given, such as scrubbing our cabin for a second time or shining the brass on the bridge for a third time because the captain thought it would be good for us. In addition, Trevor's interests were different to mine. He had or seemed to have a deep religious faith and as a consequence seemed more secure in himself than I was. His interests appeared more grounded in the ordinary everyday world than mine. By contrast to him, I seemed to be in a state of ferment, struggling with myself as I tried to come to terms with my new life, and ideas that were beginning to bother me, such as the existence of God, my place in the world, the arts, music and literature, about all of which I knew next to nothing.

As a result, in a very real sense I felt lost and that I did not have anyone with whom I could talk. I was not homesick, as after two years on the *Worcester* I had grown used to being away from home and my parents and brothers. The problem was more profound than that, and was not made easier by the fact that I was acutely aware of *the Jewish Thing*. Because of my looks, the officers suspected that I was Jewish and treated me with suspicion at best and hostility at worst. On the *Worcester* I had been one of the more able cadets, and by the time I was a senior cadet I had grown in confidence. By contrast, because of the attitude towards me on the *Waipawa*, I lost the confidence I had gained, and felt unwanted and bound down. I was lonely and behaved as if I had a burden of some kind on my shoulders, although it never occurred to me to give up.

On watch, the second officer, Mr Clarke-Lens was polite, but coldly formal, as if bored by me. Old Mick treated me well, but was too old to relate to me properly, and Mr Barry Tomlin, the fourth officer, was young and seemed to be malleable and influenced by the others. Mr Watt, the third officer, was openly hostile to me, and in return I was not very fond of him. I suspected that he was none too intelligent and disliked the way he seemed to be in love with himself. I can see him now with a silly self-satisfied smirk on his face as he stood preening himself in front of the mirror on the bulkhead immediately inside the open door of his cabin.

His dislike of me came to a head when Trevor and I swapped watches later in the voyage and I was put on the 8-12 watch with him. Initially he tried to reverse the arrangement, but when he could not, he was openly hostile. Matters came to a climax on our way home in a storm off the Panama Canal. Out of sheer nastiness he sent me to stand in the driving rain and spray on the weather side of the bridge and locked the wheelhouse door behind me, leaving me out in the weather with the wind and the rain blowing straight into my eyes, whereas the sensible thing would have been to allow me to stand in the shelter of the lee side of the wheelhouse, away from the wind, where I could have seen properly and could have kept a proper lookout.

Several years later I met him unexpectedly on a quay in a dock in Brisbane. By then I was third officer on a ship named the *Moreton*

Bay and our roles were reversed. While I was a flourishing young officer on a passenger ship, he was in a dead-end shore job, having been obliged to marry a local girl after making her pregnant.

"Well, fancy seeing you!" he said, trying to be as friendly as possible, then seeing the two gold stripes on my arm, added, "Golly, third officer already? That was very quick!"

I watched as the cogs of his mind slowly revolved and he tried to work out how I had become third officer in such a relatively short time while he had stagnated in a shore job with few prospects. I did not bother to remind him that time passes quickly and that it was already five years since we had sailed together. Instead, I felt pleasure at his discomfort. You bastard! I thought, you're pleasant enough now, but I haven't forgotten the way you treated me when I was a cadet on the *Waipawa*.

*

I wasn't the only member of the crew who felt rejected. As the ship approached Fremantle I realised that because of his age and lack of education, Old Mick was as isolated as I was. He was obviously troubled by it, as sometimes when he was on watch on the bridge on his own he was to be heard addressing the rigging and saying to himself, "I'll show yer who I am, Mister! Don't yer think yer can mess around with me, yer know."

Apparently he had started life at sea as an ordinary seaman in sailing ships and had worked his way up the hard way from the crew, *via the hawse pipe*, as the saying goes. But his career had not developed as he would have liked. Instead of progressing, after gaining the rank of chief officer he had been passed over and had not been promoted to captain.

For some reason he liked talking to me, and one day, referring to his pot belly and florid red drinker's complexion, he said to me when I went to the bridge, "I'll tell yer, Sonny, I haven't always been like this, yer know! When I was a young officer on the White Star Line I got round the girls, I can tell yer!" Then fixing me with an angry Celtic blue-eyed stare and pointing to his hair, which was either white or grey-blond, depending upon your point of view, he added, "Yer see, it wasn't always like this, yer know, Sonny. Once I had the yellowest blond hair in the whole of Ireland."

The younger officers, who were college educated like me, found his mutterings embarrassing and despised him and looked down upon him as a silly old fool, although for my part, I already realised that talking to oneself is an obvious way of relieving stress and that it is often a sensible thing to do.

Sometimes the officers played tricks on him, and on one occasion put dirt on the lens of his sextant in order to prove that he did not know how to use it properly when taking a sight of the sun.

At noon on the day after they had deposited the dirt, the second, third and fourth officers, together with Old Mick, lined up in the wing of the bridge and put their sextants to their eyes and measured the angle of the sun above the horizon.

When they had finished, Old Mick turned and looked at the others and asked, "What have you got, then, Mister?"

He was referring to the angles they had measured. After they had muttered their results, Old Mick summarized, saying, "So yer got 57° 26' Mr Clerk-Lens, yer got 57° 29' Mr Watt..., and yer got 57° 27' Mr Tomlin.... Hmm..."

Then falling into the trap they had set for him, a few seconds later he plumbed for the middle of their results, and said, "I quite agree, Mister... I got 57° 27'."

Unfortunately for old Mick the others had fabricated their results and he was left looking foolish and a liar. But it did not affect my feelings towards him. I felt sorry for him. So what if he was an old man who was no longer capable of taking a sight of the sun? His main job was supervising the crew and overseeing the maintenance of the ship, and he did that more ably than any of them would ever be able to do.

*

On the way to Fremantle I got to know some of the crew, at least superficially. Because shipping is a commercial enterprise and ship-owners like to keep costs as low as possible, despite its large size, the *Waipawa* had a crew of only sixty. By and large they were a decent bunch of men who I liked and gradually came to refer to affectionately as *the lads down aft*. Most of them came from London, but a few were from Stornoway, a town on the island of Lewis in the Outer Hebrides. On the way to Capetown one of the young men from

Stornoway began to cough blood and lose weight. A hush-hush diagnosis of the greatly feared disease tuberculosis was made. At that time there was no effective treatment for it, and for a few days fear gripped the ship, but when we reached port the young man was taken ashore and died in a sanatorium a few weeks later.

Many of the crew seemed to be tough, but as I was soon to learn, appearances can be deceptive. Often *tough men* are not as tough as they like to pretend, but instead have fragile centres and suffer from the same insecurities as the rest of us. Much later I was also to learn that the trick of dealing with these insecurities is to balance them against the fact that great endeavours are achieved by those who dare to have the confidence and determination to pursue them, and that it is the tension between confidence and insecurity that makes life so interesting and worthwhile. The prize goes to the person who dares. As a school friend of mine, Gerald Godfrey, said in a flash of youthful insight when we were out hiking one day before I went to sea: *Everything in this world is done by the doers.*

At each mealtime when Trevor and I were on day-work we washed and put on our cadet's uniform and ate in the officers' dining room where we were served by a steward named House at a small table at which we sat on our own. House was a mousy looking fellow with mousy coloured hair, and as a consequence we nicknamed *Mouse*. In the mornings in port he was so bleary eyed and trembling from the booze he had drunk the night before that he almost shook our breakfasts off its plates. He liked us but was very aggressive and hated the Chief Steward, and on several occasions showed us the eight-inch long blade of the kitchen knife with which he threatened to kill him. "I'll kill the fucking bastard if it's the last fucking thing I do!" he said, shaking with fury as he stood by our table. We tried to dissuade him, and fortunately for the Chief Steward, later in the voyage he was arrested in Melbourne for assaulting a man while ashore one night and was tried and sentenced to a year in prison.

The frequency with which Mouse swore and said the word *fucking* was typical of the language used by the crew, including me, and by the standards of the time was very strong, as very few people I knew in England said anything stronger than the occasional *bloody* or *bugger*. On the rare occasions that my father banged his finger with a hammer while doing woodwork he might say 'Bugger it!' or 'Sod it!' but I never heard him say anything stronger. At sea I gradually came to think of swearing as the salt and pepper or spice of language and a very good way of venting one's feelings. Even now, sixty years later, I enjoy a good swear and the relief it brings, and would not be surprised if, as he was once a sailor, Prince Philip knows how to swear when the situation warrants it.

*

A few days after the officers played their trick on Old Mick we arrived in Fremantle, the port of Perth and the gateway to Western Australia. In Perth, the capital of the state, I had a really close encounter with a porpoise. On my first day off I took a train into the city, and as I was standing on the banks of the Swan River looking at the black swans from which the river takes its name, a shining black porpoise swam up to my feet and looked up at me, and was so close I could see right down into its blowhole.

In Fremantle I had my first brush with a drunken sailor as I was making my way back to the ship. In those days the town of Fremantle was separated from the docks by a large railway marshalling yard over which there was a long narrow iron walking bridge. As I made my way across the bridge on my way back to the ship from the railway station I saw five drunken sailors lying unconscious at various points along its length. Some were lying face down, wearing just a vest and a pair of trousers; others were on their backs, snoring up at the sky. Later I learned that they were Scandinavians, and that in general the sailors of each nation have their own particular way of behaving when they are drunk. In what I expect is a bid to escape the depressing effects of their long dark winters, Scandinavian seamen drink themselves into oblivion and lie where they fall. On the other hand, British and American sailors become belligerent and fight and smash everything up, and Germans sing and gradually become more and more morose until finally they also sink into oblivion. I am not sure how the sailors of Greece and other countries behave when they are drunk, but from my experience of them when they are sober, I suspect that Greeks become noisy, Italians become amorous, and Spaniards sing until they fall into a deep sleep similar to a siesta.

*

While I was in Perth I visited a distant relative of my mother. We arranged to meet by the entrance to the tram station at which he worked, and on the way there I passed crowds of people leaving the station. I had not been among so many people since the ship had been in Durban, and suddenly I felt very lonely and full of doubt about myself and very self-conscious, as if the eyes of every person I passed were upon me. As they hurried or ambled by I looked at the faces of those who were closest to me, searching to see whether I could interpret what they were thinking about. They aren't troubled like I am, I thought. They are self-sufficient and self-contained, and are confident and preoccupied by practical matters such as where they are going. They are complete and untroubled. They aren't half Jewish and wondering who the hell they are, like me, and they aren't pre-occupied with wondering about whether there is a God and how they fit into the great scheme of things.

Cousin Mark, as I called him, was a cheerful tram conductor aged about sixty – a small man with big ears and a flat monkey-like face from which bright blue eyes shone out. He was a womaniser, and projected himself as a *Wacky Philandering Itinerant Australian Jewish Tram Conductor*, most of which was probably true, although I suspected that the womanizing he boasted of was at least in part fantasy. For an hour or so it was amusing to listen to him tell stories of the women with whom he had had affairs, but after a time I became tired of it, as I suspected that men like him use women as a way of feeding their messy little egos with no regard for the emotional havoc they may cause. Apart from stories about the women he had seduced, he was also full of the trips he had made back to the *Old Country*, as he called England. In the short space of seven years he claimed to have been back to Britain three times, which to me seemed unlikely for a man on a tram conductor's salary.

While I was with him he took me to see the old fashioned Australian bungalow made of wood planking and a corrugated iron roof that he shared with his daughter, and as I stood in the kitchen and looked at the stained oilcloth on the table and the filthy net curtains hanging at the windows, I decided that I did not want to see him again, although out of politeness I felt obliged to spend the rest of that day with him.

*

From Fremantle the ship swung south and then east round Cape Leeuwin and the chin of Western Australia and continued on an easterly course across the Great Australian Bight to Melbourne or *Melbun*, as Australians call it. In the Bight we rolled as much as we had on our way across the Indian Ocean, and one man was thrown against a bulkhead and broke his wrist.

In Melbourne I received my first letter from home. The arrival of mail is always a special event for the crew of a ship, and Shaw Savill was good at getting it out to us as quickly as possible. As soon as we had docked the first thing we did was collect our mail from the Chief Steward's office and settle down in our cabins in our own private worlds. My mother had written to me about the events and changes that had occurred in the lives of my brothers and other members of my family, but although I read it with interest, it all seemed very distant and far away.

Sometimes delivering mail was not easy for the Post Office. On one ship that I served on, the carpenter received a letter that had been posted near his home in Liverpool and was addressed simply to *McCullough, Gothic*. Goodness knows how the Post Office knew that the word *Gothic* referred to a ship, but they did, and the letter was delivered to him on the other side of the world in less than two weeks after it had been posted.

Melbourne was by far the biggest city I had visited so far. The streets in its centre were lined with large dignified stone office blocks and banks that reminded me of the City of London. It was also the place where there was a lot of talk about a cinema with a recently installed ceiling that had been studded with lights in imitation of the constellations of the stars in the sky. As it was new, people flocked in droves to see it and sit in darkness and look up at its so-called heavens. In much the same way, I was told I must go to a restaurant in the centre of the city that specialised in doughnuts and coffee. On its walls was a ditty that read:

As you go through life, brother

No matter what your goal
Keep your eye upon the ring
And not upon the hole

*

In Melbourne I got to know about the ruses that Australian dockers got up to at that time, as Trevor and I spent most of each day going up and down the ladders in the ship's holds, helping to supervise the unloading of the cargo. Specifically our job was to see that the work of handling the cargo was proceeding smoothly and that any delays were as short as possible. As a result I learned a lot about the state of labour relations in Australia immediately after the war.

With the cessation of hostilities and the blossoming of the economy, there was such a shortage of labour in Australia that the unions became very powerful, and in particular, the dockers became independent and did as little work as possible for as much money as they could get. In a way they were like children. At the first hint of rain they would stop work and cover the hold with a sheet of canvas and sit smoking or playing cards in the hold, even though smoking in cargo spaces was strictly forbidden. As a result, cargo that had taken only two weeks to load in London took five weeks to unload in Melbourne.

Whenever they could, the dockers pilfered the cargo. Nothing pleased them more than pilfering liquor. The *Waipawa* carried hundreds of cases of the best French brandy and several dozen barrels of Scotch whisky. To the dockers it was fair game, but for us it was minor warfare, as we tried to stop them pilfering it if possible. To help, the company stationed local security officers in the holds, but they were open to intimidation, and so on the days that alcohol was being unloaded Trevor and I were detailed off to spend part or the whole day in a hold, acting as additional security officers. Sometimes the security companies paid us for it. Even so, the cargo was not entirely safe as the dockers were wily and would arrange for a barrel to be dropped as it was being swung across the upper deck on its way over the side of the ship to the quay. Then they would gather round and collect the precious golden liquid in cups, thermos flasks, hats or whatever was to hand, and would sit drinking it until they were paralytically drunk and fell asleep.

Although the dockers were rascals, I never saw any violence on the docks in all the years I was sailing to Australia and New Zealand. As the postmaster in one of the dockland post offices in Sydney said when I went ashore to post a letter, "We're not a violent people, but perhaps because of our convict past, we are a wagon load of thieves. I suggest you nail down everything of value. You never know, even the stamps you are about to buy could be steamed off your letter and stolen! If I were you, I would register them, just in case they are steamed off before they leave the country..."

Booze was not the only thing the dockers were interested in. While we were in Melbourne, a foreman named Mick stole an expensively tailored overcoat from the cargo and got it safely out of the docks by the simple ruse of wearing it as he walked through Customs. So much for his honest appearance! I can see him now, looking like the perfect Anglo-Saxon family man, upright with blond hair, sun-flecked skin and candid blue eyes.

In general the dockers were friendly to Trevor and me as cadets, and treated us with coarse humour and referred to us as 'Mr Mate,' and pulled our legs and bantered with us about being *Pommy Bastards*, to which I learned to reply with a laugh, 'O.K., you Aussie Convicts...'

In return for working until 11 p.m., we were given the following afternoon off and were able to explore Melbourne. The *Mission to Seaman* in Flinders Street was one of my favourite haunts. It was run by a group of young Anglican priests, some of who were from England. They were a lively bunch and understood sailors and their needs, and arranged dances that brought us into contact with Australian girls. They also arranged bus trips that took us out into the Australian hinterland. Being priests, they hoped that we would be restrained with the girls and keep our mucky hands to ourselves. One Saturday they hired a bus and took a group of seamen, including me, on an outing to Ballaratt, some seventy miles west of Melbourne. On the way we passed through country that was dried-up grassland and so parched and dusty that it looked grey. On arrival we were feted by the mayor and city council and I was asked to make a speech, most probably because I was wearing a smart sports jacket, that had cost just £3 in England, and a bow tie, alas, a clip-on, as I had not yet learned the art of tying the real thing. On another occasion *The Mission* took us to Fern Tree Gully, a densely wooded beauty spot in the Dandenong Mountains about thirty miles northeast of Melbourne.

While we were in Melbourne Old Mick prevailed upon me to buy him a couple of bottles of gin, as the Australian Customs had locked the ship's duty-free liquor store while we were in port.

"Sonny!" he said, beckoning to me as I passed his cabin. "Yer know I only go ashore for Mass on Sundays. If yer're going ashore today will yer do me a favour?" And when I replied that I would, he added, "Well, Sonny, will yer buy me a couple of bottles of gin, but don't say a word to any of the other officers, if yer don't mind."

He nodded at their cabins and handed me a brown paper bag and two Australian five-pound notes.

It was an errand I often performed for him while we were in port, but about which I never mentioned a word to anyone.

*

Five weeks after arriving in Melbourne the cargo was finally discharged and, after ballasting the ship with water in order to prevent her from rolling over too far in the Tasman Sea, we set sail for Auckland in the north island of New Zealand where we were due to pick up a cargo of frozen lamb and butter and several thousand bales of wool for discharge in London.

In New Zealand I quickly realised that many places are so beautiful you can take a photograph in almost any direction and still be reasonably sure of a good outcome. The country was also so sparsely populated at that time that it was possible to motor for more than half-an-hour on a main road in the countryside without passing another vehicle. On one sunny afternoon several years later I went on an outing hurtling across the flat Canterbury Plain in the South Island on the *Lambretta* motor scooter I took to sea with me when I was second officer. It was a hot sunny day and after about half-an-hour I stopped for a rest in the shade of some trees and was stunned by the almost palpable silence. It was so thick and intense that it seemed solid enough to cut with a knife. To the north, south, east and west, the Plain stretched into the shimmering distance as far as the eye could see. Above, the dome of the sky reached down to the horizon many miles away. After about five minutes a car buzzed by, and disappeared into the distance, leaving me in utter silence once again, feeling isolated and that there was nothing between me and the frozen Antarctic, several thousand miles away to the south.

In Auckland I visited a couple of my parents' friends who had once lived across the road from my family in Wembley. After the war they had had enough of post-war austerity in Britain and in 1948 had migrated to New Zealand with their daughters, Rita and Wendy. Comfortably off, before settling down they travelled round both the North and South Islands for three months looking for the perfect place in which to live. Finally they lighted upon Titerangi, a small settlement to the northwest of Auckland, and bought a bungalow set in several acres of woodland.

The single decker bus that took me there crept down the steep tree-lined hill on the last part of the journey to their home like a cat creeping on its haunches. At the bottom of the hill it stood snorting and shaking like a wild animal, before moving off and leaving me alone, listening as the roar of its engine disappeared into the deep New Zealand silence. Looking round, I realised why the Ferris's had chosen Titerangi as their home. In Maori, Titerangi means *Fringe of Heaven*. As I took in the scene I was possessed by a feeling that I was standing at the edge of the world and was observing a morning at the beginning of time. Apart from the road, which was no more than a dirt track, the only sign of human activity was a path leading through some trees to a narrow inlet or bay on which the sea sparkled like silver in the late afternoon sun. Otherwise I was utterly alone, surrounded by row upon row of tree-clad hills that became bluer and bluer as they faded into the distance. As I followed the track up the nearest hill in the direction in which I suspected the Ferrises lived, I experienced a feeling of exhilaration and thought, 'This is great! I'm in the perfect place. I'm young, I feel so free that I could take off and sail up into the sky. I'm eighteen years old and twelve thousand miles from home in the depths of New Zealand!'

Mrs Ferris was in the kitchen of their bungalow, preparing the meal we were about to eat. I could see her through the window, moving between the table and the cooker as I approached between the trees. She was in her late forties, a middle-aged woman with a small waist, a large bosom and a sharp aquiline nose, and permed brown hair, the curls of which sat flat against her head in a style that even then a bit old fashioned and last popular in the 1940s.

At first we were shy with one another, as it was several years since we had spoken, but any awkwardness soon disappeared as we talked about the past and the things we had in common.

A few minutes later Mr Ferris came in. He had become a chicken farmer and owned six thousand chickens, which he kept in sheds hidden among the trees a few yards from the house. He was one of the first mass producers of eggs in New Zealand and was so successful that he was made Secretary of the country's Egg Marketing Board.

I loved the Ferrises and visited them every time I was in Auckland. Instinctively I sensed that they were my kind of people. I wanted to learn about books and culture and Mrs Ferris knew about such things and advised me about the books I should read and discussed them with me the next time I was in Auckland. It was from her that I first heard of Axel Munthe's book, *The Story of San Michele*, a classic about a doctor in Paris, and H V Morton's travel books entitled *In the Steps of St Paul* and *In the Steps of St Peter*, etc. Mrs Ferris also knew that the way to a young man's heart is through his belly, and each time I visited them she cooked several tiny poussin that Mr Ferris killed specially for the occasion. On one of those occasions the three of us sat down to twelve tiny birds, and I ended up with six tiny wishbones on my plate, one of which Mrs Ferris had silver plated for me and which I have to this day.

Sadly Mrs Ferris died in 1961 and after a few years I lost contact with Mr Ferris. Then, in 1981 my wife and I visited New Zealand. Twenty-three years had elapsed since I had last seen or heard of Mr Ferris and I wondered if he was still alive, and if so, where he was living? I had lost his address and did not know his telephone number, so after breakfast one morning in the hotel room in which we were staying in Auckland I picked up a phone book and searched to see if I could find anyone by the name of *Ferris*. There was just one entry, for someone named *V. Ferris*. Remembering that Mr Ferris's first name was *Vivian*, I called the number. By then Mr Ferris was in his late eighties and was very frail. At first he did not remember me, and when I suggested that we might meet, he became evasive and prevaricated, telling me that it would be very difficult. So after I had chatted to him for a while I hung up. Five minutes later, just as we were about to leave the room, the phone rang and I heard Mr Ferris say in a trembling voice, "I've been thinking. You must forgive me. I'm a very old man, but I think I remember you. It would be lovely to see you. Why don't you come over and see me today?"

Titerangi had changed and was more built up and no longer quite the Fringe of Heaven. A row of shops had been built along the ridge of the hill that led down to the tree-lined bay where only a few years before I had thought I was on the threshold of heaven. But the Ferris's house was unchanged and still among the trees, just as I remembered it from all those years before, although the chicken houses were no longer there and it lacked the subtle warmth of Mrs Ferris' hand. Otherwise, even the furnishings in the house were the same as I remembered, right down to two large Chinese vases that had stood at the bottom of the stairs in the hall of the house in which they had lived in Wembley in London in the 1940s.

Although my wife had not met Mr Ferris before, she thoroughly enjoyed the day with him. He had recently visited Japan and his grasp of current affairs and world politics was very keen, and at the end of the day we both agreed that our visit to see him had been one of the highlights of our visit to New Zealand.

*

Three-and-a-half weeks after arriving in Auckland the *Waipawa* was almost fully loaded and ready to make the voyage back to England. All that remained was for the last of the cargo to be loaded and for the hatches to be battened down. When that had been done the mooring ropes were cast-off and we headed out across the Pacific Ocean, homeward bound along the *great circle* that would take us to the Panama Canal and England.

Even today, when travel to the moon is a reality and communication with the most distant parts of the globe is instantaneous, it is difficult to comprehend the sheer size of the Pacific Ocean. It is unimaginably large. The distance from Auckland to Panama is over six thousand miles, or twice the distance from

London to New York. Plodding along at fifteen knots, the *Waipawa* took eighteen days to cover the distance – eighteen days, that is, of nothing but a watery desert and a flat horizon broken only by the occasional spout of a whale or a soaring albatross. In places the ocean was more than six miles deep, in other parts the bottom was dotted by ranges of mountains almost as high as Mount Everest, and underwater volcanoes that erupted and caused the sea to boil several miles down.

On such a long voyage life soon settled into a rhythm in which each day was the same as the one before it. Trevor and I went on day-work and worked like members of the crew, washing and painting the superstructure of the ship, or working with the lamptrimmer, splicing ropes and learning to splice wires, which is particularly difficult, as it involves weaving six stiff strands of wire in and out among one another. In the evenings we spent an hour or so before dinner doing the correspondence course the company paid for and required us to do; then after dinner, we stretched out on our bunks and read books from the library supplied by the *Seafarers' Education Service*. The authors I liked most were two favourites of the time, John Steinbeck and Somerset Maugham.

In many ways, on such a long voyage our lives resembled the lives of monks – monks of the Human Order, that is. Most of the activities that people ashore take for granted, such as going to the cinema or for a walk with friends were denied us. There were no pubs and no girls. But there were compensations. At sea our lives were deeply aesthetic. We were surrounded by the great canopy of the sky and the beauty of the sea in all its moods. Few experiences compare with the light cast by the moon on the sea at night, or with a ship slicing its way through clear blue water on a quiet sunny afternoon in the tropics.

From the captain down to the cabin boy, the ship was our mistress. We worked on her, served her and lived on her, and as a consequence had a relationship with her that is difficult for anyone other than a sailor to comprehend. But being human, we could stand only so much aesthetics and spirituality, and so after a while, as the hormones within us pulsed through our arteries, we began to feel a need to relieve ourselves and get drunk and roll around in female flesh – although at that stage of my life I was still too inhibited to contemplate doing anything practical about it.

*

The sky became increasingly dark and the atmosphere increasingly menacing as we approached the Isthmus of Panama and the Panama Canal. We sweated with the least exertion and our clothes hung dank and limp upon us. Sheets of thunderless lightning flashed eerily across the sky, lighting the gloomy space between the clouds and the sea. In a world of such gloom and menace it was not difficult to imagine how twenty thousand men had died of disease digging the canal through the tropical jungles of Central America in the late nineteenth and early twentieth centuries. When it was completed in 1914, the Panama Canal was considered to be one of *The Wonders of the World*.

De Lesseps was the first man who had attempted to build a canal between the Atlantic and Pacific Oceans, following his successful completion of the Suez Canal in 1869. But the Isthmus of Panama was very different to the desert through which the Suez Canal had been dug, and De Lesseps had been not successful. In Egypt the climate had been very dry and the land flat, and building the canal had simply involved digging a very large ditch between the Mediterranean and Red Seas. By contrast, in Panama the weather was hot and sultry, and the land through which the canal had to be dug was hilly and covered in jungle infested with mosquitoes carrying malaria and yellow fever. In addition it was necessary to construct huge locks to carry a ship up and then down 85 feet in order to get it over the hills.

The American pilot who guided us through the canal chatted to Captain Campbell in the shade of the wheelhouse as the ship edged its way between the walls of jungle pressing in on either side.

"I like British ships," he drawled, looking admiringly at the wooden planks on the fore deck and the rivets in the hull. Then when the captain asked him why, he replied, "Well, Cap'n, I go on ships of practically every nationality and I have to say that you British run them in such a way that it seems as if there is no other way of doing it. Kind-of-natural, if you know what I mean. No other nation, not even the Dutch, manages it in quite such an easy way."

He also told the captain that on some Japanese ships the officers still hit the men, despite the fact that the Second World War had been over for six or seven years, although in fairness to the Japanese I have to say that this is no longer the case and that for many years their ships have had a reputation for happiness.

Over the next few years I went through the Panama Canal more than half-a-dozen times and nearly always found the American pilots amusing. After climbing on board Shaw Savill's oldest ship, the *Pakeha*, a rusty old coal-burning tub that wouldn't go much faster than a man could walk, the pilot turned to the captain and said, "Looks a bit ancient, captain! How fast will she go?"

"Seven knots, pilot," the captain said proudly, heaving himself up in his white uniform to his full height.

"Seven knots! Gee!" the pilot exclaimed. Then, taking off his cap and turning it round and ramming it back on his head with the peak facing backwards, he said "Seven knots! O.K., captain, that's really great! Let's go! Full speed ahead!"

*

Two weeks after we had been through the Panama Canal we arrived off the southwest corner of England. After so many months away I was so excited that I could hardly suppress tears as I caught sight of the almost impossible green colour of the English countryside, as it sloped down to the sea on our port, or left hand side. Nowhere in the world – except perhaps in New Zealand – is the grass such a deep green colour. Australia has foliage that is a wonderful shade of pale lime in the spring, and I am sure Australians, who have been overseas for any length of time, feel a lump in their throat at their first sight of it. Some countries also have a characteristic odour. On one occasion I smelt the perfume of New Zealand from more than twenty miles out to sea, and I am told that after being away for several months tough Australian men have been known to shed a tear on smelling the bush of their native land from the sea.

As the ship swept up the English Channel and passed the white cliffs of Dover a barely suppressed sense of excitement passed through the crew and a newfound comradeship broke out among men who had ignored one other or had not spoken for weeks.

"Not long now, eh, Douglas?" the third mate, Mr Watt said, as we went on watch together for the last time. Apparently he had forgotten his antagonism towards me and the unfriendly way he had treated me throughout the voyage.

"No, not long now! We'll soon be there!" I replied with a gormless grin on my face.

Then it was all over and we were tied up in the King George V dock in London. I had completed my first voyage to sea and had accomplished my ambition of being a sailor and of travelling the world, but as I stood looking out from the bridge at the now deserted foredeck and bow of the ship I had a feeling of anti-climax. I had accomplished at least part of what I had set out to do and now that it was over I felt strangely empty.

Below on the quay I caught sight of my father standing near the bow. It was all a little too much. The combination of seeing him, being back in England and the voyage being over, left me feeling confused. On the one hand I was pleased to see my father looking so big and healthy in one of his double-breasted suits; on the other hand, by coming to meet me he made me feel he was boxing me in and reducing me to a schoolboy again. But I was no longer a schoolboy. I was now an independent young man. I had been round the world and had visited Australia and New Zealand and for more than four months had lived on a ship in the world of men. As a result I resented any attempt to diminish me and make me appear to be dependent, particularly as I knew that later that evening Trevor would be making his way on his own by Underground train to his home in Pinner.

My feelings were just as mixed when I went down onto the quay and shook hands with my father and led him up the gangway to our cabin. Here was the man I loved most in the world, and yet I could not tell him I loved him or put my arms round him and hug him, not because deep down I did not want to. At some level I did, but unlike emotionally demonstrable races such as Italians and Greeks, I was far too English for that, far too stiff-upper-lipped and emotionally inhibited.

A few minutes later I went to ask Mr Collins if I could go home for the night with my father. Old Mick was sitting at a table in his cabin reading letters that had been brought on board by a courier from the company's nearby dock office. At the sight of me, he put down the letter he had been reading and picked up another he had just read.

"Sonny," he said, frowning and referring to the letter. "Tomorrow morning you are to pack your bags and go on leave; then in two weeks time you are to report to the *Delphic* here in London. At the moment she's loading cargo for Melbourne and Sydney."

I was astounded. I had come to love the *Waipawa* and did not want to leave her. To me, as a sailor, she was a live thing with a soul of her own. I had served her and she had become part of me and had sustained me for nearly five months. I knew her ways; the way she moved in a heavy sea and the way she rolled in the great rollers down in the Roaring Forties of the Southern Ocean. Passengers can never know a ship that way. You have to be part of the crew to know a ship, which is why, sixty years on, I am reluctant to go on a cruise as a passenger.

As the realization that I had to leave the *Waipawa* dawned on me I became even more confused than I had been on seeing my father. On the one hand I was going home for some well-earned leave, on the other I felt empty at the prospect of leaving the ship that had been my home for so long. And then there was the question of the *Delphic*. What would her chief officer and captain be like? Would they be well disposed to cadets, as Old Mick was, or would they be pernickety like Captain Campbell or prejudiced like Mr Watt?

*

The rooms of our home in Wembley seemed smaller than I remembered, and the ceilings and walls seemed to press in upon me as I tried to orientate myself to being at home. In much the same way, my mother seemed to have shrunk and to be smaller than I remembered, although I was struck by how soft and cuddly she was when I put my arms round her and embraced her in the hallway. I was the oldest of her four boys and when I greeted my two youngest brothers they hung back shyly and stared at me with blank faces, as if they could not make out who I was – their brother, an Old Salt, a man returning from the sea.

Afterwards I wandered from room to room re-familiarising myself with their contents. My parents' hand was indelibly imprinted on everything – my mother's in the furnishings, the ornaments and the almost scrubbed cleanliness of each room, my father's in the kitchen table, bedside cupboards and other furniture he had made.

I had anticipated having a good time during my leave, but like many sailors, I could not help feeling that I no longer quite belonged at home or fitted in with life ashore. For one thing, I was at something of a loose end, as all my friends from the *Worcester* were away at sea, and my friends from John Lyon School were at work or had moved to other parts of the country. The only exception was Gerald Godfrey, a close friend from John Lyon School. He was studying law at Lincoln's Inn in London, and throughout the time I was at sea he always included me in whatever he was doing when I came home on leave. He was enjoying considerable success in his attempt to become a barrister. At the age of fifteen-and-a-half, he had made history as the youngest person to pass Roman Law at the Bar since Francis Bacon in the sixteenth century. His success was so remarkable that it had earned him a paragraph on the front page of the *Daily Telegraph*, and while I was in Australia I had even found a photograph of him with a few words beneath it in the Australian equivalent of the British magazine *Picture Post*.

In a way I was envious of him and the university friends he introduced me to. They did not have to get up early and start work at six or seven in the morning and do menial tasks such as holy-stoning decks or chipping paintwork, and they did not have to get up at midnight to go on the 12-4 watch or do the bidding of an officer who did not like them. Instead they were at university studying subjects I would like to have studied, such as English literature, economics, philosophy and religion. One had an interest in St Thomas Aquinas, another in the Koran. Two even had cars. They also seemed to have access to intelligent girls, some of whom were beautiful. On the other hand, to be fair, they had not been to Australia or New Zealand and had not experienced the beauty of a tropical night at sea or learned about men by living in the close proximity of a ship.

It was all very confusing, and to hide my feelings when I was in their company I fell back on the ploy I had adopted on the *Worcester* and hid behind a mask-like persona and pretended to be the strong silent type. That was how one of Gerald's female friends perceived me.

"Douglas, you're the strong silent type," she said, looking up at me with big liquid brown eyes. "But I suppose it's due to being in the navy. Isn't it known as the Silent Service?"

Although I tried to hide my feelings from others, I could not suppress the conflict about sex and girls that was bubbling up inside me. Physically, I was sexually mature and rearing to go, but by the standards of the day and the expectations of my parents, like nearly all young people, I was expected to be abstinent until I married. Added to this, I was still emotionally inhibited and frightened of girls, although that did not stop me fantasying about every attractive young woman I met as a potential sexual partner with whom I might jump into bed.

5

All Manner of Men

During the next two-and-a-half years I served as a cadet on the *Delphic*, the *Gothic* and the *Corinthic*, and with one exception in all that time I experienced only one episode of anti-Semitism.

The *Delphic* was in the King George V dock in London on the day I joined her – a long low graceful cargo ship of 10,500 tons. She had been built only three years before to the most modern specifications, and along with the other two cadets, I had a large comfortable cabin to myself in the officers' accommodation beneath the bridge.

m.v. Delphic in Wellington Harbour, New Zealand

Our route to Australia lay across the Atlantic Ocean to Panama and then on to Sydney. The first hint of the way the voyage was to work out came when we were about two-thirds of the way across the Atlantic Ocean. The chief officer, Mr McCann, or Jack as we called him, had gathered the other two cadets and me together on the flying bridge above the main bridge, and had shown us how to sew canvas and had set us to work sewing covers for the reels of mooring wire that were housed on the fo'c'sle.

To do this, we sat in the open with one end of the canvas tucked under a thigh and the piece we were sewing pulled tight across our knees. Sewing canvas required tough hands, as the type of canvas used on ships was almost as tough and difficult to handle as thick leather. The needles we used were three sided and had sharp edges that cut into our fingers, and the twine was like coarse string and also cut into our fingers as we strove to pull each stitch tight. To help push the needle through the canvas we used a sailmaker's thimble made of leather that wrapped round the hand with the metal thimble part of the device in the centre of the palm; hence its name *palm*. Even so, within half-an-hour our fingers and thumbs were inflamed and raw and felt as if they were on fire.

A couple of hours after we had started Jack came by to see how we were getting on.

By all accounts, normally he was a reasonable middle-aged man with fine sandy brown hair and a gaunt lined face, probably as the result of many years of smoking. Unknown to us, at the time we sailed with him, he had troubles at home that made him mean and nasty at times. He had a passion for cricket, and I expect his attitude towards us might have been different if we had played for the ship in the various ports we visited in Australia and New Zealand, but unfortunately none of us was any good at the game.

"Is that all you've done!" he sneered sarcastically, looking at the short lengths of canvas each of us had sewn. "Where on earth do you think you are? On your mother's yacht or something? In the old days a sail-maker on a sailing ship sewed three feet an hour for hour after hour, and that's what you'll be doing before the voyage is out, even if I have to make you do it!"

I watched in silence as the wind ruffled his hair and the short sleeves of his tropical white shirt. He turned his attention to Jeremy James, one of the two other cadets.

"Look how uneven that stitching is!" he said to Jeremy. "Eight stitches to the inch, my lad, or there'll be trouble for you." Then to all of us, he said, "You'd better pull yourselves together and smarten up quickly, or else you'll be doing an extra hour or two's work each day."

After he had gone Jeremy muttered under his breath, and Percy Holden, the third cadet, looked shiftily from side to side, silently wondering how he could get his own back on Jack.

The three of us were an unlikely group. Jeremy had fine chiselled features with a finely shaped nose and curly brown hair that clung to his scalp in a way that suggested that it might have been permed. He fancied himself as a lady's man and was often to be seen cultivating his looks in the mirror in much the same way as Mr Watt had on the *Waipawa*. Percy, by contrast, was a tall thin gangly youth, about 6' 4" tall, with in a long face and hollow-looking deeply set eyes that had a hunted look, while I was still long and lanky and as obsessed as ever with myself, as I tried to find out who I was.

The next hint of trouble with Jack came after we had passed through the Panama Canal and were on our way across the Pacific Ocean to Sydney. We were sitting in the sun on a hot steel deck, each dressed in only a pair of old shorts and plimsolls, chipping away at rust with a chipping hammer. It was hot dirty work and we had been at it for several hours and were covered in paint dust and flecks of rust.

"That's not nearly fast enough!" Jack said, taking Jeremy's hammer and making a show of giving the deck a few fast blows. "If you don't improve the pace at which you're working, I'll have you chipping decks every-and-all day until we get to Australia!"

A few days later we saw a different side of Jack. As potential officers we were trusted with the keys to the cargo holds. This gave us access to all sorts of valuable cargo, and at midnight each night for a week, the other cadets and one or two of the junior officers unlocked No 2 hold, and in darkness lit only by torches, slithered down among the packing cases containing cars and refrigerators until they found the consignment of four-star Hennessy cognac we were carrying to Sydney and Brisbane. Satisfied that they had reached their goal, they sat in almost pitch-blackness amidst the cargo and drank as much as they could before crawling back to their cabins at about three in the morning.

One night in a semi drunken state Percy stuffed the wrapper from one of the bottles into his pocket and instead of destroying it when he got back to his cabin, hid it under his mattress. The following morning on captain's rounds Jack pulled up the mattress to inspect under it and found the wrapper. Realising the significance of what he had stumbled upon, Jack sent for Percy later that morning, and after some initial denials, got to the truth. The question now was whether the three or four of them should be reported to the company and dismissed or perhaps even charged by the police when we arrived back in England. If they had been ordinary members of the crew I have no doubt that they would have been charged and dismissed. As it was, after some hesitation, Jack's softer side asserted itself and instead of reporting them to the captain, rightly or wrongly he settled the matter himself by giving them a warning in the hope of frightening them from ever doing such a thing again. They must have told him that I had not joined them, as despite considerable pressure to do so, I had declined, partly because I thought what they were doing was wrong, and partly because I could think of nothing more boring than sitting in darkness in the hold of a ship surreptitiously drinking stolen booze in the middle of the night.

*

Eventually after a passage from Panama lasting a few hours short of eighteen days, we arrived off Sydney Heads, the entrance to one of the world's most spectacular harbours. A heavy swell was running and the ship rolled and pitched while we waited for the pilot-boat to arrive with the pilot. I was on the bridge and from my vantage point I watched as the early morning sun rose up behind us and turned the cliffs at the entrance to the harbour to a golden yellow. Then a few minutes later they were towering over us as we steamed between them. After nearly three weeks at sea, the land looked especially attractive in the early morning light. Gentle wooded headlands sloped down to the sea, and as we rounded them, delightful little coves and inlets opened up in which in my imagination I thought a sailor might lay his head and sleep in peace. The faces of houses poked up between trees, their doors and windows resembling eyes and noses. After several miles, the Harbour Bridge hove into view on the starboard bow, looking so small it might well have been made of Meccano. As we neared the city, the density of houses of either side of the harbour increased, and we passed ferries scurrying to and fro carrying hundreds of early-morning commuters. A few minutes later we were abreast of Fort Denison, a small island on which a Martello tower had been erected at the time of the Crimean War to protect Sydney against the unlikely event of an invasion by the Tsar's armies.

We berthed at Millers Point beneath the bridge and a few hundred yards from George Street and the centre of the city, and as we went to breakfast a line of dockers came trooping on board to begin the process of discharging the cargo.

*

Three branches of my family lived in Sydney and on my first day off I decided to visit one of them. Because of the great distance between Australia and Britain, the last time any of them had been seen by my family was in 1929, some twenty-three years previously.

Today Sydney is one of the great fun cities of the world and an international centre for the arts, culture, entertainments and music, but in the 1950s it was rather old fashioned and Victorian, both in attitudes and appearance, perhaps best summed up by the elderly trams that bumped along its streets and the wrought iron balconies with which the city abounded, many of which, I am pleased to say, have been restored and now contribute to its glory.

Sophie was a distant relative by marriage of mine. I had her address, but not her phone number, and so I took a chance that she would be at home, and at about ten o'clock on a bright Australian winter's morning I caught a tram out to Rose Bay, where she was reputed to live, and arrived just in time to see a Sunderland flying boat lumbering along the harbour at the head of a huge plume of spray. Looking more like a heavy stone than an aircraft, finally, with a roar and a mass of water dripping from it, it clambered ever so slowly up into the sky.

My expectations of Sophie were dampened when I saw the bleak prison-like block of flats in which I suspected she lived. Despite knocking repeatedly on the front door of her flat, there was no reply, and so, disappointed, after a few minutes I made my way back down the stairs to the street. I was perplexed and full of questions. Was she out? Did I have the right address, and if I did, did she still live there? Or was she away, or perhaps even dead? Reluctantly, I decided to return to the city.

As I walked along the street on my way back to the tram-stop, I reviewed the little I knew about her. According to my mother, as a young woman she had lived in London and had been something of a Jewish femme fatale whose long black tresses and watery blue eyes had attracted a succession of rich lovers who had supported her and looked after her. Then in 1916, at the height of the First World War, at the age of thirty-six she had realised that time was running out and that she must either marry or risk ending up as a spinster.

At that time her boyfriend was a major in the same regiment as her brother Mark was a private whose job was to chauffeur the colonel. Mark was my uncle by marriage. In order to persuade the major to marry her, Sophie pretended to be pregnant, but when that failed to bring forth an offer of marriage, she reported him to the colonel, complaining that she was about to have the major's baby. But the colonel was not to be fooled. When the pregnancy failed to progress, he called Mark to his office and said, "Levy, I suspect your sister is nothing but a trollop and a bundle of trouble. I suggest you put her head-first down the lavatory and pull the chain on her!"

Two years later Sophie met Harry, a quiet happy forty-year-old bachelor who owned a small thriving tailor's business in the East End of London. Harry wanted to marry and was soon besotted with Sophie, and so flattered by the idea that anyone as beautiful as her might love him that he asked her to marry him. His proposal was accepted and shortly afterwards they were husband and wife. For Sophie, Harry represented security and a ready source of the money she craved. For Harry, Sophie was a disaster. His days as a happy bachelor were over. Within a short time she had spent all his money and he was deeply in debt, and so distraught that finally he decided the only course open to them was to emigrate to Australia and start a new life on the other side of the world.

As I reached the corner of the street on which I suspected Sophie lived, I saw an old lady waddling across the road towards me with a shopping basket in each hand. She was fat and small and low on the ground like a Toby jug, and was dressed completely in black and looked as if she came from central Europe rather than sunny Australia. But even so there was something about her that made me suspect that she might be Sophie. If so, how could it be that this waddling fat old woman had once been the femme fatale about whom I had heard so many stories? As she came nearer I saw that she had a bulbous nose with visible pores on it and that she was holding her fat little arms away from her body in an effort to prevent her shopping baskets bumping into her sides.

Yes, I thought, summing her up, she's Sophie, all right. So as I drew level with her, I turned and said, "Excuse me, ma'am, but I'm a visitor to Australia. You don't happen to know a lady named Mrs Symons, do you?"

She looked up at me through eyes half closed by the fat in her eyelids and said suspiciously, "I'm Mrs Symons. What you want?"

"I'm from England and I think I'm a distant relative of yours by marriage. My mother's name is Sarah," I replied, noting how pale and hot Sophie looked, and the tiny bubbles of perspiration above her upper lip.

"What Sarah...?   Sarah Morris, you mean...?   Sarah what married Joe...?"

As if she was perplexed and didn't quite know what to make of me she hesitated and looked up the street for a moment; then finally looking back at me, she said, "Well, you'd better come along with me then, I suppose."

I took the two baskets, and as I padded along beside her, I tried to fathom out how such a fat old woman could have been beautiful only a short few years before? What tricks had time played upon her that had brought her to such a sad situation, and what tricks, if any, was time already playing upon me?

Later that evening her son Gordon came home and she cooked an indifferent stew for the three of us. Subsequently I became very friendly with Gordon and the two of us knocked around together whenever I was in Sydney. He knew that as a cadet I earned very little money and often he paid for me when we went out, and on one memorable occasion at his golf club he bought me a complete second dinner after I had eaten one and said that for two pins I could eat another.

*

A few days later I visited my mother's brother, my Uncle Ben.

All I knew about him was that in 1912, at the age of sixteen, he had been sent to Australia because he had fallen in love with a non-Jewish girl and had refused to give her up despite warnings from Grandpa that something serious would happen to him if he did not. As I wrote in a previous chapter, his journey to Australia had been by sailing ship and had taken three months, and during it Ben had written to his mother saying that he was so unhappy he hoped the ship would sink and he would be drowned. But it did not turn out that way, and subsequently he had married a Jewish woman who had died after an illegal abortion, leaving him with four small sons to bring up.

I still remember the address of his home in *Brook Street, Coogee*. In 1951 it was a dark brown old-fashioned suburban Australian bungalow built of horizontal wooden planks. Now it has been completely renovated and is a modern looking up-market home with a bright façade.

My relationship with Ben was most unlikely. *He* was forty years older than I was – a fat eccentric middle-aged man who was completely bald except for a circle of white hair that sat like a halo above his ears. By contrast, *I* was still a tall lanky teenage boy. *He* was incredibly absent-minded, whereas *I* was gauche. Yet we took to one another immediately and I visited him several times on each occasion I was in Sydney. I loved Uncle Ben. He called me *Boy* and I called him *Uncle*. Each time I left Sydney he gave me an Australian £5 note, together with a bundle of hand-painted ties, many of which were too gaudy to wear. One memorable tie was decorated with a six-inches-long naked lady, standing against a green background in a posture not unlike the Statue of Liberty.

Ben wore thick spectacles and looked like Mr Magoo. And in a way he was Mr Magoo. He was short-sighted and like Mr Magoo he tended not to see things, but rather, both literally and metaphorically, to bump into them. Also like Mr Magoo, he gave the impression that life was happening to him and that he was not in charge of it. In part I think this was due to a very bad memory and the fact that he did everything at the last moment.

He owned an old Willys American car and was an atrocious driver. Every time we went out in it other drivers shook their fists at him from behind their windscreens and looked agog as he drove down the middle of the street, or drifted onto the wrong side of the road as we went round bends. But despite being eccentric he had managed to attract a beautiful girlfriend named Enid who doted on him and wanted to marry him. Enid was about twenty years younger than he was, and was very attractive, but had eyes only for him. So one evening as he was driving me along George Street on my way back to the ship I asked him why he had not married her.

"She's beautiful, Uncle," I said, as the car bumped along between the tramlines. "She loves you, and she'd make a fabulous wife."

For once Uncle kept his eyes on the road as he said, "Boy! You're right! But at my age I have to be careful. Look at her! She's many years younger than me and very attractive to men. How can I be sure I can really trust her?"

"But Uncle!" I protested. "She never looks at anyone but you. She's as loyal as the day is long!"

But he could not see it, and sadly never married her.

In 1955 he had a heart attack while I was in Sydney, and I saw him in hospital.

Deceived by feelings of invincibility, as many men are, on the morning of the heart attack he tried to work it off. For three hours he attempted to shave and get dressed, and when Enid arrived to have breakfast with him she found him collapsed on the floor. In hospital, his four sons, who normally looked upon him as a silly old fool and hardly ever visited him, arrived with their families and gathered round his bed like a flock of vultures. Enid was there, but because they were frightened she might benefit from his will, they pushed her aside. For his part, Uncle was too ill to pay much attention to what was going on. Propped up on a pile of pillows, he lay like a wounded animal, his eyes shut to the world, his thighs and abdomen covered in large purple bruises caused by the anticoagulants that were being injected into him in an effort to thin his blood and stop any further blood clots forming in the arteries of his heart.

Three days later he died, but by then I was on my way back to England.

Many months before he died he had shown me the safe in which he kept his will high up on the wall behind the clock in his office in downtown Sydney. The safe was searched after he died, but the will was never found, presumably because he left most of his estate to Enid and his sons did not like it and had found the will and had destroyed it.

Enid remained loyal to Ben's memory for the rest of her life, and seven years after he died, she visited my mother and the rest of my family in England. By then I was busy studying for a degree, and much to my shame I did not spend as much time with her as I should have done, although I did take her to see the film *West Side Story*. Over dinner before the film she told me in a voice full of love, "Your Uncle Ben was so lovely; he loved you so much. He was such a dear tender man, and was so handsome and had such lovely curly grey hair."

Although I had loved Uncle Ben, I could not help but be struck by the pathos of what she had said, as by no means could it be said that Ben had been handsome. Nor could I fail to remember that apart from the small ring of hair above his ears, he had been completely bald. But then, perhaps Enid was simply reflecting the age-old adage that beauty is a relative thing that is in the eye of the beholder.

*

When the cargo for Sydney had been unloaded, we took passage north to Townsville, a town halfway up the coast of Queensland. As we travelled further and further north the temperature rose and the sea and the islands we passed shimmered in a heat haze. Soon the great conurbations of Sydney and Melbourne were little more than a distant memory and we were in a world that was faraway and very remote. Occasional small settlements, isolated farmhouses and a few plumes of smoke were the only evidence we saw that man had touched the land off on our port or left-hand side.

As the ship approached the dock in Townsville after a voyage lasting about three days, a middle-aged man who seemed unusually well dressed to be in such an area as a dock, looked up at me from the quay as I stood twenty or so feet above him at my place on the docking station at the stern of the ship, and mistakenly identifying my uniform as an officer's uniform, shouted up at me, "Is Mr Peter Fielder aboard?"

Mr Fielder was the second officer on the *Delphic* and a dandy, if ever there was one – the sort of man who wears a white handkerchief in the top pocket of his uniform and shows half-an-inch of white cuff beneath his sleeve. Like my fellow-cadet Jeremy, and Mr Watt, the third officer who had disliked me so much on the *Waipawa*, he was a narcissist and in love with himself, although in his case, because he was friendly, it was something to laugh about rather than despise. In theory he should have been in charge of the docking procedure at the stern of the ship; but on that occasion he left it to me, and was hiding in his cabin, trying to avoid the man on the quay in the belief that he may have made his daughter pregnant when she was a passenger on a passenger ship on which he had been serving. He had told me how to answer if her father showed up, so without thinking about the morality of what I was saying, in accordance with his instructions, I shouted down, "No! I don't know on which ship Mr Fielder is serving. I'm afraid he isn't on board this ship!"

On hearing this, the head and shoulders of the man on the quay slumped and after a few second's hesitation he turned, and presenting his back to me, walked slowly away from the ship and disappeared.

In Townsville an army of huge Australian dockers, dressed in blue singlets and shorts and army-type boots, came on board, and after discharging the remaining cargo, loaded fifteen hundred tons of lead ballast from Mount Isa into the bottom of the ship. They were a tough beer-drinking lot, and for fun they competed with one another to see who could lift the greatest number of fifty-six pound bars of lead above his head. The lead was so dense and heavy that when they had finished loading it, it was no more than a foot deep in the bottom of the ship.

Today Townsville is a thriving city with air-conditioned shopping malls, restaurants and boutiques, but in the 1950s it was a hick-town that might have come straight out of a cowboy film. A strip of tarmac, a mere one-car wide, ran down the centre of the main street with strips of sand on either side of it and hitching rails for horses outside the bars. The doors of the bars were small, like the doors of bars in old films, and we had great fun rushing in and out of them, shouting, "OK, fellas! This is a raid, stick 'em up!"

Stimulated by the atmosphere of the place, I tried to become a *real* man and drink like a *real* Aussie. To be a *real* man was quite simple really. All you had to do was go into a bar an hour or so before closing time and order as many schooners and ponies of beer, as the measures of drink were called, as you thought you could drink before the pub closed at nine o'clock (six o'clock in other states). In the ensuing swill, you then drank the lot, although it wasn't easy, as usually you were so closely packed against other *real* men standing close beside you that you could hardly get your glass up to your mouth.

However, apart from such difficulties, I had other problems with being a *real* man. Try as I might, after the equivalent of about four or five pints I felt ill, and after six or seven was likely to vomit. Unable to hold his drink, not really a *real* man, you might say. If you were a High Court judge I would have to plead guilty to the charge and confess that I agree with you, my lord, and ask your lordship to take into account my other obvious unmanly vice, namely, that I react to cigarettes in much the same way. More than ten a day and I feel giddy and unwell. So, after a week or so, I gave up trying to be a *real* man, mainly because I realised there was a better way of achieving the same end, namely, by being myself.

A few days later, while we were still in Townsville, Jack told us that he and the captain had decided that while we were in port we cadets were to start work at six o'clock in the morning and every third day were to work until eleven in the evening. That meant a seventeen-hour day, followed the next day by a twelve-hour day, and after that a seven-hour day. For the first two hours of each day we were to wash the white superstructure of the ship; thereafter we were to assist with supervising the loading and unloading of the cargo until it finished at night. As that pattern of work was to continue throughout the seven days of the week, it approximated to a seventy-eight hour working week.

For fear of the Seaman's Union, they would not have dared to make the ordinary members of the crew work like that. So why were they doing it to us? Had we done something that deserved to be punished? In the end we decided that perhaps it was because of a combination of the captain's personality and the pressure Jack was under from home.

To look at, Captain Charles appeared to be benign, with kind blue eyes and a pink chubby face that reminded me of *Doc* in *Snow White and the Seven Dwarfs*. But during the time I had been at sea I had learned enough not to be deceived by looks. Having lived in the close proximity of men for eighteen months, I had learned that whilst you can gauge a person's mood by looking at their face and can tell, for instance, whether they are amused, angry or depressed, it is almost impossible to assess their character from the way they look, as a kind face can hide a wolf with a mean personality, and an ugly beaten-up-looking face can conceal a person who is gentle and kind.

As I had got to know Captain Charles it seemed to me that behind the kind persona he presented to the world was a man who probably lived in a world of fantasy in which he saw himself as a kind of Greek hero. Later, when I was one of his officers, he lent me a tome about Ferdinand Magellan titled *So Great A Captain*. I think he fancied himself in a similar vein. He told me that the most exciting time of his life had been during the war, and from his manner I surmised that ever since his life had been something of an anti-climax for which he compensated by visualizing himself as a great captain. On those occasions when reality dawned and he realised that he was just an ordinary captain, he hit the bottle for days, on account of which he was known throughout the company as *Champagne Charlie* or simply *Charlie*.

Soon the effect of working the long hours that the captain and Jack forced upon us resulted in us being chronically tired and moving about the ship like stressed-out automations. After two weeks Percy sent a telegram requesting help from the officer's union in London. A day or so later he received a reply saying that although they were sympathetic to our plight, the captain was within his legal rights as the Master of the ship and as a consequence we had to obey his lawful commands.

A few days later Jack told us to report to the captain's cabin in our best uniforms at nine o'clock the following morning.

The air in the Old Man's dayroom was still and stale and gave the place an unused feeling, and the carpet into which my feet sank as I shuffled in nervously behind Jeremy and Percy was thick and fawn and more-or-less un-trodden. The bulkheads, i.e. the walls, and the sideboard that was fixed to one of the bulkheads, were veneered with polished walnut, as was a large dining table, which was surrounded by chairs. In front of the table was a low glass-topped coffee table surrounded by a sofa and two armchairs covered in pale fawn brocade.

We waited for several minutes, wondering what was about to happen to us. Then Jack appeared and told us to stand to attention. A minute or so later the captain came in. He had been drinking heavily the night before, but apart from a rather bloated red face, he was sober and looked as benign as ever. In his hand was a book of maritime law. We listened dumbfounded as he paced up and down in front of us, haranguing us in a soft but menacing voice. However, we were too nervous to take in much of what he was saying.

For a while he rambled on about the law, referring to the book every now and again. Eventually he came to the point and the occasion took on the atmosphere of a court-martial.

"I hear you've contacted the Seaman's Union in London," he said. "Well, you know what the Romans did to their troops when they were rebellious, don't you? They decimated them, that is executed every tenth man in order to set an example to the others."

He smiled benignly and turned to Jack. "I think we may well have to do that here, Mr McCann, what do you think?" Then without waiting for a reply, he added, "I suggest we tell these young gentlemen to go below and that we'll talk it over and decide what to do with them."

With that we were dismissed to await our fate.

After we had filed out of the captain's cabin and had gone down below, we assembled in Percy's cabin. Although the captain had rambled on and had not been specific about what he intended to do to us, we knew from the way we had been stood to attention and the way he had harangued us that something unpleasant was about to happen to us, and we were all very pale and shaken, and felt very lonely and far from home. Our fait was in the captain's hands and it seemed there was nothing we could do about it. He was in such a strange mood that we were fearful that he might have us sacked and kicked out of the company, or might even attempt to make an example of one of us and have him decimated in the way that the Romans did.

"He can't possibly have one of us killed, can he?" Jeremy asked doubtfully, although as it was such a ridiculous thought he laughed nervously after he had said it.

"Just let him try!" Percy said angrily, his deeply set eyes flashing from side to side in a hunted way. He stretched himself to his full great height, and repeated, "Just let him try!"

"Personally I think he's off his rocker," I added quietly without much conviction.

We were perplexed and so could say little more. For half-an-hour we waited in limbo; then Jack came down from the captain's cabin and told us to get into our working clothes and get back to work. After that we did not hear another word about any punishment. Presumably the captain thought he had read the riot act to us and had taught us a lesson, although we did not know what the lesson was apart from the fact that we had to continue working the seventy-eight-hour week for the remainder of the time we were on the Australian and New Zealand coasts.

*

It is midday on the equator and I am sitting on the steel after-deck of the ship, wearing only a pair of shorts and a pair of plimsolls. The sun is blazing down on my back. In my hand is the chipping hammer with which I have spent the morning chipping away at rust on the deck. As a result I am covered in fine brown dust. It is hot work and rivulets of sweat have made channels in the dust on the front of my chest, but the forward motion of the ship has created a breeze that dries it before it reaches my navel. The muscles of my forearm ache from the repetitive movement of lifting the hammer and banging it down on the rust. It was the same yesterday morning and the morning before that and will be same tomorrow morning. However, fortunately the attitude of Jack and the captain has changed and we are working only normal hours now that we are back at sea.

My feelings about such work are mixed. With one part of my mind I resent being made to do such menial work; with another I don't mind, as I feel there is a certain dignity in such simple work and in knowing that I am serving the ship and helping to preserve her and keep her seaworthy. In any case, it is only a phase of my life, primarily designed to augment the number of crewmen who work on deck and also to teach me how the crew spend their days.

A few feet to my right, Percy and Jeremy are chipping away, but I do not know what their feelings are about the simple work we are doing, as it has not occurred to me to ask them. On the other side of the ship's rail, the vast Pacific Ocean is slipping by.

Because what we are doing is so simple our minds are free to wander where they will and each of us is engrossed in his own little world. For reasons that are unclear, a few minutes ago, I thought about Judy Garland. I had seen her at the London Palladium during my previous leave. When my parents told me that they had bought tickets for the show I sulked and did not want to see it, as I thought Judy was old-hat and out of date, but I changed my mind as soon as I heard her. She was unique and had the ability to mesmerise audiences, and in no time at all I was captivated and could not get enough of her....

*

I made two more voyages on the Delphic. On the first of these our cargo consisted in part of sixteen pedigree cows, a couple of prize bulls, two famous race horses and half a dozen dogs, all on their way to Australia for breeding. The cows and the bulls were housed in special wooden stalls that had been constructed on the top deck of a semi-open hold near the stern of the ship, and were looked after by a cattleman who was working his way to Australia. Sadly the heat of the tropics proved too much for some of the beasts and they collapsed and died in their stalls. The ship's doctor performed a postmortem on each of them and found them to be pregnant. It was strictly against the rules to export animals in such a condition, but presumably their owners were trying to get two animals out to Australia for the cost of one. After the post-mortems the carcasses or what remained of them were hoisted up on a derrick by the hind legs and unceremoniously dumped in the sea.

The horses were housed in wooden horse-boxes placed on the after-deck and the dogs were kept in a row of wooden kennels beside them, each separated from the others by several yards to prevent them fighting. Percy, Jeremy and I were each paid about £35 for mucking out and feeding the horses each day, and £12 for feeding and exercising the dogs.

All went well with the horses until we were about four hundred miles from Sydney when one of them, an excitable animal named Stokes that had come second in the Derby, smelt the land and in his excitement began to kick down his box. It was Jeremy's turn to muck him out that morning, and when he entered the horse's box Stokes turned round and grabbed his thigh in his mouth and in an excited state lifted him up like a doll and shook him and then dropped him upside down onto the floor of the box.

I was close by tending the dogs when Jeremy screamed. Looking up, I saw him heave himself up and his face appear in the opening above the half-door of the box.

"Jesus Fucking Christ!" he sighed and then slumped down behind the door.

Percy and I carried him out. His right knee was partially dislocated and his thigh was discoloured by a large black bruise shaped like a horse's mouth with teeth marks clearly imprinted on the skin.

The next morning Percy and I drew lots to decide who should go into Stokes' box, and as I lost, I went in. But I was prepared. As I brushed Stokes with one hand I held the other ready in a fist to punch him as hard as I could if he so much as turned and made a move to bite me. He tried it just once. Immediately I landed a straight right on the soft pad at the base of his nose. After that I had no further trouble with him. Once or twice he turned his head with the intention of biting me, but then remembered what had happened and quickly turned back, and after that I was the only person to go into his box.

*

In Melbourne, Jeremy and I went riding one Saturday afternoon. The field where we assembled with a group of local people had been trampled and was studded with hoof marks. The horses assigned to us were a clapped-out bunch standing tethered in a group with their backsides towards us. Every now and again one of them turned his head to see what sort of a group we were. It was a situation that called-out to be livened up, and out of sheer youthful exuberance and a sudden urge to show our Australian companions what an Englishman could do, I took a flying leap from behind the animal that had been assigned to me and vaulted onto its back, just as I had seen it done in cowboy films. The feat earned me a cheer from the group and a good telling off from the owner of the stables, but also brought me to the attention of three beautiful blonde girls – a pair of twins and their younger sister.

"Where did you learn to do that?" one of the twins giggled.

"From the films," I replied, embarrassed by their attention and what I had just done.

Dorothy, Anne and Shirley were different from anyone I had met before and were like a litter of playful puppies. When one of them laughed it infected the others and within seconds all three of them were convulsed in giggles. I felt that they were from a different stratum of society to me. Their home was in the centre of a dignified old part of the city known as Parliament Square. They seemed to lead charmed lives in which, a sufficiency of money was part of the natural order of things. For reasons that I could not explain, my expectations were much more limited and I felt out of place in the presence of the sort of luxury they seemed to take for granted, and in some odd way I could not but equate it with depravity. Beside them I felt like a tongue-tied clod, yet for some reason they seemed to like me, and at the end of the afternoon they invited me to their home for tea. After that I became a regular visitor to their abode. On one occasion when I was there, there were about half-a-dozen patrician-looking boys, who had been to the best schools in Australia, lounging about the house. One of them had won a scholarship to be a

Rhodes Scholar at Oxford; another was planning a career as a diplomat.

On another occasion when I visited them, the girls were lolling around in the drawing room on the first floor of their home, and were in an almost hysterical state after seeing three complete cinema programmes in a single day.

With great glee Dorothy exclaimed, "I'm boss eyed and can hardly see anymore!"

At this, the other two broke into hoots of laughter.

"I've got such a bad headache that I think I might die!" Shirley, the youngest shrieked to more laughter.

Convulsed in mirth, they crumpled onto a sofa and lay in a giggling pile on top of one another.

"I'm never going to go to the cinema again! It's given me such an awful pain in my head!" Anne shouted when she had extracted herself from the pile and had smoothed herself down.

"What, not even to see Jacques Tati?"

"No, not even to see him... Well, at least, not for a week, or till he's on again!"

Again they broke into convulsions of laughter and tears rolled down their cheeks while I looked on longingly, thinking how cuddly and yet unobtainable they were.

"What about the *Wages of Fear*? When are we going to see that?" Shirley shrieked.

At that they almost collapsed again, and Anne said, "I think we should go to the late night showing and walk home in the dark. That will really scare us!"

Sadly, their joie de vivre did not last longer than five or six years, as one after the other, two of them made disastrous marriages. Only one went on to live happily ever afterwards, or at least until she was an old lady. But before that I had gently fallen in love with one of them.

6

A Royal Ship

After three voyages on the *Delphic* I packed my bags and transferred to the *Gothic*, the ship that had been converted into a temporary Royal Yacht for the Royal Tour of Australia and New Zealand that was planned to take place later that year.

s.s. Gothic fitted out for the Royal Tour

Essentially the *Gothic* was a 15000-ton cargo ship with accommodation for eighty first class passengers. The Royal Family had insisted that she should carry cargo while she acted as the Royal Yacht and so apart from the fact that she had been painted completely white, from the outside she looked exactly the same as she had previously. Inside however, the passenger accommodation had been greatly changed. Some thirty passenger cabins had been converted into royal apartments that were kept locked while I was on the ship, except for the royal dining-room that was used by the junior officers and cadets, including me. The second officer sat in the Queen's chair at the head of the table, and the third and fourth officers and the assistant pursers and radio officers sat at the sides, with the other cadet and me at the bottom.

I ate like a king in that dining room, as I had learned that it was a good idea to be on friendly terms with the chef on each ship on which I sailed. For over a year I had better food than the captain or any of the first class passengers. When my order went out to the kitchen I could hear the steward say to the chef, "Special order for the big cadet!"

The captain on my first voyage on the *Gothic* was a happy old man named Captain Richardson, whose happy nature I ascribed to his habit of standing with his hands in his pockets playing *pocket billiards* with himself whenever he was on the bridge.

His friendly manner enabled him to deal with anyone, including the Royal Navy admiral who was seconded to the ship in preparation for the Royal Tour, although the admiral was not on the ship during the time that I sailed on her. The plan was for the ship to steam in formation with a Royal Navy escort whenever the Queen was on board. One day when this was being practised, the admiral became agitated and bad tempered. Eventually, when Captain Richardson had had enough and could not stand any more of the admiral's antics, he placed a hand on either side of the admiral's waist and frog-marched him to a corner of the wheelhouse and said, "There, Admiral! You stand there, and we'll get on with the job of manoeuvring the ship." Thanks to the captain's friendly personality, the admiral merely laughed and demurred.

In general, the first class passengers on the *Gothic* were a snobbish lot, trapped in the rigid class structure of the time. They thought themselves as superior to us. Some of them talked to us a little, but most ignored us completely. As a group they shunned anyone who did not conform to their elevated ideas of themselves. During the return journey from New Zealand on my first voyage on the *Gothic* we carried an American journalist named Mr Schultz. He did not know or perhaps did not care about the intricacies of the British class system, and instead of wearing clothes similar to those worn by the other passengers, such as grey flannels and a blazer with a cravat round the neck during the day, and a dinner suit with a bow tie in the evening, he wore garish shirts and matching shorts and sandals during the day and sometimes at dinner. When it became clear that he intended to continue doing this, the other passengers put him in *Coventry* and would not speak to him. I became friendly with him. One evening when we were chatting by the ship's rail, he said, "Gee, I like English girls and the sweaters they wear, and you know what, I like the goods inside them!" Such talk endeared him to me and other members of the crew, but the other passengers would have disapproved if they had heard him, as that is how life was in Britain and on its first class passenger ships in the 1940s and 50s.

Among the more unusual places the *Gothic* visited were the islands of Fiji and Pitcairn. In those days Fiji was an unfrequented group of islands off the beaten track, and the capital, Suva, was little more than a village of dusty streets and wooden bungalows with a few shops and one old fashioned hotel. The only form of ventilation in the hotel, apart from the windows, was a system of punkahs or short curtains hanging from the ceiling that were linked together by a chord that led back to the wall and down to the floor where a man known as a *punkah wallah* pulled them backwards and forwards to create a breeze.

The road running round the island was a dirt track along which carts and an occasional bus rattled. Apart from a few British, the people of the islands were divided into Indian traders and indigenous natives. The Indians had been brought in by the British as indentured labour in the nineteenth century. The natives were a splendid advert for the British Empire. Almost every man among them was over six feet tall with a mop of frizzy black hair that looked like a guardsman's busby, and the women were not much smaller. I was told that, as if showing-off their manhood, the men played rugby in bare feet. They also hated the Indians and openly said they would like to slit their throats if only the British would allow them to do so.

One afternoon while we were in Suva, I went for a walk along a tropical road outside the town with the other cadet, and after about half a mile we came to a river in which about a dozen naked native women were bathing. It was the first time either of us had seen a naked woman, and fascinated we stood and watched as they chattered and laughed and threw water over one another.

Pitcairn Island was little more than a rock sticking up from the floor of the Pacific Ocean. Because it was several hundred miles from the main shipping lanes of the time, in 1789 the mutineers from *HMS Bounty*, including their leader Fletcher Christian, chose it as their new home after they mutinied against their captain, the famous – or infamous – Captain Bligh. To this day the descendants of the mutineers, including people with surnames such as Christian, Young and Adams still live there. In general they are a strange looking lot, presumably due to inbreeding. Partly because of its history, and partly to give the passengers a break from the monotony of seeing nothing but sea for three weeks, the island was visited by almost every Shaw Savill passenger ship that crossed the Pacific Ocean. However, the passengers were not able to go ashore, as the steep sides of the island and the waves crashing against them precluded anything but a rudimentary harbour. Instead the islanders paddled out to the ship in outriggers and came on board and sold bananas, woven baskets and crudely carved wooden flying fishes.

*

While I was on the Gothic I sailed with two unlikely seamen, Peter Padfield, a cadet like me, and Michael Rhodes, an assistant purser. Unlike any sailors I had met before or have met since, Peter read plays by Shakespeare and Christopher Fry, who at that time was often thought of in Britain as a modern Shakespeare. Subsequently Peter left the sea and today is one of Britain's most eminent naval historians with over twenty books to his name. Michael Rhodes had started his career at sea as a ship's writer, or clerk, and had worked his way up. He read plays by Shakespeare and Eugene O'Neill, and subsequently passed A-levels and wrote a thesis about O'Neill that earned him a place at Balliol College in Oxford, from where he went on to become a highly respected Reader in English at one of the colleges of London University.

Peter and Michael were just the stimuli I needed and soon the three of us were an inseparable little group. I had a yearning to learn about literature, 'culture' and 'art', and wanted to 'improve' myself and become an educated man. Before I met Peter and Michael my idea of classical music was Strauss' *Tales from the Vienna Woods*. I had heard of Picasso, but not of Van Gough or Monet, and my reading was limited to Somerset Maugham, John Steinbeck and an *Old Worcester* turned writer named Dennis Wheatley, although I had heard of Tolstoy and had read Thomas Hardy's *The Trumpet Major* for School Certificate at John Lyon School. Stimulated by Peter and Michael, within a short time I was reading about religion and philosophy and was soon deeply immersed in Descartes, St Thomas Aquinas, Freud and Marx. I spent a month reading and re-reading the first chapter of Spinoza's *Ethics*, and in the end actually understood it and went on to read the rest of the book. I also studied and was captivated by the poetic language of the King James Bible and ploughed through most of the New Testament and bits of the Old. I bought and struggled with the Koran, but the copy provided for me by the Seafarers' Education Service was unintelligible to me, chiefly I suspect because it was an old Victorian edition.

In those days New Zealand was encouraging the development of culture, and while we were in Wellington, Michael and I went to one of the first concerts given by the country's National Orchestra, and along with the rest of the audience, were embarrassed when one of the few French horn players in the country was unable to reach several of the notes that were required of him during a solo.

My reading was mainly directed towards religion, probably because I felt insecure on account of my half Jewish, half Catholic background. My identity still bothered me and I felt insecure and still wanted to find out who I was and what life is about? At school and while I was on the *Worcester* I had tried to believe in God and had regularly attended Anglican prayers and with gusto had sung the Anglican hymns that were sung each weekday morning. On Sunday mornings I had attended the church service that was held on the *Worcester*. But although I tried to believe, such activities did not answer my needs. The more I listened and the more I read about religion the more I could not help but conclude that there is little evidence for what they teach and that religion is largely made by man in response to the knowledge that because he is mortal and knows he will die he has a need to know his place in the great scheme of things, and wants answers to the questions that bother many people, such as, "Who am I?" "What is life all about?" "How should I conduct myself?" and "What will happen to me after I die?"

To me it seemed that the way Western religions have answered these questions is by creating a God who is all-powerful, and that we have made ourselves the centre of His attention and have created the belief that He will look after us during this life and when we die. As proof of the fact that God is a creation of our minds, rather than external to us, we have made Him in our image and have endowed Him with human emotions such as our capacity for love, anger, caring and forgiveness, and have made Him even more human by referring to Him as *Our Father*.

No doubt many people will not agree with my view that religion is a psychological construct in response to man's need to know about his place in the great scheme of things. My father's answer to questions about God was to say that God is Love, but I am not sure what he meant by that, as to me Love has always meant a human emotion or feeling, and not the creator or prime mover or driving force of the Universe. Popes and bishops would also not agree with me, I am sure, as they believe in God, as do most other religious people. In a way I envy them the comfort their beliefs must bring them. My local bishop used to say that in the final analysis belief in God is a matter of faith. But to me it seems that faith is merely a mixture of upbringing, habit, hope and a blind belief in the existence of God, and that contrary to what religious people believe, the truth is that the study of religion shows it to have been fashioned by men. I suspect that if He could come back to the modern world, Jesus would not approve of the power or institutions of the Church, as He was a simple man who led a simple life, and was not a prince of a powerful institution. Personally, I suspect that it is beyond the capacity of any man or woman to know whether or not there is a God, and that if there is, He, She or It is unknowable and far more complex than the established religions would have us believe. Also, given the immensity and complexity of the Universe, if there is a God, I doubt whether He, She or It is concerned with the lives of individual men and women like me.

Today belief in God is less important in the lives of most Western people than it was a few decades ago when almost everyone believed in religion. Instead, the worship of material things and sports such as football and the cult of celebrity have largely replaced it. Strange as it may seem, coming from me, I think this is a loss, as modern society would benefit from the wisdom of The Ten Commandments, the Sermon on the Mount and the Lord's Prayer, all of which are rarely spoken about now but are superb guides by which to live.

While I was on the Gothic I also read about politics and reached the broad conclusion that basically it is the process by which we relate to one another in society. When I was young and on the ships I thought that the most successful way to achieve this was by cooperation rather than by competition, and that socialism was therefore superior to free enterprise and capitalism. Unfortunately, I did not allow for human nature and the fact that society works best when people are free to use their initiative and strive for themselves, and at the same time contribute to society. Now that I am older I appreciate that so long as the law properly regulates free enterprise and there is equality of opportunity that allows everyone the opportunity of realising their potential, competition and free enterprise are the best ways of harnessing man's energy and creative powers.

At about this time, possibly in response to meeting Peter Padfield and Michael Rhodes, but also as part of growing up and coming to terms with the world outside myself, I became aware of a sense of mission and a feeling that in some as yet unspecified way I had to do something special with my life. For the moment I was satisfied with being a seaman, but deep down I knew that one day that would have to change and that I would need to pursue a different way of life. In the meantime the sense of mission I felt energised me and lit me up and gave me a *joie-de-vive* that filled me with compassion and made me want to enquire about the world, and at times gave me a feeling of such sheer joy that I felt I might take-off and fly up into the sky.

*

As on previous ships, when we were near land Peter and I kept watches on the bridge and assisted the officers with the navigation of the ship, and on ocean voyages worked like members of the crew – holystoning the ship's wooden decks, chipping rust, painting the ship and doing more skilled work such as sewing canvas, splicing ropes and occasionally splicing wires. When we were off duty in port we played tennis with Michael or hiked in the hills around Wellington, Lyttleton, or the Bluff in the South Island of New Zealand. If nothing much was happening in the evenings we played cards in Michael's cabin with the ship's hairdresser, an old rogue named Vic Higham, who had a pointed beard and looked like Van Dyke. On one occasion Peter and I even managed to talk our way into a party of young New Zealanders who were travelling inland to spend the weekend skiing in the Southern Alps, near the mountain resort of Queenstown in the wild southern part of the South Island of New Zealand.

During the second voyage I made on the *Gothic*, the chief officer summoned me to his cabin while we were in Melbourne.

"Model," he growled, looking up from the table at which he was sitting, reading a novel. "During the outward voyage some of the bags of cement in No 3 hold broke and spilt their contents. Cement from them has solidified and blocked one of the pipes draining the bilge. I want you to take a chisel and get down in the hold and unblock it! And I don't want you to be long about it! The job has to be finished before we leave port."

The words 'get down in the hold and unblock it!' and 'I don't want you to be long about it!' were typical of the way Mr Portmann spoke to me.

Mr Portmann was an extremely muscular dour fair-haired Scot of Scandinavian decent who rarely said anything much to anybody and almost never said anything nice to Peter or me, and yet in a cack-handed way I think he quite liked me. He was the strongest man I have ever met and if for no other reason than that I admired him. On one occasion I saw him lift one end of a steel beam that probably weighed almost half a ton, in order that a seaman might slip a piece of wood under it to protect the wooden deck on which it was lying. When he was serving on one of Shaw Savill's old coal-burning ships he saved a cadet I knew from being beaten-up by a couple of tough drunken Liverpool firemen by literally getting hold of each of them by the scruff of the neck and banging their heads together and knocking them unconscious.

In theory the simplest and most efficient way of clearing the bilge would have been to employ a firm of engineers from the shore to cut away the pipe with an oxy-acetylene burner and replace it. But that would have cost several hundred pounds and would have delayed the ship by several days, as the bilge was in a refrigerated hold and it would have been necessary to remove and later replace a large quantity of highly inflammable insulating material and the wooden planking that covered it near the pipe.

The hold was over 70 feet deep and was empty and in complete darkness as I descended into it. The only light I had was a torch and a travelling light on the end of a very long electric wire. As I made my way down the ladder into the darkness it felt as if I was descending from the dome of a cathedral into its dark interior. Down, down I went, down into its vast interior, which was the size of a large warehouse. Outside, the Melbourne summer was reaching its climax and the temperature was in the nineties; at the bottom of the hold it was pitch black and insufferably hot.

The bilge was like a gutter more than two feet deep, running along the inside of the ship, and the pipe that drained it was in the bottom of it. The only way I could reach the pipe was by lying flat on the deck and extending my arm down into the bilge as far I could. Except for an hour at mealtimes and when I finished at night, for three days I lay cut-off from the world, sweating and working in darkness lit only by a small cone of light, with my chest and belly lying against the deck, chipping away as best I could, ramming a builder's chisel up and down with my arm in the hope of breaking-off bits of cement.

It was like trying to shovel the snow off Mount Everest. At first nothing happened, although by lunchtime of the first day I had begun to retrieve small pieces of cement and by the end of the day the chisel had advanced about an inch. Satisfied that I had made some progress, covered in cement dust and looking more like a snowman than an officer-cadet, I reported to Mr Portmann, who merely grunted and turned away.

By the afternoon of the second day the chisel had advanced about six inches into the pipe, and cautiously I poured some water into it to see if it was clear, but the pipe simply filled and did not drain away.

As I was about to pack up for the day I heard footsteps echoing on the ladder leading into the hold and saw a small globe of light descending towards me. At first I thought Mr Portmann was coming to see how I was getting on, but instead it was the ship's carpenter, who had certain responsibilities for the bilges.

"How's it going then, Model, boy?" he asked, handing me a bar of chocolate. "I see old Portmann's got you sorting out his mess for him? He's a bugger, if ever there was one, making you do this job. Pretty penny it would have cost him if he'd had the job done by a shore firm, I can tell you."

By lunchtime on the third day the heat was beginning to overpower me and I felt very tired. It was Saturday and in theory at lunchtime I should have been off for the weekend. But the water I had poured into the pipe the previous day was still there, and it was clear that I would have to continue. As I climbed slowly up the ladder for lunch I felt a sense of hopelessness. I had sweated several pints of fluid that morning and once again I was covered from head to foot in cement dust. The nerves in my arm vibrated and tingled from the shock of pounding the chisel up and down, and the palm of my hand was blistered. Surely, I thought as I stood on the deck at the top of the hold, blinking in the glare of the midday sun, I don't have to spend my youth working like this, slaving away in darkness in the bottom of a ship? I thought of Gerald studying law in London, and the three Australian sisters, Dorothy, Anne and Shirley, spending gilded youths little more than a mile away. But there was no way out of it; I knew that after lunch I would have to go down into the hold and start chipping away at the cement again.

At five o'clock I began to think about packing up for the day, and was contemplating the unpleasant prospect of having to face Mr Portmann and agree to work on Sunday, when suddenly I was aware that the water I had poured into the pipe had drained away and that the job was almost finished.

At six o'clock, exhausted but strangely content, I packed up my tools and reported to Mr Portmann.

"Took you long enough, then!" he growled, without looking up from the book he was still reading.

You pig, I thought, although deep down I did not care what he thought or said. I was so exhausted that I was beyond the reach of his remarks. Taking leave of him, I made my way onto the boat deck and stood watching the sun descend in the sky over the Melbourne docks. I felt relaxed. I had done the job I had been asked to do and my mind had been set free, and the sense of exhaustion I had experienced had given way to a feeling of euphoria. So what if Mr Portmann is an arrogant pig, I thought, he has no idea of the impact of the things he says. In a very real sense, I felt unassailable and that nothing unpleasant could really affect me, not even Mr Portmann and the offensive way he spoke to me.

*

The mood that clearing the pipe had induced in me lasted for several days and was in part probably responsible for an incident that occurred off Gabo Island, as we rounded the southeast corner of Australia a few days later. It was about 5 p.m. on a balmy afternoon. I was on the bridge assisting the fourth officer with the navigation of the ship. The bows of the ship were rising and falling slowly as they cut like a knife through a glassy sea. Far away on the western horizon, the hills of New South Wales blended into a blue haze that was almost indistinguishable from the blue of the sky. It was a time of magic; a time for man and a time for God. Until I was required to make the next observation of the ship's position I had nothing to do but to pace up and down and keep a lookout for other ships. Suddenly, as I did so I became aware that I was becoming very excited. A strange beam of white light seemed to be shining onto my forehead and from there to be flowing into my mind. With the light came a message. Be of good cheer, it seemed to say, you are no longer an outsider or as isolated as you think you are, but are part of the world, part of this late afternoon, part of the ship and part of everything around you. It doesn't matter how badly Mr Portmann has treated you. To be happy, all you have to do is to love him and to love everyone in the world.

For almost an hour the beam and its message kept streaming into my head, telling me that I had a place in the scheme of things, and that my future was to be one of service. It was heady stuff, and as I paced up and down, for the first time in my life I felt that I was connected to the world around me.

I cannot say how much that event consciously affected my future, but at about that time I began to realise that perhaps I did not want to stay at sea for the rest of my life. For one thing, I had observed that the life of a captain in a company like Shaw Savill was unattractive. He was responsible for everything that happened on a ship, but had nothing to do for days or even weeks at a time on long ocean voyages. At sea, the navigation and administration of the ship were divided among the officers, and any interference by the captain was resented and it was made clear to him by both verbal and non-verbal communication that he was unwelcome. "What does the old bugger want?" was likely to be whispered sufficiently loud for him to almost hear if he came onto the bridge to take sights of the midday sun or stars in the early morning or evening. Some captains responded to this by occupying their time with hobbies such as doing woodwork or painting, or on passenger ships, by entertaining the passengers. Others, like Champagne Charlie, took to the bottle. I had not appreciated this when I had chosen the sea as a career. In addition, I was now old enough to appreciate that at some stage of my life I might want to marry, and that being away from home on long voyages for months at a time was fine for a single man, but could pose difficulties for a married man.

But what sort of work could I do if I left the sea? For months I cast around trying to think of an alternative occupation. I did not want to end up in a dead-end job, but after two years on the *Worcester* and almost three years as a cadet, all I knew about were ships and the sea. Instinct told me that I would hate a shore-job such as ships' surveyor or harbour pilot, and that I would not like to be a shore-based manager in a shipping company such as Shaw Savill. Instinct also told me that I was not the type to like a desk job or pursue a career such as law or accountancy, or engineering or architecture. For a while I thought about trying to become a writer like Somerset Maugham, or to use my experience of the sea to write like Joseph Conrad, a Pole who had spent years at sea in the British Merchant Navy. But although I was bubbling over with ideas and reactions to the world, I knew I lacked the imagination to construct the plots and stories necessary to convey my ideas.

Someone suggested that I might become a schoolteacher, but Michael Rhodes said it was not academic enough and would not challenge me sufficiently. In the end I put off the decision, and instead, concentrated on trying to get my second mate's ticket, the exam that would entitle me to be an officer.

*

From Sydney the *Gothic* headed up the coast to Brisbane to collect a cargo of beef for the U.K., and I went on the 12-4 watch with the second officer, Mr Green, a small dark swarthy Welshman with rabbit black eyes and a ring of black hair around an otherwise bald head.

At mealtimes, which as always were in the royal dining room, the officers who were not on watch chatted among themselves at the top of the table, while Michael, Peter and I and the other assistant purser chatted at the bottom. At lunch one day, Mr Green interrupted the conversation, and addressing the whole table, blurted out in a loud voice, "One good thing Hitler did was to exterminate the Jews!"

Goodness knows what prompted him to say that. Perhaps the officers had already been talking among themselves about the holocaust. Immediately, Mr Ganson, the radio officer, added, "Only pity is that he didn't exterminate them all! Vermin... rats, that's what they are!"

Silence ensued and everyone looked at me and waited to see how I would react. In my chair I squirmed with embarrassment and indignation, and my cheeks felt as if they were on fire. Should I respond and accept the gauntlet that had been thrown down at me, or should I simply ignore it? It would have been easy to accept the challenge. I was bigger than Mr Green or any of the officers, except Mr Portmann, who had his own table in the passenger dining-saloon, and I could have beaten them up. But would it be worth it...? In a split second I had to make up my mind whether the pleasure of giving Mr Green and Mr Ganson a thrashing was worth risking my career at sea? At the time there were no laws against racialism and I knew that if I hit them I would be accused of assaulting an officer and would be unceremoniously drummed out of the Merchant Navy. On the other side of the table, I was aware of Michael's eyes boring into me and thought he was signalling that I should ignore the remarks as simple ignorance. In the end, my need to be accepted as an ordinary person overrode any other thoughts I might have had and I did what I had always done in such situations, which cowardly or not, was to hope I could hide my embarrassment and that I would not have to acknowledge that I was partly Jewish and apparently different from other people.

Twenty minutes later I was back on the bridge with Mr Green.

"Sorry, Bloke, I didn't mean anything. I wasn't getting at you," he said with embarrassment. He gave an embarrassed little neigh of a laugh and from then on was his usual friendly self. As I had not accepted his challenge, we were both able to ignore the incident and behave normally, but afterwards when I thought about it I realised that although it is usually dormant, anti-Semitism was and still is just beneath the surface of normal everyday life in the West.

*

After three voyages on the *Gothic*, I transferred for my last voyage as a cadet to the *Corinthic*, sister ship of the *Gothic*. Like the *Gothic*, the *Corinthic* carried eighty first class passengers, as well as thousands of tons of cargo.

s.s. Corinthic alongside a quay in Hobart, Tasmania

For the first time in the three years that I had been at sea, I was treated with respect and not as the lowest form of life in the Merchant Navy. When I was on watch the captain, Captain A.C. Jones, sometimes came onto the bridge to talk to me, and the officers treated me as one of them.

Captain Jones was a sober, middle-aged man who smoked large Havana cigars and sported a bristly grey crew-cut that stuck up from his head like the flat top of a broom. Perhaps he liked me because of a quotation from Confucius that with youthful enthusiasm I had hung on one of the bulkheads in my cabin, saying, *It is not truth that makes man great, but man that makes truth great.*

The occasions on which Captain Jones spoke to me were usually when I was on watch during the evening or the early part of the night. From his cabin he could see me using the Aldis lamp, which was like a large torch, to flash messages by Morse code to passing ships. Afterwards, sometimes he would come out to ask me about the reply I had received.

The form of these conversations with other ships followed a standard protocol, *What ship? Where from? Where bound?* plus a few comments such as *Bon voyage.* Generally only Naval ships or merchant ships from Northern European countries replied. Ships from the rest of the world were more reticent, leaving me to wonder if the officers on them were competent with the Morse code?

The first occasion that the Captain came out to ask me about a message I had received was when we were going through the archipelago of islands that separate the Atlantic Ocean from the Caribbean Sea. In his hand was a long Havana cigar.

"Tell me, Model, what was that ship we just passed?"

"The Bengal Prince, Sir. Bound from Rotterdam to Tokyo."

My only fear on these occasions was that I might not correctly have read the flickering message from the other ship and as a consequence would make a fool of myself in front of the captain. But he understood when occasionally that happened.

The chief officer, Mr Young, was a tiny bird of a man who was known as Tom. On the night before we arrived in Auckland I went to his cabin to call him at a quarter-to-four in the morning for the 4-8 watch.

"One bell, Mr Young, Sir! Time to get up, Sir. I'll be back in ten minutes," I called into the darkness.

I attempted to switch on the cabin light, but the bulb appeared to be broken and the light would not switch on. At five-to-four I went back to his cabin and called him again, and as the room was still in darkness and was permeated by the silence that suggests that someone is sleeping, I went up to his bed to shake him.

"Mr Young, sir! Time to get up, sir!" I called with a certain urgency.

At the same time I advanced my hand into the darkness and got hold of what I thought was his shoulder. Only it was not *his* shoulder. Immediately I knew I had hold of the soft flesh and silky hair of a woman. In a shocked flash I realised she could be only one person – a young woman who was travelling out to New Zealand to be married the next day.

When I was certain they were awake I made my way back to the bridge. God! I thought as I entered the wheelhouse, after witnessing that I'll never allow a woman of mine travel alone on a ship!

Goodness knows what the woman saw in Tom. For one thing, he drank heavily and reeked of tobacco. For another, he was a tiny sparrow of a man, no more than 5 feet 5 inches tall, with coal-black eyes and plastered-down thick oily black hair. Nonetheless, a few hours after she had left his bed, he stood in for her father, and dressed in his best uniform, escorted her up the aisle of the church to be married.

One evening later in the voyage Tom was so drunk that when he was going ashore he fell from the gangway and was almost crushed between the ship and the dock. Fortunately he was fished out quickly and escaped with only a fractured leg for which he was in plaster for several weeks.

The second officer on the *Corinthic* was what I would later call an *FLG* or *Funny Looking Guy*, as his face sloped away from his lips to his neck without any chin. From the hurt look in his eyes and the way he leaned backwards when he was talking to you, as if he was trying to escape, I could not help but wonder whether Mr Donald Fox, as he was called, had been beaten or in some other way abused as a child?

One day as we were chatting in the chartroom on our way home across the Pacific Ocean, he said, "Douglas, I hear you're thinking of becoming a doctor... Funny really, as I'm thinking of becoming a dentist..."

I was taken aback by what he said. For fear of jeopardizing my career with Shaw Savill I had not mentioned the possibility of changing careers or trying to become a doctor to anyone other than Michael Rhodes and Peter Padfield, both of who were no longer serving with the company.

To divert Mr Fox's attention, I pretended to concentrate on the column of smoke rising lazily from the cigarette protruding from a yellow cigarette holder he was holding between his teeth. How on earth does he know what I am thinking, I wondered, as I hardly know myself whether or not I am going to change careers?

In an effort to divert him further, I said, "Well, I wish you well. I am sure dentistry is a great career, but my mind's set on getting my second mate's ticket and staying with Shaw Savill!"

"You wait and see! As soon as I've got my Master's certificate, I'll be training to be a dentist,' he replied.

But I knew that he would not. From the way his eyes avoided mine as he spoke, I realised that the idea of becoming a dentist was just a pipedream that helped him deal with the fact that he was fed up with being at sea and away from home for months at a time.

Later during the voyage, as we neared the Panama Canal I asked the ship's doctor what he thought of someone like me trying to become a doctor and whether there were too many doctors in Britain at that time.

Dr Mackey was a frail old Scottish GP who was well into his seventies and was working on the ship as a way of occupying himself during his retirement.

"Well, the authorities ashore say there are too many doctors," he said slowly, fixing me with his watery old man's blue eyes, "but I'm sure there's always room for one more, particularly if he is good."

*

As the three years of my apprenticeship drew to a close I began to feel more confident about myself and was no longer quite so afraid of what people might think of me. The idea of being of service to society appealed to me, and one morning when the captain was due to make his rounds, in a fit of youthful idealism, with a grin I got down on my knees, and much to the amazement of the other cadet, in an act of subjugation and an attempt to be of service, I scrubbed the deck of his cabin, as well as mine.

*

The ship arrived in Liverpool and berthed in the Gladstone Dock two days before Christmas. As soon as she was tied up I asked the chief officer if Roger Bean, the other cadet and I could go home for Christmas, as apart from one officer and a watchman on the gangway, the ship would be deserted for the two or three days of the holiday. Mr Young readily agreed, but Mr Fox, who was the officer who had been selected to stay behind, said that as the carpenter was to be allowed home, either Bean or I would have to stay behind in order to sound the bilges each day, as required by law.

"But why should it be one of us?" I asked defiantly, as I stood in the doorway of Mr Fox's cabin. "That's the carpenter's job, not ours. And in any case, it will only take half-an-hour each day. Surely you don't expect us to miss one of the few Christmases we will ever have at home because of half-an-hour's work a day that isn't our responsibility?"

Mr Fox replied with his usual pained look, but was adamant, so without further ado I packed Bean off home on the next train. Then, so that my father should know what I was about to do, I phoned him and told him that as I had been away from home for four months and had not been at home for several Christmases, I was going to risk being sacked for disobeying an order, and was coming home on the next train.

My father cautioned me to be careful, but did not forbid me from coming.

On December 27th, the day after Boxing Day, I returned to the ship after a memorable family Christmas at home. As I stepped into the officers' accommodation I expected Tom to call me and tell me I had been sacked. Instead, both he and Mr Fox greeted me with smiles and asked if I had had a good time? At first I was suspicious about their intentions; then I found out what had happened. While I was at home my father had omitted to tell me that after I had phoned to say I was coming home he had phoned the company's head office in London and had spoken to Captain Meyers, one of the company's most senior managers, who after prevaricating and speaking about the needs of the Service, had finally agreed and had sent a telegram to the ship saying that I was to be released for the duration of the holiday.

It was an experience that helped to shape my attitude to the future. So long as an order seemed reasonable, I would obey it, but if it seemed inappropriate or stupid I would either ignore it or contest it.

*

With only weeks before my apprenticeship was due to finish I realised I had to make up my mind about my future. Should I continue with a career at sea and try to become captain of a large ship, or should I say to hell with it and pursue a different pathway?

The sheer audacity and ridiculousness of trying to become a doctor appealed to me, and the more I thought about it the more I was attracted to the idea, both as a challenge and as a career I might like, as it would allow me to serve society in a personal way and would stretch me academically in a way that the Merchant Navy did not. Naively, I thought that universities were places of wisdom and that if I went to one some of it would rub off on me. Now I realise that no matter how educated they may be, in the final analysis most people are ruled by their emotions and prejudices rather than by reason, and that those with prestigious degrees are just as likely to be mean or generous, and to make decisions based on their prejudices, as those who are relatively uneducated, and that people who work on the land or the shop-floor are as likely to be wise as those who have been to university.

Although I was not conscious of it at the time, I realise now that another reason I thought I might like to be a doctor was that I wished to better myself and move up, as I saw it, in society. But there were obstacles to the idea. At that time only five per cent of the British population went to university, and to think that I might be one of them seemed absurd. Which medical school, if any, would be interested in taking a sailor? All I knew about was ships, stowing cargo, ship's stability and how to splice ropes and wires and take sights of the sun and the stars. Although I had matriculated before leaving John Lyon School and therefore according to an old rule fulfilled the entry requirements to university, I did not have any A-levels. Against such a background, I felt that trying to get into medical school would be like trying to climb Mount Everest, particularly as the competition for places in medical school was so keen and only the brightest students were accepted.

And then there were my parents. What would they say after paying so much for me to be educated on the *Worcester* – probably that I was risking my future on some hare-brained scheme.

Taking courage by the hand, I decided to speak to them when I was at home studying for my second mate's certificate.

"But the sea's such a fine career. I thought you were going to be the captain of a large ship," my mother said when we spoke about it as we stood in the kitchen.

"I know, Mum," I said, trying to hide the embarrassment I felt. "But I simply can't see myself being at sea for the rest of my life. It's great when you're young, but not when you're fifty and want a home and to be at home with your wife. I know it must be a great disappointment for you and Dad, but I can't help it, I want to do something that will help society in a more personal way and stretch my mind more."

My father was more direct and said bluntly that he still had two other sons to educate, and that if I left the sea I would have to fend for myself.

Other people were just as discouraging. Dr Begg, our family doctor, said to my father as they were playing golf, "Tell him that at his age he's too old to start five long years of arduous study. By now his brain will have hardened and he won't be able to take in all the facts he will be expected to learn."

Dr Thomas, an irascible retired old Oxford don with whom my father also played golf, said, "He will want to get married and won't stick it out! In any case it will cost too much!"

Other people were just as pessimistic. Some spoke of the money it would cost and the time it would take; others that I would have to learn Latin and that the medical profession was oversubscribed.

So my days as an apprentice came to an end and I began to think about life as an officer, and the decision I might possibly make.

7

An Officer at Last

It is the hour before dawn and the sky is still dark. The ship on which I am serving is racing southeast across the Indian Ocean. Above the port bow, the planet Venus hangs in the sky like a great white orb. Further out on the bow, the moon, the second great light of the sky, shines with a ghostly grey glow that lights up the last of the night and casts a shimmering white beam across the sea on which it seems I might almost walk.

On the bridge I am preparing to take four star sights. As the junior officer of the watch I am obliged to work in semidarkness at a small table in the wheelhouse, while the first officer, the senior officer of the watch, works in the comparative good light and comfort of the chartroom. We have been on watch since four in the morning and now it is approaching five. Every few minutes I carry out the first duty of the officer of the watch, which is to keep a lookout, and walk out onto the wing of the bridge to make sure that there aren't any ships bearing down on us.

Preparing sights is a complicated business. We have decided which stars we are going to *take* or *shoot*, and are checking their positions in the sky in the Admiralty Almanac, and are using Norie's Tables to convert our findings into haversines, sines and the like. In all, it takes about twenty-five minutes. Then, as the night fades we wait for the moment when we can see both the stars and the horizon at the same time and, using our sextants, can measure the angle between them to within one sixtieth of a degree.

Using a sextant to take a sight is both challenging and fun, and in a sense is like being a cat stalking its prey. During it we use our judgement to allow for the rolling of the ship, the wind shaking our arm, the fuzziness of the horizon, the cloud that frequently obscures the stars, and the inadequacies of our eyesight and brains. It is an ancient art. Each sight is timed against one of the ship's two chronometers – clocks that have hardly changed since Kendall supplied Captain Cook with an improved version of the clock invented by the Yorkshire man John Harrison in the eighteenth century.

Fifteen minutes later I have finished my calculations and have the ship's position, latitude 11^0 15'N, longitude 60^0 07'E.

Pleased with myself, I walk into the chartroom to grab a cup of tea and a piece of buttered toast. For once I have been quicker than the First Officer.

"What's the matter with you this morning?" I tease him. "Is your brain befuddled or something? Did you not get enough sleep last night?"

"Run away, Laddie," he replies scornfully in a Scots accent, smiling without looking up from the exercise book in which he is completing his calculations. "As usual, I expect you've got it all wrong!"

Laughing, I take my tea out onto the wing of the bridge. In the east, the sky is on fire, while beneath the horizon the sun god prepares to leap from his fiery tomb. It is a time of magic – a time for God and a time for man.

*

My first ship as an officer was the *New Australia*, a strange looking vessel with the bridge right over the bow and a short stubby fore deck. She was about 20,000 tons, which was approximately twice the size of the *Delphic* or the *Waipawa*. She carried fifteen hundred emigrants to Australia and a crew of five hundred.

I was not very pleased with the lowly rank of fifth officer assigned to me or with the mean little bootlace of a gold stripe on my arm, as on practically every other Shaw Savill ship I would have been fourth officer. But there was a reason for my lowly rank. Because she carried so many passengers and crew, the *New Australia* was obliged to have two officers on watch at any one time, and I was the most junior of them.

s.s. New Australia. Note the open doors for loading stores through the side of the ship

The ship had an interesting history. Originally she had been a passenger ship named the *Monarch of Bermuda*, but a fire had so severely damaged her superstructure that she had been abandoned. Fortunately her engines had remained more or less intact, and in 1949 she had been bought by the Ministry of Transport on behalf of the Australian Government and had been rebuilt and handed over to Shaw Savill to be run as an immigrant ship.

The passenger accommodation was a warren of cheaply built cabins, each housing six people with just a bunk, a tin locker, a tiny tin wardrobe and one or two tin drawers for each person. Any heavy baggage the passengers might wish to take was carried in the hold. As a result, although the fare was only £10, most passengers had an uncomfortable voyage. Because of poor ventilation, the air on the lower decks quickly became fetid and acquired the smell of an animal house at the zoo. As a result, many people forsook their cabin and slept on deck as soon as the ship was in a warmer climate. One of my duties on the 4-8 watch was to wake those asleep on the decks and make sure they had gone below by the time the decks were due to be scrubbed at six o'clock. In part I did this by using the ship's loudspeaker system, and in part by walking round the decks and waking those who were not yet up. Prior to this I had no idea what the average middle-aged woman looked like when she woke in the morning. To see adult women stretched out asleep on the deck with their breasts hanging out of their nightdresses like so much blubber, their faces greasy and pale in the early morning light, and their legs sprawling, twisted and stubby, was a disillusioning experience for a young man who had been brought up on a diet of beautiful film stars such as Elizabeth Taylor, Olivia de Havilland, June Allison and Diana Durban.

The officers' lives were very different to those of the passengers. We were housed in considerable comfort beneath the bridge. Life for me was now much easier than it had been as an apprentice. The sense of oppression I had felt during the previous three years had gone. No longer did I feel I was the lowest form of life on the ship. Now most people on board addressed me as *Sir*. My life soon acquired a gentle rhythm. I went on watch for eight hours, slept for eight hours and relaxed and read books or studied for eight hours. I wrote long letters to Michael Rhodes and to my parents, and later to Shirley, the youngest of the three sisters I had met in Melbourne.

Because the *New Australia* did not carry any cargo and the passengers were quickly discharged, our turn-around time at each of the three ports we called at in Australia was a mere forty-eight hours and we were usually back in our home-port of Southampton in just under two months and ten days. As a result I made five voyages during the fifteen months I was on the ship. Southampton suited me well as a base, as I was able to take a bus and hike in the New Forest or visit Michael Rhodes' mother in Portsmouth, just a few miles away.

*

Before leaving England on my first voyage on the *New Australia* I decided to take a correspondence course in chemistry and physics as part of my newly hatched plan to become a doctor. The Seafarer's Education Service in Balham arranged the courses for me. However, on the day after the arrangements had been made I was filled with doubt and indecision. Faced with the reality of having to commit myself, I faltered and decided that the idea of becoming a doctor was preposterous and that the best thing I could do was not to get ideas beyond my ability, and that instead I should stay at sea and do what I knew best; so the following day I sneaked out of our home, and ashamed at being so weak, went secretly to the public phone-box in the street outside and furtively phoned the Seafarer's Education Service and cancelled the courses. For a few days I was irritable as I agonised over the decision I had made. I knew it was not really what I wanted, and several days later, I telephoned the Seafarer's Education Service and reinstated the courses. From then on I was like a guided missile, willing to sacrifice almost anything in order to realise my ambition of becoming a doctor. It was both an obsession and a magnificent dream that would require a steely single-mindedness. I was determined that nothing short of being refused admission to medical school was going to stop me from becoming a doctor and serving society in a more personal way than I was able to do in the Merchant Navy.

I was advised that I should meet my intended tutors before I left England, and so while I was still on leave I went to the home in Ruislip of Mrs Dovey, the lady who was to teach me chemistry. She wanted to assess whether I was capable of studying to A-level standard, and spent the best part of an hour explaining Mendeleev's Periodic Table of the Elements to me, and afterwards asked me questions about it. Satisfied that I had understood, she agreed to take me on. A few days later I went to King's College in London and met Dr Stokes, my physics tutor.

The way I studied was to read the books they recommended for two hours every day I was at sea, and then write answers to the questions at the end of each chapter. Corresponding across the world by post was a slow process and often I waited for more than a month for answers to my queries, but I am eternally grateful to the Seafarers' Education Service and to my tutors for the help they gave me.

Apart from studying, I also arranged to save money for the medical education I hoped to undertake one day. This involved making an *allotment* or financial agreement with a bank for a proportion of my salary to be paid into a savings account. It was an arrangement that every British seaman was entitled to make. I agreed to save three quarters of my salary; the other quarter I kept in the ship to spend while I was away and when I was at home on leave.

*

The route the ship took to Australia was the same every voyage – across the Bay of Biscay, down the west coast of Spain and Portugal, through the Pillars of Hercules or Straits of Gibraltar (with the Rock of Gibraltar to the north and the rock of Jebel Musa on the African coast to the south), along the coast of North Africa and through the enchanted waters of the Mediterranean that the Greeks, the Romans and the Phoenicians had sailed. *The wine dark sea*, Homer had called it. Usually it was calm and sometimes as flat and shiny as a sheet of steel, but at other times it was as ferocious and dangerous as any of the great oceans. At Suez, in scenes reminiscent of the Bible, I saw men in caftans, and donkeys dragging large horizontal wooden wheels round a central pole as they drew water up from beneath the desert.

After Suez, for almost four days the ship steamed down the Red Sea like an ant crawling between the deserts of Egypt on one side and the barren mountains of the Hejaz and the Yemen on the other side. Behind us lay the Peninsula of Sinai. Then it was on to Bab-el-Mandeb, the Gate of Tears at the bottom of the Red Sea, the place where our primitive ancestors are said by some to have come out of Africa to populate the world some 70,000 years ago. From there we turned left into the Gulf of Aden and proceeded east along the coast to the town of Aden, a dried-up sunburnt place of white and grey adobe houses and shops sitting on the edge of the burning Yemeni desert. In Aden we took on oil, and bartered with Arab tradesmen for leather goods and jewellery before plunging into the relatively cool waters of the Indian Ocean and heading for Colombo where we took on fresh water and made trips by taxi to the beach at Mount Lavinia or to the Buddhist Temple of the Tooth in the hills at Candy. The taxis for these trips were ancient and had elongated bonnets and tucked in backs reminiscent of the ones I had seen in Las Palmas three years before.

Sometimes we were diverted, and instead of coming back to England to collect more emigrants, we were dispatched to carry

British or Australian troops from Hong Kong, Singapore or Australia to the wars then raging in Malaya and Korea.

To get to Hong Kong or Singapore from Sydney involved taking on a pilot and making our way north to the southern end of the channel that leads through the Great Barrier Reef, a melange of more than 900 tropical islands and almost 3000 coral reefs, stretching along the coast of Queensland for 1500 miles. Many of the reefs were treacherous and skulked just beneath the surface of the water like crocodiles waiting to pounce and tear apart any ship that strayed too close. In places the channel through the reefs was little more than two or three ships wide, and for the four days we were among the reefs, the pilot was obliged to be on the bridge for most of the time and got very little sleep, as often the coral was so close that from the bridge we could look down almost vertically onto it.

The whole area abounded with evidence of the great eighteenth century navigator, Captain James Cook. Whit Sunday Passage, Daydream Island and Paradise Island – to mention but a few – were all named by him. Such was his skill that many of the depths of water and points of land on the charts we used were where he had placed them more than two hundred years before, using only the simple instruments available to him at the time.

Before we got to the Barrier Reef, while we were still in open seas off the east coast of Australia, at times we saw great whales leaping clean out of the sea. They were an awesome sight as they leapt clear of the water and left a space between their gleaming black bodies and the ocean. The noise of the splash they made as they fell back into the water could be heard for at least a quarter of a mile.

The abiding memory I have of Korea is of poverty and people so poor that they appeared to be clad in rags and to live on little more than a bowl of rice a day. Compare that with the wealth and high standard of living they enjoy today.

On one occasion we were diverted to Hiroshima and its port Kure on the island of Honshu in Japan. The approach to the port involved steaming for mile after mile among the islands of the Inland Sea, a magical stretch of water that separates the islands of Honshu, Shikoku and Kyushu. Everywhere there were steep conical hills, terraced to the top in order that no piece of cultivatable land might be wasted.

The main street in Kure was full of bars and brothels, and decorated with neon signs strung across the street and lit up in Japanese. The sign above one of the brothels was in English and read *The Fucci-u-tu*, which I will leave you to interpret, as you will.

On the day after we arrived in Kure a group of officers from the ship were taken on a conducted tour of Hiroshima. In 1954 the centre of the city was still in practically the same state of devastation and destruction that it had been in immediately after the atom bomb had exploded over it in 1945. As we wandered among the piles of debris, the Japanese people we encountered stared at us, primarily I suspect, because we were so large and – to them – looked possibly clumsy, and our group contained a nurse, and I suspect that most of them had not seen a European woman before.

One of the few structures that were still standing in the centre of the city was the steel framework of the temple over which the bomb is thought to have exploded, etched against the sky like a skeleton from which the flesh has been ripped.

After our visit to Hiroshima we were taken to a holy mountain where I became very breathless climbing the hundreds of steps up to the small temple on the top. Later the same day we visited a shrine that consisted of two tall red wooden posts standing in the sea with a decorated crossbar stretching between them. The following evening we were invited to watch a school of trainee geisha girls performing traditional dances, but I was still stupidly shy in the company of young women, and foolishly refused to go, instead, opting to stay on board and read in my cabin.

After a few months of diversions to various countries in the Far East I began to feel that I had had enough of the tropical sun and the Pacific Ocean, and on a particularly hot afternoon as I stood in the wing of the bridge as the ship cut through a calm blue sea, I found myself fantasizing, of all things, about the pleasure of walking in Liverpool on a cold grey drizzly day.

*

On the first voyage I made on the *New Australia* I invited Shirley, the youngest of the Barnard sisters to come on board the ship on the day we docked in Fremantle. She had completed her training in Melbourne as a physiotherapist and had taken a job in Perth for a year. I was now gently in love with her and was so excited and yet full of trepidation at the prospect of seeing her that I could not sleep the night before the ship arrived. Instead I lay awake anticipating the coming day. To me, Shirley was Dresden china, a princess, the love of my life; but by no stretch of the imagination was I Prince Charming. In my dreams I might hope that I was, but in reality I felt like a clod. How then could I possibly hope that she might be in love with me? Would she even turn up? And if she did so, what should I do to amuse her? The best I could think of was to invite her to tea on board. But what would I talk about? In Melbourne there had always been a bevy of boys buzzing excitedly around her and her two sisters – the three of whom I called 'the Beautiful Barnard Sisters.'

After twisting and turning for a couple of hours in my bunk I looked at my watch. Eleven o'clock. Oh God, I thought, in forty-five minutes I will have to get up and go on watch. I'll have great bags under my eyes and I'll never be able to concentrate or keep awake when the time finally comes for me to go down onto the dock to see if she has arrived. Through the porthole of my cabin I could hear the distant roar of the bow-wave as the ship slowly rose and fell in the sea and cut its way through the night, throwing water to either side of the bows in a myriad of small green phosphorescent lights.

At just after noon the following day Shirley and a friend named Jennifer came roaring down to the ship on motor scooters. Their arrival caused something of a stir on the dock, and the dockers and the crew eyed them longingly as they parked their bikes and followed me up the gangway. Both were blonde and dressed chicly in bright red jumpers and red tartan trousers with berries cocked cheekily on the sides of their heads. As I led them along the deck towards my cabin I was aware that there were many things I wanted to say to Shirley, but could not say, as I was as creased-up as ever in the presence of a girl. I wanted to touch her and tell her about the ideas that were bursting forth from me, but all I managed were a few clumsy words.

Fortunately, once we were in my cabin Shirley was so busy that apparently she did not notice my awkwardness. Her blue eyes flashed and her blonde hair shimmered as she busied herself distributing the bag of pastries she had brought with her and serving coffee from the pot the officers' steward had prepared for me. She told me that she had devised a plan for me to act as a messenger between herself and her family in Melbourne, and once the conversation had become structured in that way I felt easier and more able to cope with her until at last the moment arrived for her to go ashore, as the ship was about to sail.

"Well, Doug, I guess that's all," she said. "We'd better be running along. It's been great fun, but much as I would like to, I don't think we should stay on board when the ship sails!"

As she removed the plate from her lap and stood up in preparation for leaving I was again aware of the light from the porthole playing on her hair. How wonderful it would be, I thought, if she did not have to go, but instead, as she had hinted, could accompany me to Melbourne. Suddenly I wanted to blurt out that I loved her, but I knew that I could not, even if Jennifer had not been there.

"Shall I write to you?" I asked awkwardly.

"Of course," she replied. "I'm not very good at letter writing, but I promise I'll reply."

She touched my arm and looked up into my eyes with such a warm smile that suddenly I realised that it was possible that she might feel the same way about me as I felt about her, and that the ordinary things we were talking about were merely a cover for the things we probably both wanted to say, but dared not say.

"I'll see you down the gangway... It's been super seeing you. Drive carefully on those bikes," was all I managed to blurt out.

I escorted them along the narrow passageway that led to the gangway.

At the top of the gangway she turned to face me.

"Please don't leave it too long before you come again," she said. "Remember I depend on you as my messenger!"

I was aware of my heart pounding. There was something in her voice and the way she looked at me that told me I had interpreted her feelings correctly and that she was giving me a signal. The dear creature, I thought, she does care, she does mean it! An almost irresistible urge to break down the physical barriers between us took hold of me and I wondered if I dare risk kissing her? Following that thought, I was seized by a feeling that I wanted to undo our skins and wrap her up inside me and hug her to me until we were one, but at the same time I knew that I was afraid that she might reject me and that I lacked the courage to do even part of what I was thinking. To my mind she was still an untouchable princess, not a real woman of flesh and bones. Even so I could not resist bending forward and giving her a peck of a kiss on the cheek.

She blushed and touched my arm.

"You're such a dear man," she said. Then she was gone and I was watching as she and Jennifer disappeared down the gangway.

Later that night the second mate, Burtie Singleton, teased me about her as we stood in the wing of the bridge on the 12-4 watch and watched as the ship raced through the darkness and passed the light at Cape Leeuwin on the south-west corner of Australia.

"See you're a bit of dark horse, then, eh, Five-o! A girl in every port! Haven't got one or two to spare for me, have you?" he asked in a broad Scouse accent.

I shrugged and grinned as if to imply that I had lots of girls at my disposal, but said nothing, as inside me I knew I was not such a hell of a guy, and that for the most part it was fantasies of one sort or another that kept me going, fantasies about girls with big breasts and strong thighs, who in my imagination I could kiss and undress and romp around with as I sought the relief I so often needed.

Six days later I almost missed the ship as it prepared to leave Melbourne for Sydney. I had been fulfilling my role as messenger and had been to see Shirley's family in Parliament Square. Her mother had cooked a delicious thick tournedos steak for me, but it had taken longer to prepare than expected, and the evening rush hour was well underway by the time I finished eating and it was difficult to get a taxi back to the ship. As a result I just managed to scramble onto the gangway as it was about to be raised.

Over the following months I corresponded regularly with Shirley, but it was a case of love by proxy. For if the truth is known, in a funny sort of way it suited me not to see her too often as then I could keep her as a creation of my imagination and interpret her as I liked without the risks and commitments that seeing her regularly might have involved.

My inability to communicate extended beyond Shirley. One night on a voyage carrying troops from Sydney to Singapore I stood in the warm tropical darkness on the Boat Deck and peered through the window of the ship's main lounge at a party of army officers, dressed in mess kit, entertaining a group of army nurses dressed in white uniforms with red capes on their shoulders and little white caps on their heads. Because of the roar of the sea and the thickness of the glass in the window I could not hear what they were saying as they clicked glasses and laughed and talked animatedly. But I could see how easy they appeared to be with one another, and wondered why I was not like them. Then the answer came to me; it's because I'm a loner, an outsider. I am different to them.

*

After my first voyage on the *New Australia* I was promoted to fourth officer, and joined the first officer on the 4-8 watch. Willie Newport was a minute prematurely bald Scot with a posh Kelvinside accent and a bubbly personality that almost fizzed at times. I loved working with Willie, as he made me feel good. "I think I'll give a party…" he would say, fixing me with a mischievous blue-eyed smile, or "After we finish our watch, Douglas, I think we should get a few beers and go down to the pool for a swim. Are you going to come with me, Douglas?"

However, despite his joie de vivre, Willie had a steely side to his character. When two of the quartermasters were brought before him in Melbourne on a charge of absenting themselves from their watch on the gangway he concluded that they were drunk and incapable of performing their duties. Toby Jug, as one of them was known because of his red complexion, short rotund stature and tendency to walk on his backside, and Castle, the other, were among the most reliable and longest serving members of the crew. They claimed they weren't drunk but had simply misread the duty rota and were ashore at the time they should have been manning the gangway. But Willie was adamant and would not listen to them. Instead, he had them arraigned before the captain who fined them a week's pay and threatened them with a dishonourable discharge when we got back to England.

It was a draconian punishment, out of all proportion to what they were alleged to have done, and as I got on well with them, they came to my cabin and asked if I would intercede on their behalf. Willie was furious when afterwards I went to his cabin and said I thought they were innocent and were telling the truth.

"Douglas!" he said, rising up onto his toes and then banging his heels down on the deck as if to make up for his short stature and emphasise his authority, "Of course they were drunk! Of course they are guilty!"

"Look!" he added in an almost blind fury. "You'll learn! You're just a very junior officer. A decision has been made; they have been found guilty, and that's that! Whether we're right or wrong, we've got to stick with it. Otherwise there will be no discipline on the ship."

But I did not agree, and still do not for that matter. Why when you're in a situation like that can't you say you are sorry, you made a mistake, and that you'll do your best to rectify it?

A few days later over a beer in the second officer, Burtie Singleton's cabin, one of the other officers asked me why I had taken the crew's side and whether I was a Communist? A similar situation occurred a couple of months later and I realised I was beginning to acquire something of a reputation for being, if not a troublemaker, at least independent enough for another of my colleagues to ask if my perceived independence was because I had influence in the upper echelons of the Company?

*

After two trips Willie was transferred to another passenger ship and was replaced by an officer named Harry George who was almost the exact opposite of Willie – thin, swarthy and introspective with a few sparse hairs plastered down across the top of his bald scalp. He smoked heavily and constantly used his forefinger and thumb to pluck pieces of tobacco from the tip of his tongue. I got on well with him and sensed that deep down he was unhappy and frustrated. He had served in the Royal Navy Reserve during the war and by the time he joined Shaw Savill was too old to become a captain. He dreamed of leaving the sea but was cautious about making an irrevocable decision and used me as a sounding board for his plans. I was with him when he stayed up all night deliberating about whether to take a job as a pilot in Port Moresby in New Guinea. "Four-o," he said when we were on watch the following morning, "You've a good boy! You listened to me going on and on and as a reward I'm going to take you for lunch at the Hotel Australia when we get to Sydney... Don't worry about money, it'll be on me!"

We went on our first day off duty. We were two sailors eleven thousand miles from home and we had a great time and got thoroughly drunk. First we consumed the best part of half a bottle of gin; then we drank a couple of bottles of wine. I ate two portions of Lobster Newberg and ever since have been searching for a restaurant that prepares it in the same magical way. By five o'clock we were so drunk that we needed help to get up from our chairs and were grateful to the doorman of the hotel who ordered a taxi for us and bundled us off back to the ship.

*

The mess-room where the officers ate on the *New Australia* was a large barn of a place that accommodated about forty people – eight deck officers (including the captain, a cadet and me), twenty or so engineers, three radio officers, two doctors, three nurses, three pursers, and two passenger hostesses.

The steward who served the table at which I ate with the first officer and the officers junior to him, was a tiny weasel of a man. I doubt if Johnson would have got a job in most walks of life. He was a poor little gnome barely five feet tall, who lacked any personality and was shabby and none too clean. He was bald with a semicircle of grey dank greasy tangled hair above his ears. His steward's white jacket was usually grubby, his grey little Hitler moustache was stained brown with nicotine, and his fingernails were dirty and nicotine stained. He looked out at the world through thick-lensed spectacles that made his eyes look like small marbles. Yet unattractive as he was, for some strange reason I quite liked him or at least felt sorry for him, and was curious when he went missing for several days while we were en route from Aden to Colombo. When finally he reappeared and was serving at table again I asked him what had happened, to which he replied reticently, "I daren't tell you, sir."

"What do you mean, you daren't tell me?"

He stood silently by the side of the table, then after about half a minute a salty tear ran down the stubbly furrows on his cheeks and a minute or so later he was telling me the story of what had happened. Unlikely as it may seem, out of sheer bloody-mindedness the other three men with whom he shared a cabin were taking turns to stay up at night and keep him awake. As a consequence he was too tired to work.

The story roused my sympathy and I sent a note down to one of the men in his cabin asking if he would come to see me at eleven o'clock the following morning.

At the prescribed hour, a slim young man dressed in a clean white shirt and blue jeans knocked at my door. I welcomed him and offered him a seat, a cigarette and a can of beer. He had no idea why I wanted to see him and seemed surprised when I said, "I want to talk to you about a rather delicate matter."

I told him that I had heard from a third party that someone in their cabin was bullying Johnson and appealed to him as a responsible member of the crew to put a stop it, and was gratified to learn that after our talk, the bullying stopped at once. The man I had spoken to never suspected that the source of my information was Johnson himself, and later I got feed-back that he told his friends he was ashamed of himself and had never been so thoroughly told off at the same time as being offered a beer.

*

During the five voyages I made on the *New Australia* I served under three captains. My relationships with Captain Fisher and Captain Hart were fine, but Captain Trent and I took an instant dislike to one another. Captain Trent was the most senior captain in the Company and was later knighted, and then elevated to the House of Lords for services to the Merchant Navy. But although he was respected throughout the company, he was also known as *Miserable Mike* on account of his forlorn manner and sad brown St Bernard's eyes.

By the time he joined the *New Australia* I was an old hand on the ship and knew almost everyone on board. Probably with some justification, he thought I was a little too sure of myself, while for my part, I thought then – and still think now – that he fussed like an old woman. Even so I was not prepared for an episode that occurred on his first voyage on the *New Australia*.

We had just left Fremantle and were running west with the port behind us as we made our way towards a buoy a mile or so from the harbour prior to turning south or *left* to round the bottom left hand corner of Australia. At the same time a large Scandinavian ship, on our port or *left-hand side*, was running north at right angles to the course we were on, as she made her way towards the buoy. As a result we were likely to collide unless evasive action was taken. By the internationally agreed Rules of the Road we were the *stand-on* vessel, meaning that our job was to maintain course and speed while the other ship was required to alter course to starboard or towards the right, so as to pass behind our stern. But instead of maintaining course as we were required to do, much to the surprise of the officers on the bridge, Captain Trent ordered the helmsman to alter course to port or to the left in order to take us round the buoy and bring us onto the southerly course we would eventually need to steer to get to the south of Australia. At the same time that we altered course to port *in contravention* of the International Rules, the Scandinavian ship altered course to starboard *as required* by the Rules.

Suddenly the atmosphere on the bridge became very tense. The two ships were now steaming straight at one another's bows at a combined speed of about thirty-five knots. With every passing second the other ship loomed larger and larger and from my position at the back of the bridge I could see her bow wave becoming clearer and clearer as it foamed and bubbled along the sides of her hull. Unless something was done almost immediately we were bound to collide. As I watched I saw six white puffs of steam rise silently from the siren on her funnel, as she tried to warn us that we were standing into danger. A few seconds later the sound that had accompanied the puffs crashed onto our ears. It was now almost too late. Only the most definite action could prevent a collision. Incredulous, I looked at the senior officers to see if any of them would alert the captain to what he had done, but they seemed transfixed by the situation and perhaps were intimidated by his reputation, and so neither the chief officer nor the first or third officers said a word. Then in a pretence of inspecting the other ship, the captain put his binoculars to his eyes, and after what seemed an eternity, but in fact was only few seconds, as if breaking the spell of inertia that had seized everyone on the bridge, ordered the quartermaster to alter course to starboard and resume our original course – the course we should have maintained until the other ship was well clear of us.

For a moment nothing happened and the two ships came closer and closer, then slowly our bow swung to the right and the Scandinavian ship swung out onto our port bow, i.e. onto our left-hand side.

It had been a close call that should never have happened, and as we swept passed the other ship at a distance of about three hundred yards I could see the captain and officers on her bridge scanning us through their binoculars and no doubt cursing us as stupid English fools.

*

While I was sailing with Captain Trent I applied for places at a variety of medical schools. Using two fingers, I typed half a dozen letters of application on an old typewriter in the chief officer's office.

Bristol was the first school to reply, and offered me an interview while I was on leave. I wore my only suit for the occasion and was surprised, and indeed shocked, to see that most of the other candidates were dressed casually in sweaters and open neck shirts.

The interview was conducted in a large hall in the Cathedral Building of the University. I sat on one side of a long wooden table, and the committee, consisting of perhaps a dozen academics, sat on the other.

After a few pleasantries and general questions about the Merchant Navy, the chairman said, "Now, Mr Model, you say you've been to both Australia and New Zealand. Would you care to tell the committee about your views of the economic differences between the eastern and the western sides of Australia?"

Wow! For a moment I was flummoxed, then I remembered the cargoes I had helped to carry during the previous three-and-a-half years and the geography lessons I had sat through at John Lyon School.

"On the east coast of Australia the Great Dividing Range ensures that the prevailing south-east winds deposit a heavy rainfall," I said. "As a consequence the whole of that area is good for agriculture, that is for growing sugar and the production of beef and leather in Queensland, and for growing rice and wheat in New South Wales..." I hesitated, wondering how I was doing and what I was going to say next, then continued. "Sheep flourish in the dryer regions beyond the Great Dividing Range and provide wool... There are minerals in the north at Mount Isa. By contrast, the west is dry and the main products are gold and other minerals from the region around Kalgoorlie." At this point I gave a silent cheer for the geography lessons I remembered *Basher Sibcy* teaching at John Lyon School, and continued, "In the extreme south-west there is an area that enjoys a Mediterranean climate and is good for agriculture as it has rain in the winter..." I gave another silent cheer for *Basher*. It was surprising what you could remember when the occasion demanded!

I told them about the lead we had carried from Mount Isa and Broken Hill, and that because it was so heavy, fifteen hundred tons of it occupied little more than a foot in the bottom of the hold. Suddenly I realised I was enjoying myself and that I liked being interviewed. Today I would be nervous about such an occasion, but with the arrogance of youth, I was suddenly what I would call later *The Interview Animal*, confident and ready to be interviewed by almost anyone.

After fifteen minutes I was told I could go and that the committee would let me know by post whether I had been accepted. A week later I received a letter advising me that I was offered a place.

Many years later I did some interviewing myself and came to the conclusion that it is very difficult to discriminate properly between candidates during an interview lasting a few minutes or perhaps half-an-hour, although some authorities claim to be able to do so.

Over the following six months I attended interviews at the other medical schools to which I had applied. By and large they were ad-hoc affairs arranged to fit in with my leave and I saw only one person, such as the dean or the assistant dean. At St Mary's the procedure was slightly different. After talking to the Dean for about a quarter-of-an-hour I was directed to a small room and given an hour in which to write an essay on being a sailor, and wrote what I hoped was a humorous account of the differences between the public's perception of Jack Tar, a drunken character staggering from pub to pub, and the reality and aesthetics of a sailor's life at sea.

Probably because it was so unusual for a seaman to wish to go to university, in the end I was offered places at all the schools to which I applied, and finally chose St Mary's, partly because the staff there were so kind and said I could start whenever I was ready, and partly because it was the school nearest to my parent's home and I could travel to it easily by Underground train.

Armed with the places I set about trying to get deferment from the two year's conscription into the army or one of the other two armed forces that every fit young man over the age of eighteen in Britain was obliged to do at that time. I was not trying to dodge my obligation to serve my country and offered to sign an affidavit agreeing to do my conscription by serving as a doctor in the army after I qualified, but the government would not agree, so in the end I asked Mr Russell, my M.P., for help. I still have the letter he received from the Ministry of Labour and National Service in which it states that 'if he leaves the Merchant Navy before his liability to national service ceases (which is normally age 26) he will become available for call-up...' As by then I was already almost twenty-three and would be twenty-five by the time I finished two year's national service, and as I would be able to save so much more money towards my medical education if I stayed at sea, and would have a good chance of getting a Master's Certificate and qualifying as Master of a Foreign Going Steamship, I decided to delay going to medical school for the time being.

*

On my last voyage on the *New Australia* the ship put into Colombo to take on water, but instead of lying alongside a quay as we usually did, she was moored to buoys about half a mile from the shore, and loaded water from a convoy of barges that ran back and forth between the ship and the shore. As the junior officer of the watch, I was on the bridge for much of the time we were there.

Taking on water that way was a slow process, as some of the barges were delayed. Captain Trent found that irksome and was impatient to be off, and on several occasions came onto the bridge to see if he could chivvy the process along. But we were in the hands of the bargemen and the company's local agent, and there was nothing he or anyone else on the ship could do about it. Finally, after about five hours he stormed out of his cabin at the rear of the bridge and in a fury began screaming at nobody in particular, and banging his fists up and down in the air above his head. A moment later he leaned over the dodger in the wing of the bridge and shrieked at a Singhalese waterman on the foredeck, some twenty feet below, and told him to get a move on. Such an outburst did not fit with my concept of a captain, let alone the commodore of the company, and in disgust and embarrassment, full of youthful indignation I walked onto the other side of the bridge. A few seconds later the captain followed me, and looking red-eyed and furious, told me to go down onto the foredeck and speak directly to the waterman. But it did not make any difference. Already more water had been loaded than either the captain or I realised, and an hour later we were able to sail, and were only a few minutes behind schedule.

Later during that voyage, after all the emigrants had disembarked, we were ordered north to Brisbane to pick up Australian troops for Korea. The agreement between the ship and the Australian army stated that the only gangways we would be expected to provide were those needed when the ship was in port. We were therefore surprised when without warning, while we were still well out to sea, off the mouth of the Brisbane River, we received a radio message saying that an Australian general and his party were coming out in a launch and would be boarding the ship in the next few minutes, to check the quality of the accommodation provided for the troops.

Immediately I was summoned to the bridge, as apart from being a watch-keeping officer, I was in charge and responsible for the preparation and slinging of the gangways. From my experience I knew it would take almost an hour to rig a proper gangway from its stowed position, as it weighed well over a ton, and blocks and tackle would have to be attached to it, and it would have to be swung out over the side of the ship. Because of this I suggested to Captain Trent that the general should be advised to delay his visit until a gangway was ready. Nonetheless a few minutes later a launch bearing the general appeared on our port side. I hurried down into the bowels of the ship and opened a door in the ship's side and shouted down to the crew of the launch that we would be as quick as possible, but if the general chose not to wait, he could come on board almost immediately by climbing a rope ladder we could lower over the ship's side. The general chose not to wait, and a few minutes later the khaki cap of an army officer appeared at the top of the rope ladder we had hastily lowered from the door. A second or so later, a middle-aged man with red flashes on his lapels and a baton in his hand, scrambled on board.

The general had climbed almost twenty feet up the side of the ship and was breathless and clearly needed a few moments to gather his composure. While I was welcoming him on board and he was recovering, Captain Trent suddenly appeared from the bridge and unceremoniously pushed me aside and began to apologise to the general and brush him down with a clothes brush he had collected from his cabin. Again I thought the captain's behaviour was unbecoming of the master of a large ship, as it made us appear responsible for the general's discomfort, when in fact the problem was of the army's making.

*

At the end of my fifth voyage on the *New Australia*, the chief officer, Mr Welsh, sent for me and told me he was recommending me for promotion to third officer. I was therefore disappointed when we docked in Southampton and I received a message from the company's head office saying that after a week's leave I was to report back to the ship for another voyage as fourth officer. Determined to do something about it, I wrote to Captain Meyers, the Marine Superintendent at the company's Head Office in London, to ask if I could have an appointment to see him. Captain Myers was not used to young men asking for promotion, but he listened with good humour as I told him why I thought I should be promoted; then telling me that he liked my keenness, he said he would do his best for me, but could not promise anything. A few days later he phoned me at home while I was still on leave.

"Model," he said. "Congratulations! You're to report as third officer to the *Ceramic* in two weeks time! It'll be a rushed job. As you know, like the *Gothic* and the *Corinthic* on which you served as a cadet, it's a first class passenger ship, and as an officer you'll have to have mess kit made for you before you go."

I put down the phone with mixed feelings. Perhaps, when all was considered, I had not been wise to ask for promotion, as I had heard about Captain Austen, the captain of the *Ceramic*, and had sworn I would never sail with him. Throughout the company he had a reputation for destroying officers, and because he smiled as he did so, was known as *The Smiling Bastard*. Compared with him, it was said that Captain Queeg in the fictional story *The Caine Mutiny* was a gentleman.

8.

The Smiling Bastard

The captain of the *Ceramic* lived up to his reputation from the first day of the voyage, and smiled from ear to ear as he told us off in words that issued from his mouth in a tough Scots brogue like bullets fired from a gun. Physically, he was like a pale ginger version of Popeye, with tiny brown eyes, and forearms that bulged like inverted Indian clubs from beneath the short sleeves of his tropical white shirts.

s.s. Ceramic, one of the four passenger 'ic' ships belonging to Shaw Savill, i.e. Athenic, Ceramic, Corinthic and Gothic

The route he chose to New Zealand took us across the Atlantic Ocean to Panama, and then across the Pacific Ocean to Pitcairn and Wellington. From the first day he dominated us with his rituals. He had a ritual for everything – for altering course, for reacting to reduced visibility caused by fog or rain, for entering port, for hoisting flags, and even for the way we should hand over the watch.

The ritual for altering course is probably the simplest to explain. On other ships the officer-of-the-watch would check the new course on the chart, tell the helmsman to steer it, and then finally check that he was actually steering it; and that would be an end to the matter. But not with Captain Austen. Although the officer-of-the-watch on the *Ceramic* was supposed to be in charge of the navigation of the ship when he was on the bridge, in fact he was not, as strange though it may sound, with Captain Austen the officer did not know from hour to hour where the ship was going. Normally, before leaving Britain, the second officer would draw the courses in pencil for the whole voyage on the charts. But on the *Ceramic* the officer-of-the-watch was expected to work with an unmarked chart, waiting for the captain to appear from his cabin at the last moment to draw a line representing the course for the next few miles. When we got to the end of that line and were about to spill off it, he would appear again and draw the next line, and so on.

But that was only the beginning of the ritual for altering course. If the line he had drawn on the chart involved altering course to, say 270^0, i.e. due west, the officer had to go into the chartroom and repeat the course to the captain, saying "Course 270^0, Sir." He then had to check the newly drawn line on the chart, and assuming it was correct and did not pass over any rocks or other hidden hazards, he had to hurry out to the wheel-house and give the order to the helmsman to steer the new course, saying, "Helmsman, put the wheel over to starboard and steer 270^0." The helmsman then had to say, "Helm to starboard. Steer 270^0, third officer," or whatever rank the officer carried.

The officer had to stand over the helmsman to make sure he turned the wheel the correct way and that he brought the ship onto the new course and steered it correctly. Once on the new course, the helmsman had to repeat the course back to the officer by saying, "Steering 270^0, third officer."

Immediately that had been done, the officer had to run up the ladder leading from the wheelhouse to the flying-bridge and check the new course on the magnetic compass, and then come down and report both the gyro and magnetic courses to the captain, saying "Ship steering 270^0 by gyro, Sir, and 277^0 magnetic." Only when all that had been done was the ritual over. If any part of it was not exactly as the captain required, he would become angry and an embarrassed smile would cross his face and the bullets would come flying from his mouth.

Sometimes the captain's rituals misfired. Normally, ships flew their national flags only in port or when entering port. But not on the *Ceramic*. On that ship the ensign was hoisted everyday, even when we were in the middle of the Pacific Ocean thousands of miles away from anything or any prying eyes.

On the voyage before I joined the ship, my predecessor Peter Purdy quickly ran foul of the captain. Purdy was partially deaf and sometimes failed to hear what was being said to him on the bridge, particularly if the wind was howling. So early during his first voyage on the *Ceramic* he decided to avoid being repeatedly told off by the captain, by saying *Yes, Sir* to everything the captain asked him, and then checking it afterwards.

On the morning in question, as the ship was steaming across the Pacific Ocean, the captain came out of his cabin at five-past-eight and looking aft saw that the ensign had not been hoisted. In a fury he walked over to Purdy and the bullets began issuing from his mouth.

"Mr Purdy, have you had the ensign hoisted this morning?"

Because of the wind, Purdy did not hear what the captain had said, and so in keeping with his plan, he replied, "Yes, Sir."

The captain looked aft and checked again, but could not see an ensign. Turning to Purdy once more, he said in a menacing voice, "Mr Purdy! What do you think I am, a bloody fool?"

Again Purdy did not hear, and replied "Yes, Sir."

The captain was not amused.

"So you think I'm a bloody fool, do you, Mr Purdy?" the captain fumed.

Again Purdy replied, "Yes, Sir."

The captain could hardly contain himself, as apart from giving Purdy a telling-off or reporting him to the company at the end of the voyage, disciplining an officer was difficult at sea. So, seething and smiling menacingly to himself he turned and stomped over to *his* side of the bridge and spent half-an-hour pacing up and down, fuming and cursing against the unfortunate Purdy.

*

By the time the ship reached Trinidad to take on oil, the captain had most of the officers, including me, in a state of nervous anxiety - the exact opposite of the effect he should have had, which should have been to help and encourage us to make sensible decisions.

One of my jobs as third officer was to calculate the *trim of the ship*, that is the depth of water we were likely to draw at the bow and the stern after we had loaded or unloaded cargo, or in this case, oil. The purpose of the calculation was to make sure that the bow would not be sticking out of the water, and that the stern would not be so shallowly immersed that the propellers would be exposed and not function properly after cargo or oil had been loaded.

We arrived in Trinidad in the late afternoon, and anchored a few hundred yards from a sandy beach surrounded by palm trees. After dinner I performed the calculations for the first time, and concluded that the weight of the oil we were about to take on board would result in us sitting on the bottom of the harbour, or at best having only about a foot of water between the bottom of the ship and the seabed. I should have reported my findings to the captain, but as it was the first time I had done the calculations, and as by then I was frightened of the captain and the bawling-out he would give me if I was wrong, I was paralysed into a state of indecision, and instead of telling him what I had found, I simply repeated the calculations.

By the time I had reworked the calculations three or four times it was midnight and the captain was asleep and I was reluctant to call him for fear of incurring his wrath. In the end I did nothing, but was unable to sleep and lay awake for most of the night, wondering if we were already aground? The next morning I watched nervously when the pilot came on board, and the anchor was heaved up and the order given *Slow ahead* on the engines. For a full minute the ship remained stationary and the only change to be seen in the sea were the clouds of mud churned up by the rotation of the ship's propellers. Then, to my relief, the ship began to turn slowly and nose her way out of the anchorage. She had not gone aground after all, but by then that was hardly the point. I realised I was unable to tolerate Captain Austen, and later that day I wrote a letter that I posted to the Company from Panama, requesting a transfer to another ship as soon as we arrived back in England.

When we were almost at the Panama Canal I went to the chief officer's cabin, and over a drink discussed the dilemma I had faced about whether or not to call the captain. Mr Lindop was a slim willowy young man who seemed to be out of place on the bridge of a ship. Instead, he looked as if he might be more comfortable in a corduroy jacket, reading critically acclaimed biographies and novels and appreciating art and poetry. Like me, he was making his first voyage with Captain Austen, and the captain was wearing him down and the circles under his eyes were becoming darker and darker as the days progressed. Giving me a tired smile that revealed two rows of perfect white teeth, he sympathised with my dilemma, but said I should have called the captain.

"Humour and drink are the only ways of dealing with our situation," he said languidly, as we raised our glasses. "Here's to all the poor devils who are obliged to serve on the *Ceramic* with the appalling Captain Austen."

*

Ships arriving at a foreign port were and still are required as a matter of courtesy to hoist the national flag of the country they are visiting, and so as we approached the Panama Canal, we were ready to hoist the American flag, as the Canal was then under the control of the U.S.A.

The Americans had and still have a very different attitude to their national flag than the British have to theirs. On one occasion I had used the Red Ensign, or the Red Duster as we affectionately called our flag, to wrap myself in when it was cold on the bridge, and on another occasion had actually seen it used as a duster to give the brass compass a final polish. By contrast, the Americans viewed their flag with respect bordering on holiness. A person desecrating the

Stars and Stripes risked a prison sentence and a fine of $1000; and if the flag touched the ground, it was considered to be contaminated and had to be burnt.

No wonder then that the captain went purple with fury when Lansbury, the seaman who had been detailed-off to go down onto the foredeck to hoist the Stars and Stripes, purposely dropped it on the deck and stamped on it in full view of the American pilot who had come on board the ship a few minutes earlier. It was not the first time Lansbury had been in trouble. He had already been fined for a misdemeanour despite the fact that the voyage was as yet only two weeks old.

"Seems you've got a spirited young seaman down there, Captain!" the American pilot drawled laconically as the episode unfolded on the deck beneath him. "I wonder what problem he has with our flag."

That was as far as the matter went so far as the pilot was concerned, but the captain did not see the matter in quite the same way. A few hours later Lansbury was up on a charge, standing to attention in the captain's cabin, and was fined three days' pay. Later when we were alone on watch together, Lansbury told me he considered the fine good value for the embarrassment and trouble he had caused the captain.

Although unacceptable, Lansbury's behaviour was simply a response to the tyrannical way the captain ran the ship. Normally the captain's rituals did not affect the crew as much as they affected the officers, but they did impinge on their lives to an extent.

One morning when I was on watch after we left Panama, the captain leaned over the dodger in the wing of the bridge, and looking down onto the foredeck, saw two seamen talking to one another as they painted the handrails at the side of the ship.

"Mr Model," he said, coming over to where I was keeping a lookout and quietly enjoying the morning. "Send for the chief officer immediately, if you don't mind!"

When Mr Lindop appeared a few minutes later, bullet after bullet came flying out of the captain's mouth. "Mr Lindop! There are two men down there working together and talking. Never allow two men to work together, Mr Lindop. They'll waste time talking. Separate them immediately."

As much as he disliked having to do it, Mr Lindop had no alternative but to go down onto the foredeck and separate the men.

Fortunately, there were no other unpleasant episodes for a week or two and life on the ship settled into its usual gentle rhythm as we made our way across the six thousand miles of the Pacific Ocean. At Pitcairn we stopped just long enough for the passengers to buy souvenirs and for the islanders to bring out mail for posting in New Zealand, and by the time we reached Wellington, it was almost Christmas and the height of the southern summer.

The ship was securely moored alongside one of the town quays; and on Christmas Day, which was a Sunday, as he always did on Sundays, Len Northfield, the assistant purser, a dapper young man with curly brown hair plastered down close to his skull with brilliantine, took the official logbook up to the captain's cabin for the captain to sign.

"Come in! What do you want?" the captain snapped in response to Len's knock on his door.

"Good morning, Sir" Len replied politely. "May I extend the compliments of the season to you and wish you a happy Christmas."

Captain Austen swung round from his desk and looked at Len as if he was looking right through him.

"That's quite enough of that!" he snapped. "Here, hand me the log book and get out!"

Visibly shaken, Len stepped forward and quietly handed the logbook to the captain.

Earlier in the voyage, one of the officers had received an equally hostile response when he greeted the captain as he walked into the wheelhouse at just after 8 a.m. one morning while the ship was still crossing the Pacific Ocean.

"Good morning, Sir," the officer said.

The captain's response was immediate and to the point.

"Who asked you for a weather report?" he snapped.

I spent Christmas on a beach opposite Kapiti Island with the second radio officer and a couple of girls from a family I knew who had emigrated from the suburb in which I lived in London. It was a pagan affair. The girls bought a Christmas hamper, to which we contributed, and during the day we swam and lazed on the beach, eating turkey and Christmas pudding and drinking wine and verbally stalking one another and flirting for all we were worth. One of the girls had designs on me, but by then I had learned enough to deal with such situations by simply pretending I was not aware of them.

When the radio officer and I got back to the ship in the evening we learned that the crew had given the captain a very special Christmas present. During the night of Christmas Eve a group of them had cut all the mooring ropes, leaving the ship secured to the quay by only two wires. It was a serious crime that placed the ship in considerable danger. If a strong wind had blown or the tide had been unusually strong the wires might have snapped and the ship might have drifted across the harbour and been wrecked on the opposite shore. The captain was visibly shaken when he was told about it, but failed to understand why it had happened.

"Why on earth would anyone want to do that?" for once contrite, he asked Mr Lindop.

An inquiry was set up, but for lack of evidence failed to find the culprits or reach a conclusion.

*

One day on our way back across the Pacific Ocean to England I went onto the bridge to relieve the second officer for lunch. The weather was fine and the ship was on automatic pilot, meaning it was being steered electronically, rather than by a man. Above us small tufts of white cumulus cloud sailed across a pacific blue sky and tumbled off the edge of the horizon.

Knowing that the captain was in the dining room, the only member of the crew on the bridge, other than me, asked if he could go off for a few minutes to have a smoke.

"OK, bugger off, but don't be longer than ten minutes," I said in a way he recognised was friendly.

He gave me a knowing grin and left the bridge. Five minutes later a dense rainstorm appeared out of nowhere and within a few seconds visibility was so poor that it was impossible to see beyond the fo'c'sle. On most ships, a rainstorm of that type occurring thousands of miles from anywhere would have been ignored in the knowledge that it would be over in a few minutes. On the *Ceramic* things were different. Captain Austen had a five-point ritual for dealing with poor visibility, even in the middle of an empty ocean. First the officer-of-the-watch was required to send the man on the bridge to get another member of the crew to go to the fo'c'sle as quickly as possible to act as an extra lookout. Then the man from the bridge had to return and steer the ship manually. The officer was also required to warn the engine room and ring the engine telegraphs to *Standby*, and to switch on the radar and call the captain.

In the event I did none of these things, as I had allowed the only member of the crew with me on the bridge to go for a smoke, and I was alone and could not set a lookout or put a man on the wheel, and in any case, I knew that only a minute or so before the ocean had been devoid of ships or any other visible sign of life.

Down in the passenger dining room, the captain had just started the main course of his lunch when he saw the rain beating against the windows. Excusing himself from the passengers at his table, he dashed up to the bridge and looked at the steering wheel to see if the ship was being steered manually. It was not ... Then he turned to the engine telegraphs to see if they had been put on *Standby*. They had not been ... Next, without saying a word, he walked over to the radar to see if it had been switched on. It had not been ... From the radar he stepped forward to one of the windows of the wheelhouse and looked forward to the bow to see if a lookout had been posted. None had been... Finally he turned to me and erupted in an explosion of terrible anger. There was no embarrassed smile on his face now. He was too angry for that. He was a raging bull. His complexion was purple, his little eyes were more piggy than ever and his body was visibly swollen and puffed up in fury. "What the hell have you been doing?" he roared. "Don't you know what you're supposed to do when we get into rain!"

I thought he was about to have me clapped into irons, and was so frightened by his rage that I stood transfixed to the spot while he raged on and on. Then unable to cope anymore, without warning, I began to laugh hysterically. I had not intended to laugh, and I certainly did not intend to be insubordinate or rude. I simply could not help myself. The situation was so serious and I was so scared that

I lost control of myself and simply reacted at an unconscious level. In theory I might have cringed or run away. Instead I just laughed and laughed, until in the end, I laughed so much that it hurt. And the more I laughed, the angrier the captain became until suddenly he stopped ranting and raging and stood silently, almost foaming at the mouth, staring at me with his arms clenched tightly by his sides.

The situation was relieved by the arrival of the second officer back from lunch. Immediately I went below and sat in my cabin, waiting to hear whether I was about to be hanged or clapped in irons. But much to my surprise nothing happened. Although I did not appreciate it at the time, I had witnessed a seminal event. Without intending to, I had got the better of the Old Man. Not understanding why I had laughed, he had been rendered impotent and did not know what to do with me, even though I gave every appearance of provoking him and being insolent. So instead of punishing me as I expected, he simply paced up and down the deck outside his cabin for two hours, muttering to himself, while for my part, I sat waiting in expectation of the punishment I was sure was about to be meted out on me.

At ten-past-four there was knock on my door and I braced myself for the inevitable. But it was only the second officer coming in with a grin on his face.

"What on earth have you done to the Old Man?" he asked. "He's really upset. I've never seen him like this before. You've wrecked his afternoon nap. He's pacing up and down, muttering to himself in a highly agitated state. I reckon you must have done something pretty awful. He looks as if he is going to have a fit or collapse."

I heard nothing more about the incident, and it was not until a couple of days before we arrived at Panama that I spoke to the captain again.

At eight o'clock in the evening, while we were still about five or six hundred miles from the land, I went onto the bridge to take over the watch from Brian or BV Smith, the fourth officer. Subsequently Brian went on to become professor of Business Studies at a university in New Zealand, but that evening he was an agitated young man running his fingers nervously through his hair because of the behaviour of a ship on our port bow.

"See that ship over there," he said, looking towards the silhouette of a ship a mile or so away on our port or left-hand side. "It's slowly getting nearer and nearer and is supposed to get out of our way, but it hasn't. I've been watching it for three-quarters of an hour, and it's gradually coming closer and closer. I don't know what to do? We're the stand-on vessel, but the Old Man's got me into such a state that if I stand-on. and don't alter course, I know he'll come out of his cabin and give me a bollocking, and ask me why I haven't taken evasive action. Similarly, if I alter course when we're supposed to maintain course and speed, he'll bawl me out for taking action and putting the ship in danger."

I could see that BV was in a state. To the other officers, the captain was still worse than Captain Bligh of *HMS Bounty* or Captain Queeg of the *USS Caine*, but following my confrontation with him in the rain I knew I had the better of him, and as a consequence I was no longer frightened of him.

Calmly I took in the scene. To the north of us, beyond the ship that was causing BV to be in such a quandary, tropical lightning was playing on the bottom of clouds. Beyond the lightning a curtain of black rain was obscuring the horizon. How extraordinary, I thought in a detached way. For months the Old Man has ruled us with fear and a rod of iron, and now I really don't give a damn what he gets up to. So looking at BV, I said, "OK, BV. I think I understand the situation. You go below and have your supper. I'll watch the ship for another half-an-hour and if it continues to get closer and doesn't take any evasive action I'll call the Old Man and ask him if we can alter course to starboard and go round in a circle behind her."

Half an hour later I called the captain, and for once he was polite and stood quietly by as we altered course away from the other vessel and went round in a circle behind her.

But the following day he was back on form and up to his old tricks as we approached the Isthmus of Panama. At six o'clock in the evening he appeared on the bridge and instead of drawing a course on the chart that would take us five or ten miles clear of our landfall, he drew a course that would take us right over it. When BV saw that the course would result in us running aground, he nipped off the bridge for a few seconds to tell the second officer.

"The Old Man's off his rocker," he said, excitedly. "In his Night Order book he's left orders to call him at two o'clock in the morning, so he can draw the next course on the chart, but anyone can see we're going to hit the land and run aground an hour or so before that."

Excited by the prospect of running aground before the Old Man was called, the officers who were not on watch gathered in the second officer's cabin for a celebratory drink.

"Here's to one o'clock!" someone said.

"Shouldn't we point it out to him?" someone else asked.

"No! Not bloody likely! It will serve him right if we run aground! He knows perfectly well what he's doing. I suggest we go to sleep with our life-jackets on!"

We laughed and had a drink to that. Then someone suggested that we should put *X marks the spot* on the chart where we were likely to run aground.

We had another drink to that, then the second officer said, "What about swinging-out the life-boats in readiness?"

"I think I'll sleep in my lifeboat!" I replied.

We all laughed again. We were having a great time. We hated the Old Man so much that in a strange sort of way we half hoped that we would run aground. But of course, we did not. Wily to the end, the Old Man appeared on the bridge at eleven o'clock, three hours before the time he was due to be called, and drew a new line on the chart that took us clear of the land.

*

Two-and-a-half weeks later, as we approached the English Channel I went onto the bridge for one of my last 8-12 watches of the voyage, safe in the knowledge that as a result of the letter I had sent from Panama, I was likely to be transferred to another ship when we arrived back in England. All I had to do now was a watch that night and another the next morning; then I would be free to go home and shake-off the dust of the *Ceramic* and her hateful captain. But before I could do that we had to pick up the pilot at Start Point in Devon and then make our way up the Channel to the mouth of the Thames.

Even by the standards of January, the weather was foul as we approached Start Point. A cold damp wind was blowing out of the east and was throwing sheets of rain across the windows of the wheelhouse. When I ventured out onto the wing of the bridge I could see lines of rain streaking down towards me in the glare of the green and red navigation lights. Not a night to be stirring from your cabin, I thought, as I felt the full force of the wind pushing me backwards. Visibility was down to about a mile and the temperature wa just 3^0 or 4^0 above freezing. Shit a fucking brick, I said to myself, as I huddled into my Burberry, there must be better ways of earning a living than standing a watch in this fucking lot. Not that I really minded; I was simply giving vent to my feelings, and making a little symbolic protest. In next to no time I knew I would be at home, and in the meantime there was the fun of making the landfall and navigating the ship through the crowded waters at the mouth of the Channel.

At nine o'clock a fuzzy white line on the left hand side of the radar indicated that we were approaching land. England, I thought! I'm the first man on the ship to see home! Home is the sailor from the seas...

A few minutes later the lookout on the fo'c'sle rang three bells to indicate that he had seen a ship dead ahead. In the murky darkness, with my binoculars I was just able to make out two tiny twinkling white lights, one above the other. A fishing trawler out in this dreadful weather, I thought...

Gradually the angle that the lights made with our bow increased and, after a few more minutes, the black outline of a small ship became visible on our starboard side. At the same time, in keeping with the idea that it was a trawler that was fishing, its top white light changed to green.

We were on a fishing ground. In the next half hour five or six more vessels showing similar lights appeared out of the darkness and after a few minutes passed down one or other sides of the ship without me having to alter course or take evasive action. Then another appeared fine on the starboard bow, a couple of miles away. At the same time Captain Austen came out of his cabin. For a moment he stood in the wing of the bridge with his binoculars clapped to his eyes, then turning to me, he snapped, "Mr Model, alter course to starboard immediately!"

The order placed me in a difficult position. Because of the vessels we had already passed I realised that the vessel we were now dealing with was a fishing trawler and that it would pass down our starboard side without us needing to take evasive action, and that if I followed the captain's order and altered course to starboard, that is to the right, we would pass right across its bow and risk colliding with it. What should I do...? Follow an order I knew to be wrong...? Do as I was told and say nothing, and risk colliding with the other ship?

There was not much time for discussion. A decision had to be made almost immediately. Most probably, I thought, the Old Man has not allowed enough time for his eyes to adjust to the darkness, and as a result he has not interpreted the tiny specks of light correctly. Perhaps he will respond reasonably if I speak to him politely... So, before telling the helmsman to alter course to starboard, I walked over to where the captain was standing, and said quietly, "Captain, if you'll excuse me, sir, she's a fishing vessel showing two white lights vertically one over the other; if we alter course to starboard now we'll pass right across her bow."

The captain put his binoculars to his eyes once more. "No, she's not," he snapped. "She's showing two horizontally separated white lights above a red light. She's an ordinary steamer and we're crossing her. She's the stand-on vessel; it's our job to get out of the way. Alter course to starboard immediately."

I put my binoculars to my eyes once again, but saw only two white lights vertically above one another. We were now in a *Caine Mutiny* situation. As it says in the film of that name, *Captain, I'm sorry, but you're a sick man. I'm relieving you of command of this ship...*

I was furious. I could feel the blood pumping in my neck and my pulse beating in my ears. You swine, I thought, you fucking bastard, I'll fucking teach you to give me a wrong order!

Barely managing to control myself, I said, "Captain, I'm going to do what you say, but I'm telling you now that if we hit that ship I'm going to make an entry in the logbook that I disagreed with your order and advised you against it! If instead, we maintain our course and speed you'll see the uppermost white light change to green and she will pass down our starboard side. If we go across her, you'll see the uppermost white light change to red if we haven't already hit her!"

The captain looked through his binoculars again. "Mr Model," he said, "I'm giving you a lawful command!"

Lawful command, my fucking arse...

In a fury I walked into the wheelhouse and said to the helmsman. "Put the bloody wheel over to starboard... No, it's OK, Lansbury; it's not your fault. It's something else that's made me mad!"

I watched as the ship heeled over, and the other ship came hurtling towards us. I felt as if I was a member of an audience watching a disaster slowly unfold in front of my eyes.

We were now barely five hundred yards from her and her bow was racing towards our bow. It was not difficult to imagine the life going on in her cabins and the panic and cursing on her small bridge.

"Put the fucking wheel over harder, Man, or we'll hit her!" I yelled at Lansbury.

The ship heeled over another ten or twenty degrees and our turn tightened. Then, perhaps a minute later, the other ship crossed onto our other side and the uppermost white light on her changed to red. Triumphant, I stormed out of the wheelhouse and went over to the captain, who was still in the wing of the bridge. "There!" I said to him. "I damn well told you she would show a red light when we'd crossed her bow!"

She was so close that despite the darkness and the mist, I was able to see her silhouette and the white lights shining from her portholes. She was much smaller than we were, and from my elevated position on the bridge, I was able to look down onto her as she slipped closely by our port side. As she did so, I heard the clockwork throb of her engines beating against the darkness of the night, and could see the black shadows of her masts and superstructure against the blackness of the sea and the night sky.

Then she was astern of us, and the red light on her port side had disappeared, and all she was showing was the all-round lower white light. The danger was over, but I was still very steamed up.

The captain was also obviously deeply affected by the incident. Normally he would have stayed on the bridge until we made land, particularly as the weather was so bad and the visibility was so poor. Instead he went into his cabin and stayed there until almost the end of my watch. Then he did a very strange thing. Just before the second mate appeared on the bridge to relieve me at midnight he came out onto the bridge in preparation for the landfall and handed me a tot of whisky, and said in an affable voice, "Good night, third mate. And thank you for all you've done during the voyage."

*

We docked in London during the afternoon of the following day and amid all the excitement of packing to go on leave I learned that the captain's wife had came on board, and at dinner that evening I watched as, accompanied by the chief officer and the chief engineer, the two of them interacted at his table. No longer was the captain the dominating figure he had been throughout the voyage. Instead, to my amazement, his wife talked for the two of them, while he sat subdued and strangely quiet for a man who had ruled the ship with a rod of iron and was known as *the Smiling Bastard*. Could it be, I wondered as I watched them, that he is simply a browbeaten husband who compensates for the frustrations he suffers at home by being a tyrant when he is at sea, or is the responsibility of being a captain the thing that makes him behave in the way that he does?

It was not a question I had much time to think about that night, as I had to pack my bags, and the following morning proceed on leave for two weeks before joining the *Moreton Bay*.

9

A Life of Riley

The day of the jet aeroplane had not yet arrived and passenger ships were still the main means of travel between one side of the world and the other. The *Moreton Bay* was one of those passenger ships, a grand old lady of the seas that carried 514 tourist-class passengers as well as a full load of cargo. She had been built by Vickers at Barrow-in-Furness in 1921, and was thirty-five years old at the time I joined her in 1956. In keeping with her age, she had an old fashioned straight up-and-down bow, an overhanging counter stern and a tall narrow yellow funnel. In a way she looked like a small version of the *Titanic* or a ship from a faded old photograph. In her public rooms the furniture was made of old fashioned, heavy, dark mahogany wood. In places the paint on her hull and masts was over an inch thick. She creaked like an old lady, and her bulkheads – many of which were constructed of tongue-and-groove planking – had been painted so many times that the paint on them was no longer smooth, but was bumpy and uneven where dust and hairs had caught in it before it dried.

Bay Class ship, i.e. Esperance Bay, Jervis Bay, Largs Bay & Moreton Bay

Many of the passengers she carried were unattached single young women and as a consequence *the Bay-Boats*, as the class of ships to which she belonged was known, had a reputation for great fun, and it was with a sense of anticipation and relief at having escaped from the *Ceramic* and the clutches of Captain Austen that I joined her in the King George V dock in London on an overcast grey winter's day in February.

As soon as the last of the cargo had been loaded we headed east down the River Thames and then south and west round the southeast corner of England to Southampton, where we picked up the passengers. Once they were on board we set sail for Fremantle by way of the Mediterranean Sea and the Suez Canal. By now I was an experienced watch-keeping officer and knew many of the landmarks along the way, and although I was only twenty-three, being in charge on the bridge and navigating the ship for eight hours each day offered few problems. Over the years I had developed an approach to navigating that was to influence the way I worked for the rest my life. If the weather was fine and I could see the coast or the peaks of distant mountains I preferred to use my judgement and feel my way like a cat, and navigate by taking bearings of landmarks, such as distant peaks and lighthouses observed with simple instruments such as an azimuth, rather than relying on complex technology, such as radar. It was a matter of temperament really. If the radar was on when I went on the bridge, I would say, "What the hell is that fucking thing on for?" and walk over to it and switch it off. I was not being arrogant. It was simply that I felt it was artistic and more fun to use my judgement, rather than to allow a machine to dictate what I should do. It was the same when many years later I was no longer at sea. I always preferred using my own observations and judgement, rather than relying on technology.

With the exception of the captain, all the officers were new to the ship. The captain, George Heyward, was an easy-going man and so long as we, the officers, had enough sleep to perform our duties efficiently and did not drink too much he encouraged us to take part in entertaining the passengers. To make sure that we had enough sleep, one of the few rules he insisted on was that we should be off the decks and in our cabins by 10 p.m.

As we steamed across the Bay of Biscay, on our second day out the officers who were not on watch met in the fourth mate's cabin for a drink, and it was not long before we were discussing how we could set up a meeting with some of the girls on board.

We were an assorted group. I was third officer. The chief officer was married and immediately declared no interest in the social life on board. The second officer had just been re-instated in the company after being dismissed for an unknown misdemeanour. The fourth officer was a callow young man with a creamy white complexion and strawberry-coloured red cheeks set in an unused-looking face that suggested, probably correctly as it turned out, that he had hardly been touched by life. The fifth officer, a chap named Ned, was a well-meaning Scouser from Liverpool who had worked his way up from the crew and was making his first voyage as an officer. He was an unpolished rough diamond who scuttled about in a baggy uniform with his backside close to the deck. Within a few days he was very popular and liked by everyone on the ship.

By the time we had rounded the northwest corner of Spain Ned had got to know a group of girls on B-deck, and within a few hours had invited them to his cabin for a pre-dinner drink. Because of this, we christened him *The Tamer of B-Deck*. One of his favourite sayings was "You know, Man, there are so many girls on this ship all you have to do is turn-on a tap and out they come, hot and cold running – mainly hot!"

Unfortunately Ned had a sad career. Although he had obtained his Second Mate's certificate, he did not really understand what he had been taught and as a result taking sights and navigating the ship was almost beyond him. At first his difficulties were met with sympathy, but after a while his colleagues became impatient with him, and after some years he went into decline and became an alcoholic.

The first time the girls he had invited came to his cabin they wore party dresses and sat in a row on his sofa, while we sat on the bunk opposite them and plied them with gin and tonic until it was time for dinner and they went to eat in the passenger dining saloon. After that, coming to one or other of our cabins for a pre-dinner drink became almost a normal part of the day. Frequently it was not easy for them to get into our accommodation, as they had to contend with a group of old spinsters who took it upon themselves to act as the arbitrators of public morality by sitting in a row of deckchairs outside the entrance to our accommodation and making caustic remarks as the girls passed by, in much the same way as the old hags who shouted and squawked during executions in the French Revolution.

Within a few days we gradually paired off, and I found myself with a girl named Gwen who was travelling back to Australia after seeing *The Old Country*, as she called England.

Ned was pleased with his work, and one evening after the girls had gone to dinner and we were sitting in our mess, having our meal, he said to me, "You look grand with Gwen, Man! You make a splendid couple."

But I was not so sure. The permanence implied by what he had said, made me shudder. The sort of girl I wanted was not Gwen. For one thing I suspected she was on the lookout for a husband; for another, she was too passive and too ordinary for me. Although she was neat and reasonably slim, already there was something settled and matronly about her that suggested that the seeds of middle age had already began to grow in her, and I have no doubt that if she is still alive today she is more than a little dumpy. What I wanted was a girl with dash, a girl who was intelligent and spirited with an enquiring mind, a girl who would stimulate me and be an equal partner, a girl like Shirley Barnard, the physiotherapist, who I still wrote to and visited whenever I was in Australia.

Sometimes I considered asking Shirley to marry me, but she had turned up too early in my life and I knew that if I did so it would end my dream of becoming a doctor – and I had no intention of letting that happen. Even so, at times I could not help but wonder if all the waiting and hassle implied by the dream was worthwhile, or whether it might not be best to call it a day and forget the idea of becoming a doctor, and instead settle down to a 9-5 shore job, as so many of my colleagues and friends eventually did.

To reassure myself and strengthen my resolve, when the ship docked in Port Said I bartered with one of the Egyptian traders who came on board and bought a navy blue leather attaché case with a fold-over clasp, and like a bride collecting a *bottom drawer*, stored it in the bottom of my wardrobe in the hope that one day I would be able to use it to carry my books to medical school.

*

Instincts are innate drives we cannot resist that are placed in us by Nature to ensure the continuity of the race. The need to survive is the most basic instinct. The desire for pleasure is another. All animals, even organisms consisting of just one cell, like the lowly amoeba, seek pleasure and move towards pleasurable stimuli and away from noxious ones; and for all our sophistication we are not very different.

The urge to reproduce is part of the instinct for survival as it ensures the continuity of the species. To make sure that it happens and that the species is preserved, Nature has very cunningly combined the reproductive instinct in us with the pleasure instinct and has made the sexual part of reproduction so pleasurable that no matter how cerebral a man or a woman may be, or how much they may wish to be celibate, as occasionally I thought I might like to be, very few people can resist the urge to seek the pleasure of sex. That is how it was for me one evening as the ship passed Malta. As the girls were leaving Ned's cabin to go for dinner I made a grab for Gwen's hand. My heart was pounding in my chest as I said very quietly so that the others would not hear, "Gwen, how about a drink in my cabin when I come off watch at midnight tonight?"

I waited anxiously for what seemed like an eternity for her to reply. It's now or never, I thought, aware of a thumping like a drum in my ears. Either I find out about women now, or I don't.

"Are you sure it'll be all right?" she hissed. "Are you sure nobody will know?"

"Yes, I'm sure! It will be very late and very dark and everyone will be in their bunks."

I left my bedside lamp on when I went on watch, and wondered if she would be there when I came off the bridge at midnight.

*

The night was black and the decks were in almost complete darkness as I made my way down from the bridge at the appointed hour. The few lights that were on cast a weak yellow glare, as if they were not quite up to the job of keeping the night at bay.

I wondered if Gwen would be in my cabin, and if she were, what I would do? Make love to her, I supposed. But how…? How should I go about it, and what should I do if she refused me? As I opened the door of my cabin, I felt very uncertain of myself and wondered whether, before it got out of hand, it might not be best to back out of the predicament into which I might have landed myself?

She was sitting on the sofa. Her eyes didn't leave me as I walked in. Immediately I sensed that she was as anxious as I was – it was clear from the rigid upright way she was sitting and from the look of uncertainty on her face.

"How are you? Been here long?" I asked, noting that for some unearthly reason I was whispering, as if what we were doing was part of a conspiracy.

I noted the way the light cast by my bunk-side lamp created a halo of light around her dark curly hair.

I offered her a gin-and-tonic, and as she picked it up I noticed with distaste that her hands were large and her fingers were thick like the fingers of a peasant.

I sat in the chair by my desk and attempted conversation. I knew what to do, but did I dare do it? And if so, how should I translate my intentions into actions? Although she had come to my cabin I was still afraid that she might rebuff me. What would I do if that happened? Accept defeat; slink away? Or should I perhaps take a risk and persist?

I tossed a few clumsy words across the chasm-like space between us. I had to get across that space. But how…?

As I spoke, she seemed to grow further and further away and the distance between us seemed to grow larger. Oh Christ, I thought, I'll never manage it; I'll never be able to get across the space between us. The more it preoccupied me, the more I seemed to be immobilised and rooted to the seat of my chair. I became aware of the thumping again, this time at the back of my head. Then finally, after a few more irrelevant comments, I blurted out, "Do you mind if I come and sit next to you over there?"

I was ready to retreat if she said *No*. But she seemed to consent, and so I slid across the space between us and sat down beside her on the sofa.

"You're a lovely girl," I said, gently stroking the back of her neck.

I leaned towards her and somehow our lips came into contact, but my knowledge of how to kiss was far from perfect, and I was aware of my hot breath streaming down my nostrils, and realised that I had still to learn how to breathe when kissing.

I liked kissing her. It made my lips tingle and swell, and my tongue feel as if it was on fire, and after one or two more attempts, I became bolder and explored the roof of her mouth with my tongue.

I put a hand on her blouse and felt the softness of her breast. At first she resisted, but then she seemed to yield, and so I put my hand down the front of her blouse and gently lifted her breast from her bra. I could feel the weight of it cupped in my hand. It was so perfectly round and soft, so exquisitely warm and inviting...

I kissed her breast, and then I kissed her on the mouth again, and as I did so I placed my hand on her knee and became aware of the hard shiny surface of her stocking. Then she stiffened and pushed my hand away.

"No, please, darling, you mustn't do that."

The word *darling* grated on my mind and annoyed me. *Darling* was a special word; a word that was reserved for special relationships, not a relationship like this. My mother and father called one another *darling*...

I put my hand back on her thigh and slid it up towards her groin. She offered a little token resistance and made a half-hearted attempt to push me away once again, but I ignored her and pushed on upwards along the shiny firm surface of her stocking. Then I was above it and on the soft skin at the top of her thigh. The velvety softness of her groin and the frill of her panties passed beneath my fingers, and a moment later I was in soft pubic hair and a few seconds after that I was at the soft centre of her. For a moment her body stiffened and I thought she would push my hand away; then she lay back and relaxed.

I was there! I had won! She was mine! I've got to the place where I want to be, I thought triumphantly, the place where I belong, the place where every man longs to be.

I was no longer an ordinary rational man. I was a predatory animal with its prey in its grasp. I was preparing her like a succulent meal. Nothing was going to stop me. No, nothing, nothing at all...

"I hope you know what you're doing! Just you be careful!" she hissed.

All my doubts had been banished and the rest came naturally.

A few minutes later we lay locked together in movement. Then suddenly I was aware of her making little noises beneath me. A moment later I felt an irresistible urgency. At the same time an explosion occurred inside me and a great flash, like a white light, spread out from my loins to the furthest parts of my fingers and toes, as every pleasure nerve in my body fired at once.

I had never experienced anything as powerful and pleasurable before. Great waves of joy, like waves of hot molten lava, surged over my body. Then a huge eruption occurred in my pelvis and a most wonderful rushing feeling of ecstasy surged over me.

Oh, God! Oh, No! Oh, Yes! Oh, Wow!

Apart from sheer physical pleasure, I was aware that I was in the grip of something bigger than me, and knew that I was fulfilling the purpose for which I had been made. Although I had taken precautions, I had, so to speak, placed my seed in the body of a woman. Our body fluids had mixed and we had become one. This was what I was made for, I thought, the thing for which my body was shaped. I was no longer a person with arms and legs. I was a vehicle of Nature's intention, a primordial man performing the act that was intended to replicate the race. I had placed my genes inside the body of a woman, as it were. Ever since the beginning of time men and women had been doing that to one another in order to ensure the continuity of the race. Without its compulsion and urgency there would have been no stream of humanity, no Adam and Eve, no Him and Her, no Male and Female. All my life I had been travelling towards this point, and now I was there I wanted to swim and, if necessary, to drown in a sea of it.

Suddenly my thoughts were disturbed and I became aware that Gwen's hair was wet and that there were beads of perspiration between her breasts. Looking into her eyes, close up against mine, I saw that they were deep blue and had a distant look, as if she was in some far off place.

She must have become aware of me looking at her.

"Hello, darling," she said. "Was that your first time?"

"Was I all right?" I asked, ignoring the way she had used the word *darling* again.

"You were wonderful!" she sighed.

"I wanted to please you. It was as if I had a need to do so."

She laughed. "I think I love you," she said.

At two o'clock I went out to the toilet situated along the corridor outside my cabin.

"Tea, sir? Would you like some tea and toast?"

It was Lambert, the night steward, a man aged about fifty. He had been sitting, with the lights out, in the officer's dining room, looking along the corridor that ran passed the officers' cabins.

I thought that tea and toast would complete the night in splendid style.

"Do you mean it?" I asked. "Is it really possible to have tea and toast at this ungodly hour?"

Lambert smiled.

"You know, sir," he said very softly. "I was young once myself, believe it or not."

*

Now, these were the days of youth... days of quiet sunny mornings on the bridge of the ship and hot tempestuous nights in my cabin with Gwen. Through her I had tasted the forbidden fruit and had found it to be sweet. I had experienced one of the great mysteries of life, and as a result felt tremendous relief. Among the things I learned from her was that to be a good lover it is necessary to please your partner, and that sex is largely a matter of affection and kissing and stroking and caressing and touching of skin.

I was twenty-three when I lost my virginity – old by today's standards, you may say. But I am not sorry I had waited so long, as I appreciated the significance of what had happened much more than if I had been sixteen.

*

The other officers slept with their girls. The second mate learned that his girl was a nymphomaniac, happy to sleep with anyone and as a result she quickly became known as *The Bike*, as anyone could ride her. Apart from the second officer, the ship's doctor, a man aged about thirty-five, was foremost among her customers. We called him *The Snide* because we disliked his oily manner and sleeked-down black hair. The Snide was almost as promiscuous as the Bike, and one night as the Second Mate was making his rounds after completing the 12-4 watch, he passed the Snide's cabin and looking in through the open window saw the Snide naked, heaving up and down on a woman who was lying naked beneath him on his bunk, just a foot or so beneath the window. The Second Mate watched for a moment as the Snide's buttocks pumped up and down, then unable to resist the temptation, he put his hand through the open window, and with his palm gave the Snide an almighty slap on his bare backside. He did not wait to find out the result of what he had done, but ran-off into the night as fast as he could.

None of the officers was more of a rogue than Aus, an Australian engineer with whom I became friendly. Aus was a good guy, a rough-as-guts Australian from the backwoods behind Sydney, but he was good tempered and was a much better shipmate to have on a long voyage than one or two of the superficially better-mannered English officers with whom I sailed. He was on the 4-8 watch, and when he had finished in the engine-room in the evening, he liked nothing more than to come up onto the bridge to see the stars and talk to me for an hour or so before going to one of the numerous parties that were taking place in various parts of the ship.

Although we were very different, we were drawn together by our common interest in girls and sex and were soon great buddies. Night after night he amused me with tales of the girls he had slept with, or probably more correctly, fancied he had slept with. On the voyage to Australia, he struck up a relationship with a middle-aged Dutch lady who was returning home to her husband in Melbourne after visiting her mother in Holland. She was a good twenty years older than Aus, and seemed too refined to have a relationship with such a tough guy as him, but they seemed to get along well together. "I don't think her Old Man's up to it," Aus confided to me one night as we stood on the bridge while the ship trundled across the Indian Ocean. "Lady or not, she likes what I do to her." For her part, when I talked to the Dutch lady, she said coolly but not without affection, "Yes, Aus is a nice boy. A bit rough, you know, but he means well and has a heart of gold and is nice underneath it all."

Later in the voyage, when we were returning to England, Aus met an English girl who would not sleep with him. "Damn it!" he said, as we stood in the darkness looking over the dodger of the bridge while the breeze ruffled our hair. "She's the first girl I've met with whom I can't get away with it. She'll let me do anything above the waist, but not an inch below it. You know, if I'm not careful, I think I may fall in love with her and, you never know, I may well ask her to marry me."

*

Gwen came to my cabin almost every night for the rest of the voyage to Melbourne, and although I was always aware that our relationship could never be permanent, I grew quite fond of her. In a way, I suppose you could say I used her; but then, she also used me, as she was looking for both a husband and a shipboard romance. After leaving the ship, for a while she wrote long dull letters to me in a laboured hand; and for a month or so I replied with letters that were probably equally dull and uninspired, because when all was said and done, the truth was that all we had in common was what had happened on the ship.

*

Fremantle was our first port in Australia. On the night of our arrival, the second officer was the duty officer and the officer in charge of supervising the discharge of the cargo. With the exception of the chief officer, who was relaxing quietly in his cabin, the rest of the officers, including the captain, and many of the passengers were ashore. At about eight o'clock, as the second officer was making his rounds of the ship, he noticed that the quartermaster was absent from his post at the top of the gangway, even though it was very important that he should be there, as it was used by both the passengers and the crew.

The quartermaster in question was a member of my watch, who I knew as Ginger. On the voyage out he had been a good worker, but now he had left his post, and against all the rules of the ship, had gone to a passenger's cabin. Half an hour later he was still missing. When eventually he re-appeared the second officer told him he would be on the captain's report the following morning. Ginger had been drinking heavily and was incensed by the second officer's manner and words, and leaving his post once again, he followed the second officer, as the latter made his way back to his cabin in the officers' quarters.

As he hurried along the main passenger deck to catch up with the second officer, Ginger's bearing was sufficiently unusual to arouse the attention of the Master-at-Arms, whose role on the ship was to act as a policeman and keep order among the crew on behalf of the captain and the chief officer. On the *Moreton Bay* the Master-at-Arms was a retired police sergeant.

Three people were now hurrying towards the officer's accommodation – the second officer followed at a decreasing distance by Ginger, who in turn was followed by the Master-at-Arms.

A few seconds after the second officer entered his cabin, Ginger knocked at his door and entered without waiting for an answer. An argument ensued. Hearing this, the Master-at-Arms knocked and entered. What happened next depends upon whom you listened to, but there was little doubt that the second officer and the Master-at-Arms set upon Ginger and beat him up. When it was over, they were unmarked, but both Ginger's eyes were black, and there were contusions on his head and neck, and bruises due to kicking, on various parts of his body.

Having severely beaten-up Ginger, the second officer then telephoned the Australian police and had Ginger arrested and taken to a police station in Fremantle where he was charged with assaulting a ship's officer.

The next morning, bedraggled and looking beaten-up, Ginger was arraigned in court and sentenced to six months in prison. Apart from involving a custodial sentence, the sentence meant that he would miss the ship when it sailed to Melbourne, and that he would be dishonourably discharged and his career as a merchant seaman would be over.

When they heard about it, the crew were incensed, as they felt that as he had been both beaten-up and sentenced to prison, Ginger had been punished twice for the same offence. The crew also had other grievances about the way they had been treated on the way out from England. In the heat of the Red Sea potatoes that had been loaded in a frost in London, had gone rotten and it had been necessary to shovel them over the side. In their place everyone on board, including the passengers, had been served rice. But the crew did not like rice; only Chinamen ate that. Meat and potatoes were the staple diet of Englishmen at that time.

The crew also felt that the Master-at-Arms had treated them savagely on the way out from England. The combination of these facts, namely the beating and sentence that Ginger had received, the Master-at-Arm's viciousness, and the lack of potatoes, combined to create a situation on the ship that was like a powder keg about to explode.

I was the duty officer on the evening that Ginger was sentenced to prison, and after I had been on deck for an hour, supervising the discharge of the cargo, I went back to my cabin at about eight o'clock, and had just sat down in my chair when I heard screams and shouts in the after-part of the passenger accommodation.

Slipping on the heavy industrial gloves I wore when going up and down the holds, and picking up a large torch in case I needed a weapon, I made my way to investigate what was happening. The scene in the foyer of the after passenger accommodation was utter mayhem. Under the bright lights that illuminated the place a group of women were standing, screaming and looking transfixed at a trail of blood leading to a doorway that led down a ladder to the deck below.

"Get the police!... There's been a murder!" one of them shouted.

I tried to establish what had happened, but the women were so hysterical that it took me three or four minutes to appreciate that the Master-at-Arms had been found by a crowd of sailors returning from the shore, and had been chased through the passenger accommodation, and had been beaten up. He had fought back and had escaped, but had sustained several cuts to his head.

Leaving the passengers, I followed the trail of blood through the door and down the ladder in the hope of being able to help the quartermaster, but the trail soon petered out; so turning back, I retraced my steps up the ladder and made my way to the gangway on the main passenger deck. Everywhere passengers were standing about open-mouthed, dazed and bewildered.

At the top of the gangway a large crowd of drunken sailors was milling about and swaying like trees in the wind. Many were dressed in dirty singlets and trousers, their hair dishevelled and their faces pumped up and bright red with alcohol. Others were gesticulating wildly and shouting, their eyes red and staring with pent up anger. A few were sitting like zombies on the deck with their backs against the bulkhead and their legs stretched out in front of them.

It was a frightening scene, but instead of getting out of the way and going to safety, a large crowd of passengers were standing round them, staring like ghouls or moths attracted to a light that was about to burn them.

"For God's sake, please don't stand there gawping?" I shouted at them. "For safety's sake, go back to your cabins!"

A few passengers moved away, but many stayed.

The rules about the way the crew were to use the gangway were clear. As they came on board they were expected to proceed forward quickly and quietly to their accommodation in the fo'c'sle, and under no circumstances to hang around and annoy the passengers.

My instinct was to try to control them, but I was just one man against twenty – an officer, a symbol of the authority that had sent Ginger to prison. Should I follow my instinct and try to get the better of the situation, or should I slink away to safety as quickly as possible, excusing myself to myself by saying that I was going back to my cabin to phone the police?

Rather foolishly I stepped into the melee and shouted, "OK, lads, you can't stay here! You know the rules! You have to go forward!"

At my words, the melee stirred like a swarm of angry bees, but fortunately no one made a move to attack me. One or two voices were raised against me, and just as matters appeared about to be getting out of hand a member of my watch appeared at the bottom of the gangway.

O'Leary was a big Irish sailor with a broad chest. Now drunk, he lurched up the gangway, holding onto its side rails with both hands to steady himself. At the top he staggered, and on seeing me, shouted in a broad Irish brogue, "Well, if it isn't me ole' frien', the t'ird mate!"

Without realising it, O'Leary, or Paddy as I called him, had saved the situation. Throwing himself against my chest and putting his arms round my neck, he collapsed in a drunken heap against me. Immediately the atmosphere changed and the menace went out of the situation. Taking advantage of the opportunity Paddy had presented to me, I shouted, "OK, Paddy, OK lads, let's go forwards!"

With Paddy draped round my neck, like the Pied Piper, I led the melee forward, first along the passenger deck, then down the ladder onto the foredeck, and finally into their accommodation.

Once there, the men became quieter and three or four of those who were more sober came forward to speak to me. They asked if a dozen of them could wait at the top of the gangway in order to petition the captain on Ginger's behalf when the captain came back from a dinner he was attending ashore. I suggested one man, and in the end we compromised on three.

By now a squad-car with five Australian policemen had arrived at the ship and was parked at the bottom of the gangway, but the policemen refused to come on board, saying that they were too greatly outnumbered by the crew to be able to do anything useful.

Then I made a stupid, potentially fatal mistake. About an hour after I had led the crew forward, I went back along the foredeck to their accommodation to see if everything was quiet. It was a foolish thing to have done. Their mess-room was in almost complete darkness, and as I walked in a voice called out of the gloom, "It's an officer, let's get him!" Then fortunately, a moment later another voice said, "No, it's the third mate! He's all right! Leave him alone!"

Realising that it was not a place for an officer to be, I decided to get out as quickly as possible. But I did not want to lose my dignity by running, and so taking a tight grip on my torch and telling myself not to panic, I turned and feigning a calm I did not feel, hurried out slowly, wondering all the time whether something would be thrown at me, or whether perhaps someone would jump on my back.

An eternity seemed to elapse before I reached the raised safety of the passenger deck. Then, as I approached the gangway, I saw the captain coming on board. Captain Heyward was a man I admired – sober and one of the sanest captains in the company. Within three or four minutes he had grasped the situation and agreed to see the delegation from the crew and to do what he could for Ginger the following morning.

But the court was adamant; Ginger could appeal, but an appeal would take several weeks and in the meantime he had to stay in prison.

The crew were now even more incensed than they had been the day before, and in a show of solidarity with Ginger, refused to take the ship out of harbour when the time came to depart for Melbourne. Strictly speaking, their refusal to obey a lawful command of the captain meant that they were now mutineers. But Captain Heyward appreciated that it would be difficult to accuse the whole crew of mutiny, and was wise enough to allow them to vent their feelings so long as they did not harm the ship or the passengers. Eventually, after sitting around for almost two days, the crew tired of their protest and quietly agreed to take the ship out the following evening.

But even when we were at sea and were on our way round the southwest corner of Australia to the Great Australian Bight and Melbourne, the atmosphere on the ship remained one of menace and potential violence. The crew were sullen and withdrawn, and the passengers were frightened. Gwen and the other girls were reluctant to come to our cabins and required a great deal of reassurance.

The Master-at-Arms had not been badly hurt and after the attack had fled to the engine-room and had hidden for some hours amongst the ducting that conveyed the propeller shaft to the stern of the ship. Afterwards he was very careful in his dealings with the crew. The second officer was equally careful. For a week he confined himself to the bridge and the area immediately around the officers' accommodation and did not venture near the fo'c'sle. At night he locked the door of his cabin and for protection slept with a piece of wood under his pillow.

When we arrived in Melbourne, the headline in one local paper read *HELL SHIP ARRIVES*. In the accompanying article it stated that one of the officers had contemptuously referred to the passengers as 'peasants'. The captain said that there was only one officer on the ship who would have done that, and that was me! But as I had been praised by the police and the company manager in Fremantle for the way I had handled the crew, the captain merely laughed, and along with the rest of the officers, treated it as a joke.

In Melbourne the situation remained tense. Although more than a week had elapsed since the attack on Ginger, the crew were still resentful, and the atmosphere on the ship was still full of venom. Then an incident occurred that threatened to make matters worse. On their way back to the ship with a few bottles of beer and a couple of bottles of wine, several sailors were stopped at the customs post at the entrance to the dock and their alcohol was confiscated. They were furious, and because I was the duty officer, one of them came to my cabin to speak to me. To me it seemed that the crew might mutiny again, so after I had spoken to the man, I went up to the captain's cabin and explained to the captain what had happened. The captain agreed that the situation was ugly, and as all the other officers were ashore, he volunteered to stand in for me as duty officer while I went to the customs post to see if I could defuse the situation by retrieving the men's alcohol for them.

"And three-o," the captain said, as I left his cabin. "I want to see you when you get back. Come up and have a drink. I want to talk to you."

It was eight o'clock in the evening by the time I got to the customs post and the docks were quiet after the activity of the day. Like many people in Melbourne, the customs officers knew about the trouble on the ship, but at first fell back on protocol and refused to give me the alcohol. Then, after I appealed to them and explained what a difference to the feelings of the crew it would make, they relented and handed me the brown paper bags in which the drink was contained.

The crew were grateful. "OK, third mate," one of them said, "We know you, and appreciate what you've done."

"That's OK," I said. "But I want you to know that all the officers look upon you in the same way as they look upon each other. We're all members of the crew. To us you're the lads up for'ard, and when all's said and done, we're all simply sailors many thousands of miles from home."

Afterwards I went up to the captain's cabin.

"Come in, three-o!" the captain called out, as I knocked at his door. "Come and sit down and relax... What will it be...? Gin and tonic?"

I settled back in one of the deep armchairs in the captain's day room and while he bent over the drinks cabinet, I looked at the polished walnut panels with which the bulkheads were covered and the thick woollen carpet that covered the deck.

The captain handed me a drink, then threw himself into one of the armchairs and hoisted a leg over its side. At the best of times Captain Heyward was a gaunt-looking lanky man with a shock of grey hair. Now, after the worry of the previous few days, his face looked positively haunted.

"I don't mind telling you, three-o," he said, "I'm worried. I've never known such trouble on a ship... Cheers! Good health, and here's an end to it!"

I watched as he started to fidget with his glass and the crystal in it glittered in the light from the lamp on his desk. On the bulkhead behind him was a painting of an old-fashioned sailing ship, and another of an apple orchard, both firmly screwed to the bulkhead so they would not slide about as the ship pitched and rolled.

"You know," Captain Heyward said, running his fingers nervously through his hair. "I'm beginning to form a plan. I think one of the officers should talk to the whole crew and try to establish a common bond between us. You seem to get on well with the crew. What do you think?"

I agreed.

"Only trouble is," the captain said, "who is going to do it...? I can't... because if it fails, I will have lost my authority."

"And I can't," I said. "I'm far too young and too junior."

The second officer could not do it, as he was the source of the trouble. That left only the chief officer. The only problem with him was that although he was very competent, he was quiet and reserved and the captain thought that to inspire the crew required someone with a more forceful personality. Nonetheless, he decided that the chief officer should do the job.

The next morning the crew were mustered on the foredeck and the chief officer addressed them from a vantage point on the passenger deck. As a result, like snow melting in the sun, the poison that had enveloped the ship for so long melted away and within a few days the relationship between the officers and the crew was normal again.

*

The voyage home was uneventful for the most part. After Gwen left the ship I had reservations about the way I had behaved on the voyage out. Strange though it may sound, although I had enjoyed myself with Gwen, my conscience, which I could never escape, and still can never escape, left me feeling guilty and that I had let myself down. In my heart of hearts I knew that I had used Gwen in a cold calculated way, and that I had behaved in a way that was contrary to the way I had been brought-up. Probably because of that way, I knew that there is more to relationships than screwing around in the way I had done. Although I did not have a clear idea of it at the time, in a vague sort of way, deep down I felt that real men do not use women and copulate randomly, as I had done, but instead, arrange their lives so as to have a deep lasting relationship with just one woman who fulfils all the roles for them that a woman might fulfil, just as they fulfil all the rolls for her that a man might fulfil. Thus, although I could not put it into words at that time, I sensed that in such a relationship, a woman is her man's companion, lover, wife, best friend and strumpet, just as he is her best friend, lover, companion, protector, stand-up clown and husband.

As a result of these feelings I decided I would be friendly with all the passengers and would play deck tennis and fool around in the swimming pool before dinner each evening, and would study chemistry and physics in the afternoons, but would have nothing to do with any particular girl. One or two of the other officers, including the Snide, did not share my scruples – or perhaps inhibitions – and behaved in exactly the same way on the voyage home as they had on the voyage out.

However, I was not left in peace for long. At nine o'clock on a particularly dark evening as we made our way across the Indian Ocean from Colombo to Aden a woman appeared in the wing of the bridge after I had been on watch for about an hour, and said out of the darkness, "I know this is highly irregular, but the captain has sent me up to get a weather report. He wants to know what the weather is going to be like for this evening's dance."

I peered into the darkness and saw that the person addressing me was a slim middle-aged lady wearing a taffeta dress that rustled as she moved.

"Well! How nice! You're welcome," I said innocently, unaware that she was such a nuisance to the captain that he had sent her up to me in order to get rid of her. "It'll take me about five or ten minutes. Come and have a look at the bridge while I collect the data."

I set about reading the barometer, the wet and dry thermometers and the direction of the wind, and when I had finished, wrote the results on a piece of paper and handed them to the lady.

She did not appear to be in a hurry, and so we stood facing forward into the tropical night. and I kept a lookout and listened as she told me about her time as a wren during the war and the ships she said she had served on.

After about ten minutes she said, "Do you think it's going to rain tonight?"

"No. I'm sure it'll be all right for the dance," I replied.

She gave a little embarrassed neigh of a laugh. "You've been very sweet," she said. "But you know the real reason why I've come up here, don't you?"

"To get a weather report," I replied, like the innocent fool that I was...

"No, you silly boy!" she said, laughing again. "I've come to make love to you! The captain's knows I'm crazy about you and that this is one way of getting to meet you."

I was completely taken aback. And to think that I went to the bother of reading the barometer and the wet and dry thermometers, I thought!

Casting around for something to say and a way to get out of the predicament into which it seemed the captain had landed me, I stammered, "Would you like to steer the ship?"

As I led the woman into the wheelhouse I was horrified at the idea of making love to her. Who on earth does she think she is, I thought? I am just twenty-three. She's old enough to be my mother. Making love to her would be like committing incest or making love to an aunt...

I handed her over to the helmsman who seemed only too delighted to instruct her in the art of steering the ship. "Here, madam, let me show you," he said, standing behind her with his arms round her so he could still control the wheel.

She was in no hurry to return to the party. At ten o'clock she shared the tea and toast that the ever-faithful Lambert brought up to the bridge for me, and at midnight was still there when the Second Officer appeared, creased and grumpy from his bunk, to take over the 12-4 watch.

A startled look crossed his sleep-crumpled face, as he almost bumped into her on his way into the chartroom and saw her sitting on the chart-table with her bottom partially covering the chart.

"Good God! What on Earth is this! A woman on the bridge!" he snapped angrily.

There was now only one way to get rid of her, and that was to play the perfect gentleman and take her down to my cabin for a drink and then afterwards escort her to her cabin and say goodnight. So, as soon as I had handed over the watch, I led her down from the bridge and along the corridor to my cabin. Full of expectation, she sat on the sofa with a drink in her hand and waited for me to make a move. But I was having none of it. A couple of decks up, I had no doubt the captain was laughing his head off as he contemplated the situation in which he had landed me, and the idea, as he saw it, that I would do my duty. But I had other ideas. She might want me to make love to her, but *I* did not want to make love to *her*. For a while I made an effort at polite conversation, but it was not a success and the atmosphere between us became increasingly tense until in the end the words we said to one another went more or less unheard.

Finally, I said, "I've got to get up early in the morning, so if you don't mind, I'll escort you down to your cabin as soon as you've finished your drink."

The lights in the passageways glared as I walked behind her on the way back to her cabin. Outside the door, I bent forward and gave her a peck on the cheek and wished her goodnight, and then stepped back and watched as she opened the door and disappeared without so much as a backward turn of her head.

The next morning the captain and the chief engineer were waiting for me as I walked into the officers' dining room for breakfast. Knowing smiles were exchanged and the captain said, "How did you get on then last night then, three-o? Good night, eh? Did what England expected of you, did you?"

"Certainly!" I replied, grinning in an attempt to bluff my way out of giving a direct answer. "I had a great time. Never a dull moment!"

There was only one repercussion of that night. When Clarissa, as the woman was named, left the ship in Malta, the captain asked her whether she had enjoyed the voyage?

"It was all right," she replied sulkily, as they shook hands at the top of the gangway. "The only trouble was the men. They were no damned good! No damned good, at all!"

*

But I have got ahead of myself. Before we got to Malta, something of world importance happened in Egypt. After an overnight passage through the Suez canal, we arrived in Port Said to learn that Colonel Nasser, leader of the Egyptian people, had nationalised the canal.

It was a brilliant move that completely out-foxed the British and French. Port Said was in uproar as we steamed into our berth. Crowds of Egyptians dressed in kaftans were milling around, celebrating in front of the Canal Company's Headquarters. The British and French flags had been hauled down, and the green flag of Egypt had been raised. But nobody harmed us, although the officials who came on board advised us not to go ashore.

Later the British and French retaliated by withdrawing their pilots in the belief that without them the Egyptians would not be able to operate the Canal. But the Egyptians were more than up to that.

Piloting a ship through the Canal was not as difficult as the British and French had led the world to believe, as the water on either side of a vessel acted as a cushion that held the ship in position almost as surely as if it was held by ropes. Realising this, the Egyptians recruited captains from their own Merchant Navy and from sympathetic non-aligned countries such as India and Yugoslavia, and trained them as pilots, and within a few weeks were getting ships through the canal as efficiently or more efficiently than the British and French had ever done.

*

From Port Said the ship sailed to Malta, where at midnight when my watch was over, I went for a ride in a horse-drawn carriage with a young passenger I had met while playing deck tennis a few days earlier. Elizabeth had a beautiful English speaking voice, and at that time I was fascinated by women with voices like hers.

My intention was that the ride should be an innocent occasion. While Valetta slept, the horse click-clopped its way through deserted streets that had been turned an ashen white by the glare of a full moon. Inside their houses, the burghers of the town slept peacefully in their beds, while inside the carriage, in a little world of our own, against all my intentions, I found myself in a clinch with Elizabeth. The temptation was too great and when we got back to the ship I forgot my plan to be friendly but nothing more with the passengers, and swept her up to my cabin and made love to her all night.

The next night, by which time we were abreast of Gibraltar, I expected her to be in my cabin when I came down from the bridge at midnight, but for some reason she was not there. The following night she turned up. The pattern repeated itself until we arrived in Southampton, where, as I was walking through the foyer in the passenger accommodation, I saw her talking animatedly to one of the assistant pursers and realised from the way they were laughing and leaning towards one another that they were probably more intimate than might at first appear.

When she had left the ship, I asked the assistant purser about her.

"I thought you knew," he said, surprised. "I knew she was sleeping with you. She liked us both, and when she wasn't with you she was with me."

Call me a hypocrite if you like, but I was disgusted in what I expect might be called a priggish way, as my mind filled with a picture of him lying on top of her, making love to her in his bunk. In my mind's eye, I could see the look on her face as she watched him and submitted to him. The little whore, I thought, the little bitch; she made love to him just a few hours after I had made love to her. When I made love to her it was O.K., but if someone else did just a few hours later, it was, well ... little short of or akin to prostitution.

*

At the end of the voyage the officers had a collection for the ever-faithful Lambert, and gave him £25, which was more than most people probably earned in two weeks in those days. When I presented it to him, he said, "Thank you very much, sir, and if you don't mind me saying so, sir, I thought you looked lovely with that young lady on the voyage out."

*

As soon as the ship was tied up in London I was told to proceed home on leave. My father was not very pleased when unintentionally I hinted to him about the girls I had known and the life I had led on the *Moreton Bay*. But his disapproval did not last long, and when Elizabeth phoned he left a message for me saying that she wanted to see me while I was in London. But I did not reply, as my pride had been hurt, mainly I suspect because I was, and indeed still am, narrow minded in certain respects and, in any case, I did not like being two-timed.

10

Beginning of the End

It is two o'clock in the morning and the world is in darkness. I am just twenty-four years old, and am now second officer and am on the 12-4 watch, pacing up and down on my own in the wing of the bridge as the ship races across the Indian Ocean. For some inexplicable reason I feel incredibly excited. Above me the stars hang like great white orbs from the celestial sphere, so close that I feel that if I reach up I can grasp one. Perhaps it is because I am young that I feel such an intense, almost physical sense of elation and that something tremendously exciting is about to happen, and that I might take-off and fly up into the sky. There are no girls or wine or beer here, nor any need for any of those things. There is just me and the sea, and the ship racing through the night, and a feeling that the boundaries between the person I am, and the world around me, have been broken down and have disappeared, and that invisible tentacles are flowing out from me and are connecting me with the world in such a way that I feel part of it and part of eternity.

At that moment it seemed as if life might go on forever. Now that I am old, I know that it will not, and that life consists of just three short phases – childhood and youth, when it seems as if life is for forever, middle age when you know that it is not, and old age when you can see the end, and if you are wise, are getting ready for your demise.

As I write this in my room in London, I look out and see heavy white clouds lumbering slowly across a blue sky and wonder why I don't feel quite the same sense of joy as I did when I was young? Now when I look at myself in a mirror I hardly recognise myself. I am so old and grey that I look like a man in the negative of a photograph. Prompted by that realization I look at myself again and ask, am I really me? Can it be that the man who was so full of zest when he was young and an officer on the ships, the man who had such thick black hair and clear pink skin is now old, baggy and bald? Surely we are two different people. If I go on fading like this shortly there will be nothing left of me and I shall have disappeared and will be remembered only by my family and a few friends. Then, in their turn, they will have gone, and I shall have completely disappeared, and it will be as if I had never lived.

And yet now, when I am old, bald and baggy, inside I feel almost as young as I did when I *was* young. And that is the conundrum of old age. Emotionally you feel you are the same or almost the same person you were when you were young, and yet, at the same time, you know you are not. Your body has decayed and all the knowledge and wisdom you have accumulated during your life is about to be extinguished. It is as if we are ghosts that flick across the stage of life and then are gone, or moths that flutter around a flame that is about to consume them.

But to return to the time when I was young and at sea – Oh, God, it was good to be alive then and watch the ship racing through the night!

*

Tempting, as it would have been to make another voyage on the *Moreton Bay*, I felt that enough was enough and that I should get on with my career. If I were to have any chance of getting my Master's Certificate before I was twenty-six and hopefully proceeding to medical school I would have to take my First Mate's Certificate immediately. So knuckling down, I proceeded to study hard for three weeks.

While I was studying I lived at home with my parents. Michael Rhodes and his brother David, who by then was a medical student at St George's Hospital Medical School, often came for Sunday lunch. Normally when the family was alone we ate in the kitchen and kept the dining room for Sundays and when we had guests, such as Michael and David. When they were with us my father presided over the occasion like an old lion surrounded by his cubs. He was naturally empathetic towards the young and looked upon us with a kindly eye as, seated round the dining table, we became hot under the collar and aired our views about matters such as politics and religion.

Instinctively he knew that we were the future and understood the ferment going on within us and that we wanted to change society and the world, just as he had when he was young.

His early life had not been easy. Six feet two inches tall, he was the epitome of the 1930s idea of a tall, dark, handsome man; so handsome in fact that my mother, who was plump and mumsy, to say the least, often wondered aloud to us why such a handsome man had chosen her? But we knew why, and so did he, as she was soft and warm and was a natural home for the doubts and anxieties that racked him and, despite his good looks, prevented him from realising his potential. As a boy he had been brought-up by a father who believed that beating a boy with horse-reins was the best way of moulding him. At the age of fourteen his father, who was an old fashioned Victorian who believed in *WORK* – in capital letters – had taken him away from school and forced him to work as a labourer on the small dairy farm that he owned. My father hated it, as he had a good brain and was academic and wanted to be a historian. As a result, he was frustrated and felt that he had been a failure. But who is to say what is failure and what is success – a man who has had a phenomenally successful career at a cost to his family, or a man who presides over a happy family and raises four boys, three of whom go on to have successful careers?

My mother was the background against which our lives and our Sunday lunches occurred. Although she was warm and mumsy without any side, she was also strong and intensely loyal, and as a consequence people liked her. We lived in a large flat over the drapers-and-haberdashery business that she ran. Because she was so friendly, without necessarily intending to buy anything, many customers popped in for a chat, and some for a cup of tea. She was not highly educated but had a fund of common sense, and when our Sunday conversations became too cerebral she would chip-in with comments that would bring us all down to earth. She also produced delicious meals of roast lamb with mint sauce, or roast beef with horseradish and Yorkshire pudding. Her specialities were rice that had first been boiled, and then baked in the roasting pan alongside the meat, and served as a vegetable; and baked jam roll served with custard, the thought of which makes me drool to this day.

Apart from my parents, I also had three brothers – Richard, born before the Second World War, like me; and David and Martin, born ten and twelve years later respectively. From the time I was a small boy, the money my mother earned in the shop helped to pay for our schooling and the luxuries we enjoyed. Because she was so busy, she had help with the housework but was such a workaholic that when Mrs Pink, the lady who helped her, had finished cleaning the flat, she would re-polish some of the things that Mrs Pink had already cleaned. She had an obsession with cleaning the windows. Risking life and limb, every other morning she would clamber onto the window seals, and leaning out of the window, would reach as far as she could with her arm and polish them while holding on to the window frame with her other arm. Commenting on this one day, a man who lived in a house opposite the shop, said to his wife, "There is only one bloody thing that makes me madder than you scrubbing our doorstep every day, and that's that bloody woman over there polishing her windows every other morning!"

*

As soon as I had obtained my First Mate's Certificate I was promoted to second officer of my old ship, the *Delphic*, the ship on which I had served as a cadet. The last time I had seen her I had been at sea for less than two years. Now, within the short space of five years, I was one of her more senior crew, responsible to the captain for the management of the gyrocompass, the navigation of the ship, and for compiling accurate plans of where cargo had been stowed.

On the day that I joined her the ship was lying in the Royal Albert Dock on the east side of London. Today the Royal Albert Dock is a long rectangle of calm water, as flat as a garden pond, lined on the south side by City Airport and on the north side by rows of new apartment blocks and the University of East London's Docklands Campus. By contrast, at the time of which I am writing, it was one of the busiest docks in the world and hummed to the sounds of men wheeling barrows loaded with carcasses of meat or other goods, men shouting directions to one another, lorries moving to and fro, and cranes on long legs, looking like tall birds, dipping and raising their beaks as they lifted or lowered cargo from all over the world into or out of more than thirty ships.

And now, sixty years later, what has happened to all that activity? Gone. Gone. Gone. Like so much else and so many people that I knew.

*

As I walked round the officers' accommodation I was visited by ghosts of the past. Neither Jeremy nor Percy, the cadets with whom I had sailed on the *Delphic* previously, were still with the company, and the cabin I had occupied for over a year as a cadet was now occupied by a young New Zealand cadet named Jimmy Miles. Mr McCann, the chief officer who had hounded me and stood over me as I chipped decks or sewed canvas when I was a cadet was now captain of another Shaw Savill ship, and his place had been taken by a mild mannered young man named Pat Carden, who was only three or four years older than I was.

From the officers' accommodation I wandered out onto the deck and looked at the places I had painted when I was a cadet. They seemed to have lasted well enough. There was no rust on the ventilator that led down into No. 2 hold, and the winches behind the bridge, adjacent to No. 3 hold were pretty good too. From there I wandered aft and looked at the deck, where dressed only in a pair of shorts and plimsolls, I had sat chipping away at rust for days on end only a few brief years before. How strange, I thought, how times have changed... Now I have two-and-a-half gold stripes on my arm...

The only person who was not new to the *Delphic* was the captain, Captain Charles or Champagne Charlie. I was sorting through charts in the chartroom when he came out to see me. Despite five more years of heavy drinking he still looked as innocent and chubby as *Doc* in *Snow White*, and certainly did not look like the man who had made me work seventeen hours a day just a few years previously.

He shook my hand with just the right amount of disdain, as if to say *he* was the captain and I was one of *his* officers, and pointed with his forefinger to the track on the chart he wished the ship to take on its way across the Atlantic Ocean to Curacao in the West Indies and then on to the Panama Canal.

While we were talking I asked him if he would allow me to bring a motorbike with me if I bought one, and to my surprise, he agreed.

It was a decision not without risk for him, as if I was injured in a road accident while in Australia or New Zealand it might have proved difficult to find a replacement for me. Having obtained his permission I bought a Lambretta, and so far as I know, was the only officer in the company to take any form of transport with him.

*

The Second Mate

I was determined that the cadets should be well treated and I became friendly with Jimmy, the cadet from New Zealand. Jimmy was a rough-cut diamond who had left school early. He had a good sense of humour, and so I 'adopted' him and called him *Kiwi* and treated him as a minion of mine. "Hey, Kiwi, come here! I want you!" I would shout from my cabin, and he would come laughing to see what I wanted. Sixty years later we still keep in touch. In the interval between then and now he had a successful career and was Master of several ships.

Before we left London he found a bolt of canvas laying on No. 1 hatch and for £5 sewed a canvas cover for my bike, which I then stored in an open hold at the rear of the ship. The chief officer was upset when the lamptrimmer told him that a bolt of canvas that he had left on No. 1 hatch was missing, and having seen the brand new cover on my bike, he asked me if I had taken it, but thinking that Jimmy and I might get into trouble if I told the truth, I told Pat that the cover had been made specially for me ashore before we left London.

*

As second officer I was on the 12-4 or *Graveyard* watch, and soon became used to getting no more than three-and-a-half hours sleep at a time and even liked it, as during the afternoon and the small hours of the morning the ship was quiet, as the captain and most of the other officers were either having an afternoon nap or were sleeping in the middle of the night and within reason I could do more or less as I liked on the bridge.

But first I had to catch up with correcting the charts that my predecessor had neglected to correct. Each week the Admiralty published a directive known as *Notice to Mariners* that contained a list of alterations that had to be carefully entered in Indian ink onto the dozens of charts that the ship carried. It was tedious work, and for the previous six months my predecessor had omitted to do it.

By Christmas Day I had had enough of correcting charts. By then we were in the middle of the Pacific Ocean, eight thousand miles from home and a thousand miles from the nearest land, and almost every man on the ship, from the captain down to the cabin boy, including me, was more-or-less drunk. In a way I suppose it was an irresponsible way to have behaved, but when you have been away from home on a watery desert for more than three weeks in stinking hot weather, with no distractions other than reading, it is understandable that a man should celebrate a festivity such as Christmas by getting drunk. Even allowing for the fact that we were in the tropics the weather was unseasonably hot and sticky, and our white uniforms hung on us like dank rags. At dawn each day for a week the sun god had leapt from his fiery tomb, and as if climbing a ladder, had risen at a merciless rate in the sky until he stood right overhead and was shining his rays directly upon us.

After a small Christmas breakfast, I started drinking at eleven o'clock, and by the time I went on watch at noon my head was spinning and all I wanted to do was to lie down, but I knew that I could not, and so I wandered about the bridge like a drunken butterfly, touching this and inspecting that and looking at the distorted image of my face in the brass cover of the compass binnacle. Eventually the seaman who was on the bridge with me attracted my attention. He was wandering up and down in a zigzag line in the wing of the bridge, singing to himself in a drunken stupor.

"Hansford!" I shouted, swaying as I walked towards him. "For Christ's sake, man, shut up, and either walk up and down in a fucking straight line, or else fucking well stand still in the corner."

Hansford stopped walking, and swaying slightly, gave me a drunken grin. "What do you mean, Second Mate?" he asked. "I *am* walking up and down in a fucking straight line!"

He put his heels together, and like a tree that has almost been felled and is about to fall down, he fell over backwards and landed sitting on the deck with both his arms extended behind him. For a moment he looked stupidly ahead as if he might cry, then looking up at me, he said in a slurred drunken voice, "Happy fucking Christmas, Second Mate!"

Half-an-hour later I was sitting in the dining room during my lunch break, pulling crackers with the other officers, and despite the temperature and the fact that I had to go back to the bridge in half-an-hour, was eating hot turkey and Christmas pudding washed down with copious volumes of wine.

"Gadsby!" I said, leering across the table at our table steward, at the same time as taking some cheese and pouring myself a glass of port. "You horrible worm of a fellow! Come and pull this cracker with me!"

The abuse implied by what I had said was carefully calculated in such a way that Gadsby would not take offence. As a Scouser, i.e. a Liverpudlian, he had a great sense of humour and simply laughed, and his pumpkin-like face became rounder than usual. If it seems strange that I talked to him as I did, it is because by one of those peculiar quirks to which human relationships are prone, he knew that the insults the third officer, Phil Griffin and I hurled at him were all part of a game and that really we liked him.

But it was not the same when the engineers, who sat at another table in the dining room, tried to do the same a few days after Christmas. On New Year's Eve, Gadsby knocked at the door of my cabin.

"Mr Model," he said when I called him in. "When you and Mr Griffin call me an oaf or give me some other insult I know it's a joke and that there's something special between us, and that's perfectly alright. But now the engineers have started doing it, and I don't like it at all, Sir. Not one little bit! They're a load of grease monkeys as far as I am concerned, and I'll nought put up with it!"

He left me with no alternative, and at his request I asked the engineers to desist from teasing him.

*

A few days later we arrived in Suva, the capital of Fiji, and the following day I put my motorbike ashore and set off with the ship's doctor sitting behind me. My intention was to circumnavigate the island, a distance of about three hundred miles, but after the first mile or so the road became little more than a bridle path and we could not go at more than 20 mph, and I realised that we would be unable to do more than a few dozen miles that day.

Soon the road became very narrow and rough, and for a short distance tall grasses and tropical trees pressed in on either side.

After a while the road widened and the vegetation fell away, and a land of green and pleasant fields and coconut palms opened up before us. Poking up behind the fields were rows of low undulating green hills, their summits outlined against the sky by the silhouettes of trees that looked like hairs sticking up from a hairy man's arm.

A few minutes later we were on our way up through the hills and on reaching the crest looked down to our left over a forest of trees, the top of which looked much like a green carpet of seaweed on the bottom of the sea. Beyond the forest, about three or four miles away, the grey and red tin roofs of the buildings of Suva poked up through the trees, so small and far away that they might have been part of a town built for ants.

Beyond the town, in the far distance an indistinct milky blue blur marked the point where the blue of the sea blended with the blue of the sky. The Pacific Ocean, I thought, the Ocean of Peace...

"Look!" the doctor called out, pointing to an area of sea between the town and the horizon. "Just beyond the town you can see the surf breaking over the reef."

I looked carefully and saw a white line like a thin pyjama cord stretching round the island, where the surf was crashing onto the reef exactly as the doctor described. Inside the reef, the waters of the lagoon were a pale chalky blue. Outside, the ocean was a deeper colour. Immediately opposite the town, looking no more than about an inch wide, a gap in the reef indicated the channel through which the *Delphic* had passed as it entered port. As I looked I could see a cloud of mist and spray hanging over the reef, and in my imagination thought I could hear the roar of the sea as it crashed onto it.

A mile or so further on we came to the first of several human settlements we were to encounter that day. Straddling the road for a couple of hundred yards, were several large shaggy-looking huts or houses built of palm leaves. A native dressed in khaki shirt and shorts stood in front of one of the houses that had been built on a piece of land dotted with palm trees. To our surprise, when we asked him the way he replied in perfect English and told us that he was the local schoolmaster.

"Let me give you a drink and show you the house I am building," he said in a deep guttural voice. "I am getting married, and like many bridegrooms here, I am building the house that my wife and I will live in."

Like nearly all the natives he was tall and very black and had a splendid physique and frizzy black hair that in his case had been cut short.

He led us into his house and gave us each a half coconut-shell full of water that he took from an earthenware pitcher.

"It's good water and safe to drink," he said, the whites of his eyes flashing in his coal black face.

The hut was rectangular and surprisingly large, perhaps thirty feet long, and every part of it was made either of bamboo or palm leaves. Outside it looked shaggy, but inside the walls were made of fine smooth basketwork. Proudly our host explained that he had achieved this by folding and weaving the leaves in such a way that the green part of the leaf formed the shaggy outside of the building, while the stalks and stems were folded and woven to form the smooth inside. Instead of windows, there were large rectangular openings in the walls. The floor was raised on stilts about a foot above the ground, and was covered with mats made from the stalks of palm leaves. The partitions that divided the house into rooms were made in a similar fashion.

After we left the schoolmaster we spent the rest of the day motoring from one settlement to another without meeting anyone who spoke English. At about half-past-four in the afternoon, as we were making our way back to Suva after getting no further than about thirty miles from the town, we came to a group of huts we had passed in the morning, and heard the distant sound of singing. Intrigued, we dismounted and walked across a patch of open grassland towards the sound and eventually came to a compound covered by a flat roof made of woven palm leaves under which about a hundred natives were sitting, singing and swaying to the sound of music provided by a battered old flute and a drum made from a hollowed-out tree trunk.

At our appearance the music and singing stopped and the whites of a hundred pairs of eyes swivelled round in our direction. While they continued to stare silently, an urgent conversation took place between a coal-black young Fijian man dressed in only a sarong, and a thin grey-haired old man who was sitting cross-legged in a corner of the compound, holding a black ebony stick, the top of which had been embossed with a silver crown that the British had given him to signify his position as chief.

Eventually the coal-black young Fijian stepped forward and spoke, and we quickly gleaned that he was the only person in the place who spoke English.

"Boss!" he said in a slow deep guttural voice, "We are celebrating the third day of the New Year and the chief says you are to join us!"

He signalled to us to sit on the ground in the centre of the gathering, and said, "Boss! You drink this!"

He laid two half-coconut shells on the ground in front of us, and another young man filled them with a white liquid that looked like watered-down milk.

"Kava!" the young man said. "You drink it, Boss! Very good! Very strong!"

I was aware of the whites of two hundred eyes staring at us as we lifted the coconuts to our mouths and took a sip. The liquid looked like semen and tasted foul, but I knew that now was not the time to argue about it or to be rude, and so, hoping that it would not upset me if I drank it without letting it touch my lips, I took another sip and then another.

The dancing resumed and under cover of the noise that followed, the doctor said, "Not the best brew I've ever tasted!"

The chief then said something and the dancing stopped and everyone sat down.

"Boss! Now you dance for us!" the young man said.

I told him we could not dance; but to no avail. The chief wanted us to dance, and so dance we had to. Getting up from the earth on which we were seated, we shuffled round one another to the beat of the drum and the general approval – or disapproval, I'm not sure which – of the assembled crowd.

After a minute or so of gyrating about and making fools of ourselves, we sat down again.

The chief spoke once more and immediately two thick-lipped fuzzy-wuzzy girls stood up and came forward from the back of the crowd.

"Boss!" the young man said, "These two girls yours for the night!"

I looked at the girls, who were each at least six feet tall, and I looked at their thick black lips and their dirty sarongs and the dozens of bangles round their arms and necks. Christ, I thought, we're really in trouble.

"They've all got endemic gonorrhoea," the doctor whispered.

"Don't worry, Doc. My mother wouldn't like this!" I replied very softly.

We were now in a very difficult situation. To decline the girls would be interpreted as an insult. On the other hand there was no way we could possibly accept them.

"I think we should tell them the ship's sailing in a couple of hours," I whispered to the doctor.

I explained to the young man that the ship was leaving, but either he did not understand or he pretended not to understand.

"No, Boss! It will be all right. We invite you. You stay here for the night!"

In the end we were obliged to stand up and make it clear that we were about to leave. But although we shook hands with both the chief and the young man and waved a polite farewell to the crowd, we were aware that their attitude towards us had changed. We had declined the greatest hospitality they could offer us and we could hear their disapproval from the tone of their whispers.

As we stepped out of the compound I had just one thought in my mind – to get back to the bike and the road to Suva. But to do so we had to go across the patch of open grassland we had crossed an hour before, and also had to start the engine and get away before a spear landed in our backs.

The sun was setting as we drove into Suva. Back on board the ship, the officers and the English stevedore in charge of unloading the cargo, were highly amused by our story.

"You know how they make kava out in the villages, don't you?" the stevedore said. "By chewing the root of the kava plant and spitting it into a bowl and pouring water over it and allowing the saliva in the mixture to ferment it. I don't want to worry you boys, but you've probably each drunk half-a-pint of natives' saliva."

As he spoke I could feel the foul taste of the stuff welling up in my mouth and felt nauseous, but it was too late to do anything about it. Almost two hours had elapsed since we had drunk the wretched stuff and it was now well into our systems.

Later I told the chief steward about our adventures.

"But what about the girls? Where are they, what did you do with them?" he asked after I had told him the story of the kava. "Only a couple of bloody fools would turn down an opportunity like that! Where can I get a bus out to the place?"

*

Two days later we sailed from Fiji to Sydney to discharge the remainder of our cargo before proceeding up to Brisbane to take on a load of beef. On the way to Sydney the lamptrimmer got into trouble over the carpenter's cough. The ship's carpenter smoked heavily and had a chronic smoker's cough, and like the crocodile in Peter Pan, who could always be located by the tick of the clock it had swallowed, the carpenter could always be located by listening for his cough. He coughed all day and he coughed all night. He coughed when he was eating, he coughed when he was on the toilet, he coughed when he was relaxing in his cabin, and one day he coughed over the lamptrimmer's food as the two of them were eating lunch in the petty officer's mess.

Normally, the lamptrimmer, Dick Brencher, was a mild mannered young man with a ready laugh, but after almost a month of the carpenter's cough, he had had enough. Suddenly his temper snapped and losing control of himself, he picked up a fork and banged it down for all he was worth through the back of the carpenter's hand, pinning it to the wooden table.

For his trouble the lamptrimmer was fined a week's pay for assaulting a fellow member of the crew, but the sympathies of everyone on the ship were with him, as we all knew that in the close proximity of a ship good manners and consideration for others are the key to good relationships and that it was not enough for the carpenter to claim he could not help himself over his cough.

*

Following our visit to Fiji my motorbike became the first thing to go ashore when we arrived in a port and the last thing to come on board before we sailed. In Brisbane, on one of my days off I motored south to the Gold Coast to visit an immigrant from Britain named Bill Hancock, the son of one of my mother's customers.

At the height of the Second World War Bill had run away from home at the age of twelve, and had joined the Merchant Navy in a bid to help the British war effort. On his first voyage he had been torpedoed twice, and as a consequence, because he was so young, he was famous by the time he arrived in the United States. After the war, by which time he was aged about twenty, he decided to move to Australia, and had ended up on the Gold Coast to the south of Brisbane. In those days Australia was, and probably still is, a place where you could get on and make a lot of money if you were lucky and had the right entrepreneurial temperament. Bill had both luck and the right temperament, and was soon a wealthy young man.

Today the Gold Coast is one of Australia's most highly developed vacation spots, full of hotels, nightclubs and restaurants, but when I went there in 1956 it consisted of just one or two hotels and cafés set in a series of sand dunes. Even the road into the place was half-covered in sand.

Bill had bought a café and several plots of land there, and for £300 offered to buy an adjacent plot for me. If I had followed his advice I would now be a multi-millionaire, but I did not, as I am not a gambler and was frightened I would lose my hard earned savings and would jeopardize my chances of being able to support myself at medical school.

*

While a cargo of beef was being loaded in Brisbane I decided that, in order to find out how it is prepared, as a meat-eater I should visit the abattoir alongside which we were lying.

The Meat Works as it was known, or *The Slaughter House*, as it should have been known, was a large flat-roofed white building close to the river and surrounded by fields in which some of the cattle about to be slaughtered were held.

Cattle were brought to the abattoir by a railway running up to the door of the building. Inside, the roar of machinery and the hissing of steam made it almost impossible to be heard. The cattle to be slaughtered straight away were herded through the door and up a long narrow sloping ramp until they were about ten feet above the ground. To encourage those that faltered or stumbled, small electric shocks were delivered from wires sticking out from either side of the ramp. Frightened and snorting, their eyes wild and red with fear, the animals were so closely packed together that, as they ascended the ramp, some were forced to put their heads up over the backs of those in front of them, while others had their heads forced down between the hind legs of the beast ahead of them.

At the top of the ramp, a large pasty-faced muscular Australian stood hidden on a small platform with a sledgehammer ready in his hands. As each animal advanced towards him he swung the sledgehammer at the front of its skull, and with a thwack that was audible above the noise of the machinery, hit it in the middle of its forehead with the spherical end of the hammer. The result was a deep red indentation just above the animal's eyes. Stunned, with a clatter of hooves, usually the animal stumbled and fell against the sides of the ramp, immediately in front of the animal coming up behind it. Occasionally, if the first blow was inaccurate, a second or even a third blow was delivered to the head.

As each animal fell, another man standing on a platform at the side of the ramp, stepped forward and secured its hind legs to a chain suspended from a conveyor belt that was moving slowly overhead. A trap door in the bottom of the ramp then opened, and as if it was being hanged for a crime it had not committed, the animal dropped through the door to be brought up with a jerk, upside down, suspended from the chain by its hind legs. Still only stunned, but usually not yet dead, it was then delivered to two men waiting in rubber overalls and aprons beneath the ramp. Hanging with its hind legs up towards the roof and its head down close to the floor, what once had been a cow was then dispatched. As it swung from the chain, the two men stepped forward with large knives and deftly cut the jugular veins on either side of its neck. Gallons of blood gushed out from the animal's neck in a dark red torrent that smelt hot and sour, and in a few seconds it was exsanguinated. Nothing was wasted. Once the animal's throat had been cut, the men who had wielded the knives took up hoses and brooms and, after hosing themselves down, swept the blood into gutters from which it was conveyed to be used for making fertiliser.

As the corpse of the animal passed further along the conveyor belt, other men stepped forward and made cuts in various parts of its body and began to skin it. Soon it had been reduced to little more than a fatty white carcass, swinging to and fro in time with the movement of the conveyor belt. Then its front legs were hacked from its body, leaving it looking like little more than a white sack.

I did not stay to see anymore. I had seen as much as I could take and got out of the place as fast as I could. I felt nauseated and wanted to vomit. The expressionless look on the face of the pasty-faced man with the hammer, and the torrent of blood, were more than I could take. As I came out into the bright sunlight, I could still taste the sick sour smell of blood on my tongue and could still hear the distressed snorts of the animals as they climbed the ramp. Looking at the grass and the trees surrounding the factory, I wondered what sort of men could work in such a place and what they said to their families when they arrived home at night after their day's work? "I watched the terror in the eyes of a couple of hundred cows I slaughtered today by cutting their throats?"

For six months I could not eat beef, although by one of those strange idiosyncrasies to which humans are prone, I was able to eat chicken and lamb.

*

Not all the blood from the slaughterhouse was used for products such as fertiliser. Some washed out into the river at the bow of the ship and streaked the muddy brown water red and attracted sharks that provided sport for the crew. Using a meat hook attached to a length of chain that in turn was attached to a wire that led to a winch, the bo'sun and several sailors amused themselves by trying to catch the sharks. I watched from the bridge as a shark thrashed around in the water, fighting and struggling before finally being hauled on board and left to die on the deck. The largest shark the crew caught was about ten feet long, but even the smallest ones had mouths lined with rows of sharp triangular teeth. The crew cut up the sharks and used them as bait to catch more of their fellows, and dried their bones in the sun to take home as souvenirs.

*

From Brisbane the ship sailed across the Tasman Sea to New Plymouth on the west coast of the North Island of New Zealand to pick up a cargo of cheese and apples for London.

In New Plymouth I phoned the nurses' home and asked if any nurses would like to come down to the ship for a party. Like all the young men on board, I had a great need. The hormones coursing through my arteries made me randy, and so in each port we visited, either the third or fourth officers or I would phone the local nurses' home. Sometimes the nurses obliged and came down to the ship; at other times, they did not.

When several thousand tons of cheese and apples had been loaded and we were almost ready to sail, a telegram was received telling us that a vessel owned by Port Line, a rival company of Shaw Savill, was racing from Auckland to pick up a large consignment of lamb that we had hoped to pick up in Lyttleton on the east coast of the South Island. The race was on, and when the last of the cargo had been loaded, the hatches were battened down as quickly as possible and we put out to sea. However, unfortunately the pressure to win the race proved too much for the captain, Champagne Charlie, and he retired to his cabin and proceeded to get drunk.

Apart from the captain, several other members of the crew were also drunk, as during the two weeks we had been in New Plymouth they had formed liaisons with local Maori women and did not want to leave them. Among them was a tall young seaman named Baker who, we learned later, was last seen swaying and shouting to his girlfriend when the ship was about a quarter of a mile from the shore.

The route to Lyttleton lay through the currents of the Cook Strait between the North and South Islands of New Zealand. At four o'clock in the morning I went off watch and was soon fast asleep in my bunk and knew nothing of the drama unfolding on the bridge. At five o'clock Baker was reported to be missing and the chief officer, who together with the fourth officer, had replaced me on the bridge, ordered a search of the ship. But Baker was not to be found and it was assumed he had jumped overboard and had tried to swim back to his girlfriend. Another possibility was that he had fallen overboard in a drunken stupor somewhere along our route through the Cook Strait and that there was a slim chance that he might be found if the ship turned round and retraced its course. However, that would have meant losing the race for the cargo in Lyttleton.

The chief officer went to ask the captain if we should abandon the race and turn back to search for Baker. But Champagne Charlie was lying in a drunken stupor on the sofa in his cabin and could not be roused. Uncertain what to do, the chief and fourth officers decided to continue on to Lyttleton – a decision with which I disagreed when I got up at just after eight o'clock, although like them I suspected that Baker had jumped overboard and had attempted to swim ashore while we were still close to New Plymouth.

When we arrived in Lyttleton we were told that the Port Line vessel had not yet left Auckland and that we need not have raced to get there. For weeks afterwards we wondered whether Baker had made it ashore, but he was never heard of again, either in England or New Zealand. Later, when we arrived back in London the captain was summoned to attend a coroner's inquest into Baker's death. During it we expected him to be asked why he had not ordered the ship to be turned round, but apparently the coroner did not appreciate the nuances of the situation and so did not ask the appropriate questions.

*

On the voyage home to England the ship's doctor was a middle-aged New Zealander named Colin Swallow. Colin was working his passage to Britain in order to study for the FRCS, the Fellowship of the Royal College of Surgeons. Essentially, he was a general practitioner who had become interested in surgery while carrying out emergency operations on wounded troops in the back of a lorry close to the frontline during the war against Rommel in North Africa. After the war his interest in surgery had grown, but he needed the FRCS before he could become a fully-fledged independent consultant surgeon.

Although he was almost twice my age, it was soon clear that our minds worked in much the same way and in no time we were great friends and he became my mentor. Because he did not represent the type of authority my father represented, I was able to talk to him about difficult subjects more easily than I could with my father. He was interested in my plans for going to medical school, but warned me about several possible negative consequences of doing so.

"This may not sound very romantic, and you may not like it," he said, smiling shyly as we sat in my cabin over a pre-dinner drink. "Marriage is a market. When you are eighteen or so, all the goods, that is all the girls, are available and on display for you to chose from, but if you go to medical school at the age of twenty-six you'll be well over thirty by the time you qualify and are ready to marry, and by the time you've finished your house-jobs you'll be almost thirty-five. By then all the best goods in the market will have been snapped-up."

Smiling still, he took a cigarette from the silver cigarette case he always carried and after tapping the end of the cigarette once or twice on the case, slipped it into his mouth and lit it.

"Mind you," he said, ignorant of the fact that within a few years' cigarettes would be the cause of his death, "there will be girls available when you are ready, but in the main they'll be divorcees and widows coming onto the market for the second time. Many of them will be nicer and more understanding as a result of their experience, but you'll have to be sure that is what you want."

On another occasion he gave me more advice of a similar sort. "There will probably be several girls with whom you think you *could* live, but the question isn't *who you can live with*? The question is, *who is the one you cannot live without*? There is usually only one lady in that category, and for me she is my wife Betty."

Such advice was more acceptable than that from another friend, who said it was as easy to fall in love with a rich girl as a poor one, and subsequently went on to do just that.

*

For want of something better to do on the long voyage home across the Pacific, along with several other officers, I decided to grow a beard in the knowledge that even though the captain did not like it, there was little he could do about it as growing a beard was an accepted tradition in both the Royal and the Merchant navies.

For a week or so our faces merely looked dirty, but gradually our beards began to take shape and provide a topic of conversation at the breakfast table, such as, "Do you sleep with it inside or outside the bed covers?" or "How many times a week do you wash your face?"

Inevitably Colin teased me about it. "You know why men grow beards, don't you?" he asked; then without waiting for a reply, added. "Because they've got something to hide. It's the same with most people who wear sunglasses indoors. Unless they have a real ophthalmological problem, they're hiding and think they cannot be seen!"

*

While we were taking on oil in Curacao, Champagne Charlie went on another of his benders. The following morning he was still drunk and the chief officer stood in for him on the bridge as we left Willemstad, the capital of the island. At eight o'clock, as I was shaving, I looked out of the front porthole of my cabin and was amazed to see the land on the 'wrong' side of the ship. Instead of being on the port or left hand side, as it should have been as we ran east along the south coast of the island, it was dead ahead or even slightly to starboard, that is, on our right hand side. Thinking that something must have gone wrong with the gyrocompass, I grabbed my shirt, and half shaven rushed up to the bridge.

The scene in the wheelhouse was one of utter calm. Nothing was out of place. Phil Griffin, the third officer, had just come on watch and was standing in the wheelhouse looking over to port where the captain, who had apparently regained consciousness, but was still drunk, was standing with Colin. At first I did not realise what was happening, so I walked out onto the wing of the bridge and was amazed to see Champagne Charlie leaning over the side of the ship with his left arm extended, giving a hand signal, as if he were turning left in a car.

"There, Doc!" he burbled in a drunken voice, leaning precariously out over the sea some sixty feet below. "See what I mean! Just like driving a car! You see, I'll take us pretty close to that lighthouse over there!"

Dumfounded, I looked at his crumpled white uniform and pink bloated face, and then I looked enquiringly at Phil as if to say, *what the hell's going on here?*

"Don't worry," Phil whispered from the side of his mouth. "I'm keeping an eye on the old bastard and watching what he does. We were heading much closer a minute ago. I think he'll take us clear."

I stayed on the bridge long enough to hear Champagne Charlie give an order to the helmsman that would take us about a quarter of a mile clear of the land, and when I was satisfied that the danger was over, I went down to my cabin and finished my shave.

*

Normally, as the officer in charge of navigation I would have asked the captain about the route he wished to take across the Caribbean and out into the Atlantic Ocean, but for the next two days Champagne Charlie was flat-out drunk on his sofa with two bottles of gin by his side. So I decided on the route I thought we should take.

At noon on the third day Charlie appeared in the chartroom, but was unable to support himself and plonked his chest down on the chart, and said in a hoarse voice, "Everything all right, then, two-o? Where are we?"

To look at, he was pitiful sight. His head was bright red and looked as if it had cooked in the sun. Gin seemed to ooze from the pores of his skin. His eyes were swollen and bloodshot and his shirt and shorts were dirty and stained; and from the look of the white stubble on his face it was clear that he had not shaved for several days.

God knows what he felt like; he looked like something one might find on the floor of a cowshed.

I showed him where we were on the chart, and with a grunt he went back to his cabin for the rest of that day. The following morning he appeared in starched clean whites, looking bright and shaven, and when the ship's position had been plotted at noon, he took over command of the ship as if nothing had happened and told me about the rest of the route he wished to take.

In retrospect, I think he became drunk in response to the stress he had felt about the possibility of the ship running aground as it approached Curacao; so I was not surprised when he went on another bender as we approached Ushant off the northwest coast of France. This time he was aggressive as well as drunk, and Phil Griffin was worried when I took over the watch from him at midnight. Visibility was down to about a mile and the radar was on, although except for a ship on the starboard quarter, nothing was to be seen on the screen.

"He's as drunk as a skunk and muttering to himself, and I think he might well do something silly like trying to take us in to find the land," Phil said, as he handed over the watch to me. "And in his present mood it would be difficult to stop him if he tried to do something silly like that."

"Don't worry, Phil," I said. "I won't let him do anything stupid."

I sipped the tea that one of the sailors had made for me, and walked out onto the wing of the bridge where, because the wind was blowing from behind at exactly the same speed as the ship was travelling, everything was quiet except for the throb of the engines. Fortunately that is how it remained for the rest of the night. Champagne Charlie paced up and down on his side of the bridge for a while; then retreated to his cabin for a drunken sleep.

*

In Hamburg, the radio officer and I went ashore for the afternoon. By then our beards were several inches long and we looked like a couple of pirates.

Our intention was to have a bit of fun and visit the red light district of the city, known as the Reeperbahn, where there was a famous street of whores known to sailors throughout the world as *The Street of a Thousand Arseholes.*

To enter the street we had to go through a tall steel barrier that had been erected across the road in order to keep cars out. Inside the barrier, on either side of the road was a row of cottages with latticed windows behind which girls sat, offering their wares. It was all very quiet and civilised. If you fancied a particular girl, you signalled to her and she opened a pane in the window and discussed the price and any other questions you might have. If after considering the matter you decided you did not like the offer, you were free to wander along the street to the next window and so on. We did not even get as far as discussing the price. When we approached the girl in the nearest window she exclaimed, "Nein, nein! Not vith viskers!"

Hurt, we went to the next window.

"Nein, nein! Not vith viskers!" the next girl said, repeating what we had already been told.

After five refusals we realised we must look pretty dreadful, and so turning to the radio officer, I said, "Sparks! If a tart won't have us, there's only one fucking thing to do, and that's to go back to the ship to shave the fucking things off!"

Back on the ship I hesitated, as I wanted to arrive home with my beard intact, so I could show it to my parents, but the reception we had received from the girls was still reverberating through my mind, and so taking a pair of scissors and looking at myself in the mirror, I hacked away and watched as my face reappeared and a pile of black hairs accumulated in the washbasin.

11

End of an Era

After four voyages on the *Delphic* I was transferred to the *Carnatic* for what I hoped would be my last voyage before taking my Master's Certificate in time to start the academic year at St Mary's Hospital Medical School.

The *Carnatic* was a cargo ship that was just over a year old when I joined her in the London docks, and my cabin was so large I could have held a dance in it.

m.v. Carnatic in Wellington Harbour, New Zealand. Note the lower red part of her hull, indicating that much of her cargo has been discharged. When fully laden the hull sunk deeper in the water and the red disappeared beneath the surface of the sea

From the day I met her captain I realised we were unlikely to be friends. Captain Osborne or Obesity Osborne, as he was sometimes called on account of his great weight and protruding belly, was a snob with a pucker Oxford accent that he used to intimidate people in order to get his way, as many middle class people in Britain did at that time, although in fairness to him, I have to say that when he retired from the sea he did good work as a voluntary lay pastoral assistant at his local church.

He had never met an officer who wanted to take a motorbike to sea, and when I asked him before we sailed if I might take mine, he become more pompous, and sticking out his belly further than usual and truculently protruding his lower lip, pronounced that I could not. Possibly because I had asked such a question, he took a dislike to me; while for my part, I found it difficult to accept his pomposity.

My first real brush with him came when we were off the Galapagos Islands on our way from Panama to New Zealand. He became cross because I did not call him when I sighted the islands, even though we were still some twenty-five miles from them.

However he was reasonable when we were in Auckland a few weeks later and I asked him if the fourth officer and I might fly to New Plymouth for a weekend with friends – in reality a girl I knew there. His belly shook and he looked down his nose and waffled pompously, but in the end he grudgingly agreed that we might go, even though strictly speaking officers were not supposed to fly when they were abroad, as it would have been difficult to replace them if they were injured or killed so far from home.

The girl in New Plymouth, whose name was Janice, worked in a travel agent's office and had been given a couple of complimentary airline tickets as a perk. I knew she had her eye on me as a potential husband, and rather disrespectfully when speaking of her, referred to her jokingly as having *Wedding Bell Tinnitus*, meaning that she had wedding bells ringing in her ears. Nonetheless, the offer of flying for the first time and having a weekend away was too good to turn down and so on Friday afternoon the fourth officer, Michael Grump and I reported to the airport.

Michael was as posh as the captain, but much more friendly. He was the type of English officer who wore a white handkerchief in the top pocket of his uniform jacket and always had half an inch of white cuff protruding beneath the bottom of his jacket sleeve. He could be annoying. At breakfast he had a habit of rattling his spoon against his teeth as he ate his cereal, and after a month of it on the voyage out I found myself waiting for it to happen each morning, after which I could willingly have killed him for a few minutes. However, he could be amusing, one of his favourite sayings about sex being, "It isn't the size of the weapon that counts, but the power of the shot that is important!"

New Zealand was still rather parochial in those days and the airport at Auckland closed at half-past-four in the afternoon. The plane we were due to fly in was an old Dakota of the type that had been used during the Second World War. The back of its fuselage rested on a small wheel on the ground and as a consequence it sloped up to the front at an angle of about thirty degrees, making it a climb to get to our seats.

"That was like climbing a mountain," Michael joked when we were seated and were trying to work out what to do with our seat belts. "I hope the pilot knows what he's got to do!"

"Do you think they'll issue us with parachutes?" I quipped, trying to hide the anxiety I felt.

A few minutes later the engines started with a roar that was like the roar of a horde of angry hornets and very different to the whine of a modern jet engine. Then we were bumping along the grass runway, and a few seconds later were in the air, and in no time at all were looking down on buildings that appeared to be no larger than houses on a Monopoly board. At five thousand feet or so the plane levelled off and I relaxed in the naive belief that if anything untoward happened we would be able to glide safely down to the ground. Later I decided that flying as a passenger in an aeroplane is basically boring and does not compare with standing on the moving deck of a ship.

For most of the weekend we necked on the beach with our respective girls. In the telegram Janice had sent inviting us, she had told me that she had *someone very nice* for Michael. In the event Audrey turned out to be an unmarried spinster not a day under forty, with a mouth that turned down at the corners like the mouth of a fish, and a voice that rasped so hard it could have cut through steel.

I was not much luckier. Janice was in serious mood, as she suspected I was about to leave the sea and she wanted me to understand that if I married her I would be her *first*.

"We'd make such a lovely couple," she said. "I'm sure I would make you happy."

For my part, I explained that while I appreciated the honour she was doing me, I was more interested in the possibilities of the present rather than events at some time in the unspecified future. She had something I wanted, but did not want to part with it; I had something she wanted, but was unwilling to give it, and so in the end neither of us got what we wanted.

*

On the voyage out to New Zealand I had become friendly with the third officer, a softly spoken slim ginger-haired Scot. After almost sixty years Colin Paterson and I are still firm friends. Of all the people I have known, Colin is the one whose thought processes seem most closely akin to my own. As a consequence, even if we have not seen one another for a year, we pick up the threads of our relationship as if the last time we met was only the previous week.

One day, while we were in Auckland, I went into his cabin and saw a beautiful girl sitting on the sofa opposite him.

"Where on earth did you find such a beautiful creature?" I teased him.

From the way she was dressed and was holding herself I could see that Helen was the sort of dignified girl I might have liked for myself. But for Colin she posed something of a dilemma, as he also had a girlfriend in Scotland, a Scottish lass named Sheila, who by all accounts was as lovely as Helen. Colin agonised over the dilemma the two girls posed for him, and a few nights later, while we were still in Auckland, he switched on the light in my cabin at about half-past-one in the morning and woke me from a deep sleep.

With a supreme effort I heaved myself up to consciousness, wondering what on earth had happened and why he had woken me at such an ungodly hour.

"Douglas," he said, towering over me and looking down at me as I lay in my bunk. "I'm sorry to wake you, but I'd appreciate a word with you if you don't mind. I would like to know if you think it's possible to be equally in love with two girls at the same time and to want to marry them both?"

With a great effort I sat up. My eyes did not seem to be functioning properly. The light hurt them and for some odd reason I felt a compulsion to keep them shut. Shit, I thought, as I tried to concentrate. What on earth is Colin talking about being equally in love with two girls at such a crazy hour of the night? Is he stupid, or something?

Through the clouds of returning consciousness I remembered my mother telling me that there is only *one* right girl and that it is usually obvious who she is after you have known her for a little while. I also remembered that Colin Swallow, the doctor from Palmerston North in New Zealand, had told me that the girl to marry is not one with whom you think you *can* live but *the unique one* without whom you *cannot* live.

I put this to Colin.

"Umm, I'm not sure..." he muttered doubtfully. "The trouble is I feel I can't live without either of them..."

Colin did not reach a decision that night, but a year or so later he did and married Sheila, the Scots girl, and having now known her myself for more than fifty years, I have no doubt that he made the right decision.

*

Love was also on the mind of another young man on the *Carnatic*. Tony Goodman was the second engineer, and had a reputation for chasing anything wearing a skirt. A few nights after Colin had woken me, he switched on the light in my cabin at 1.30 a.m. and said, "Hey, you bugger, get out of bed! I want a word with you!"

Once again I was in the middle of a deep sleep and my eyes hurt and my mind felt as if it was being wrenched from my skull as I struggled up to consciousness. Rolling over, I looked, or more correctly, *tried* to look at my wristwatch. Half-past-fucking-one! Jesus Christ, I thought, there must be an emergency. The ship must be on fire... or perhaps there's been an explosion...

With the taste of sleep still in my mouth, I managed to say, "Tony, what's the matter?... What the fuck's up?... Is the ship sinking or something?"

But Tony wasn't interested in what I was thinking.

"Get-up, you bugger! I want to talk to you," he insisted.

I swung my legs over the side of my bunk and stood swaying and blinking in my pyjamas. Then I stumbled to my chair and flopped down into it. Perhaps Tony had received a telegram from home telling him that his mother had died, or perhaps he had suddenly come into money...

"So? I said, rubbing my eyes and yawning, "What on earth's happened?"

"Something fantastic! That's what's happened! I've just been to a dance, and I've just met the girl I'm going to marry!"

"Arrrh, shit, come-off it, Tony! It's half-past-fucking-one in the morning! Couldn't that have waited till breakfast?" I replied.

"No! No!" Tony said, leaning towards me and placing his shiny forehead and his thick black brylcreemed hair so close to my face that it almost touched my eyes. "She's coming down to the ship for a drink at noon today, and I want you and that bugger Paterson next door to be in my cabin at ten-to-twelve in your best uniforms. And there's to be no swearing. She's a lady! You're to be on your best behaviour. No words like fucking or bastard or bugger-off!"

Just before noon Colin and I and the third engineer mustered in Tony's cabin, dressed in our best uniforms, and sat waiting and feeling rather stupid as we expected nothing would come of Tony's great love and we would all be left feeling embarrassed. But it was too late to question him, as he had already scuttled off to the gate at the entrance to the dock and was waiting for his truelove to appear.

"I bet she won't turn up," the third engineer said.

"And if she does, she'll probably look like the back of a bus!" either Colin or I said. "You know how he is! Any port in a storm. I expect that as usual he was drunk and didn't know what he was doing."

We practised trying to behave ourselves. Then a few minutes later we heard footsteps coming along the corridor and saw Tony standing outside the door, proudly ushering in a young woman with long dark hair reaching halfway down her back.

As one we rose from our chairs and waited to be introduced. She was both beautiful and dignified, and we wondered how on earth Tony had got hold of her?

In keeping with Tony's instructions, we did not swear and we did not cuss, and the occasion went-off with the all the decorum that Tony had hoped for.

A few months later the young woman, whose name was Fay, travelled home on a Shaw Savill ship named the *Mataroa* on which Tony's father was the chief steward, and a few weeks later she and Tony were married and lived happily together in London until Tony passed away a couple of years ago.

*

The *Carnatic* arrived home in London in the middle of August, and as soon as she was moored I went to my cabin and waited to be told that I was to proceed ashore to study for my Master's Certificate. Officially the course for Master's was supposed to last three months, but if I was to start at St Mary's in five weeks time I knew that even if I started the course the following day I would have only three weeks in which to study before being obliged to take the exam. In preparation for it I had taken some textbooks with me on the *Carnatic,* and as well as studying chemistry and physics, had tried to teach myself the theory of the gyrocompass, Ship Master's business, and how to swing and correct a magnetic compass.

But the Company did not want me to go for my Master's Certificate. Instead, it had other plans for me.

"Captain Lockheart wants you to make another voyage before coming ashore to study for your Master's," Captain Hoare, a semi-retired alcoholic, who worked in the Company's London Dock Office, said as he sat on the sofa in my cabin and eyed the bottle of duty-free whisky I had saved to take home to my father.

As I had already waited five years to start my new career, I was determined not to spend another year at sea. It's now or never, I thought, I'm going for Master's no matter what they say. So working myself up to a pitch, I said to Captain Hoare, "I'm terribly sorry, but you'll have to tell Captain Lockheart that I've decided to go. I have earned my three months study leave and I'm going to take it."

On the following Monday morning I started the course for my Master's Certificate at the Sir John Cass School of Navigation in Aldgate. The Principal was doubtful about my chances of passing the exam after only three weeks' study, but was sympathetic and suggested that I should hop from class to class as suited my needs.

Three weeks later, at ten o'clock on a Monday morning I presented myself at the examination hall, and for a week sat with several dozen other candidates, answering papers on Navigation, Ship Master's Business, Ship Stability, the gyrocompass and radar. The last exam was Meteorology on Friday afternoon. I felt confident about it except for constructing what is known as a Synoptic Chart, that is a chart that shows concentric, approximately circular lines of barometric pressure, similar to those shown during Weather Forecasts on television. So, at lunchtime on the day of the exam, as we sat eating our sandwiches in a park close to the examination hall, I asked Jim Glyde, an old friend from the *Worcester*, who was also taking the exam, how a Synoptic Chart was constructed.

"Don't worry!" Jim said. "It's such a big task to construct a Synoptic Chart that it wouldn't be fair to ask it. They tried it once several years ago and haven't done so since."

"I know," I said. "But just supposing they do, I'd be up the creek without a paddle. If you don't mind, I think you'd better explain it to me."

For fifteen minutes I listened as Jim told me how the charts are constructed from numerous small packets of numbers sent over the radio by Morse code. If I remember correctly, the packets contain information about the day of the week, the latitude and the longitude at which the data applies, the barometric pressure and the wind direction at that position.

At two o'clock we filed into the examination hall for the final time. There was just one question on the examination paper – construct a Synoptic Chart over the North Atlantic Ocean from the data printed on the examination paper. Beneath the question were rows and rows of small packets of numbers arranged in columns. Thanking my lucky stars that I had talked to Jim, I set to work and two hours later handed in my answer, aware that but for Jim I would not have been able to write a thing.

A few days later I reported for the Oral exams. These were the most discriminating part of the examination process, and were incomparably more difficult than any of the numerous oral exams I subsequently sat at medical school. For one thing they lasted for well over an hour, compared with ten to fifteen minutes in medicine. For another, they were much more searching.

Unfortunately I was assigned to Captain Thompson, the most feared examiner in London, a bad tempered, ginger haired man, who on the day I met him was wearing an old baggy brown tweed suit.

Bemoaning my bad luck, I sat in front of him and waited for the onslaught to begin, but to my amazement he was unexpectedly conciliatory, and after putting me at my ease, led me over to a large table on which numerous small models of ships were laid out, each painted with a different set of navigation lights. Some bore the lights of ships under way, others the lights of fishing vessels or vessels towing another ship, or vessels in distress. Others showed the lights of vessels standing into danger or vessels at anchor, or laying buoys.

"You're in a ship heading north-north-west," Captain Thompson said. "And you see these lights three points out on your starboard bow. Tell me what type of ship it is, what possible courses it's steering, and what action, if any, you would take…"

He plonked one of the models on the table between himself and me.

"By the Articles stated in the Rules of the Road, the vessel is showing the lights of a large steamship underway and is heading in a direction between the following points…"

Seven or eight models later he led me through to the compass room where a ship's magnetic compass was standing in a binnacle, complete with Flinders' bars, hemispherical spheres and magnets in a little bucket. Pointing to the compass, he said, "You've got fifty minutes to correct this compass. See what you can do."

He walked away and left me to it. So far he had not been nearly as ferocious as I had expected. In fact, if the truth is known, I had been lucky and had enjoyed myself.

The results of the exams were published on the following Monday. Feeling empty and full of doubts rather than hope, I joined the queue of candidates waiting in a Dickensian office in Aldgate to find out whether or not I had passed? The results were given out by a clerk, who was standing behind a counter. As each man in turn stepped forward, the clerk asked him his name.

"Burroughs," the man at the front of the queue replied.

The clerk looked down at a list on the counter.

"I'm sorry, you failed... Next! Tell me your name?"

The unlucky Burroughs turned and slunk away.

"Robertson," the next man replied

Again the clerk looked at the list.

"I'm sorry, you failed... Next! Tell me your name?"

The unlucky Robertson turned and walked slowly away, his eyes fixed to the ground.

"Ainsworth, the next man replied."

"Congratulations, you've passed!"

The clerk turned to the row of wooden pigeon holes on the wall behind him, and reaching into the one marked 'A,' drew out the relevant certificate, which looked like an old fashioned blue or black covered passport, and handed it to the lucky recipient; then turning back to the list, the clerk said, "Next! What's your name?"

I watched as three of the six men in front of me were told they had failed, then forlornly realised it was my turn. The moment of truth has arrived, I thought, stepping nervously forward. Either I have completed my career at sea on the crest of a wave or I have failed ignominiously.

"What is your name?" the clerk asked.

"Model," I replied

The clerk looked down the list.

"Congratulations! You've passed!"

Relieved almost to the point of anti-climax, I took the certificate and made for the door.

After weeks of doing nothing except swotting for twelve hours a day I had forgotten what ordinary life was like and did not know what to do with myself. Outside in the street people were going about their business, cars and buses were passing by, office workers were going for lunch, but somehow I did not seem to be part of it. I was as cut off from them as surely as if I was standing behind an opaque glass window. For want of something to do I walked to the Sir John Cass School and left a message for the Principal, thanking him and his staff for their help. Then to pass the time before going home, I went to the canteen in the School and asked for a cup of coffee, and sat down at one of the tables to drink it. Except for two men at an adjacent table, I was the only person in the place and could not help but hear what they were saying.

"Did you hear about the bloke who passed Master's after only three weeks at the School?" one of them said.

"Well, what do you expect?" the other replied. "He's a Jew, and you know what Jews are like, don't you!"

As I listened I felt an icy dagger pierce my chest and experienced the same old pangs of anxiety and the same old feelings of rejection that I had experienced when I was at school and when I was a cadet... Will I never be free of it, I wondered; will I never be accepted as the ordinary person I am?

With mixed emotions I made my way to Aldgate Underground Station. On the one hand I was full of satisfaction at having obtained my Master's Certificate and having completed my career at sea in grand style; on the other hand, I felt rejected because of what I had heard and what I was, and the way my success had been interpreted by men who only a few weeks before might well have been my shipmates. Deep down I knew that over the years I had been damaged by the anti-Semitism to which I had been subjected, and that my mind was scarred as surely as if it had been cut with a knife. But even so, nothing could detract from the satisfaction I felt at having obtained my Master's Certificate.

*

So my days at sea came to an end. With the exception of the anti-Semitism I had experienced, I had had a great time. Few people are lucky enough to have a youth like mine. True, on the *Worcester* I had been subjected to Victorian discipline, but I had flourished and been happy there despite the Spartan conditions under which I had lived. Although it had not always been easy being an apprentice in Shaw Savill, I had learned how to deal with adversity, and in general terms I had been at sea during the years when life in the British Merchant Navy had been at its best. While I was at sea Britain still had the greatest Merchant Fleet in the world and the living had been good. I had been paid to travel the world at a time before countries had almost been reduced to a common culture by Globalization, when Australia was still Australia and Japan was still Japan. I had been housed, fed and looked after like a fighting cock. The Merchant Navy had been a magic carpet on which I had been conveyed to places that most people probably only dream of. I had completely circumnavigated the world six times and had sailed back and forth half way round it on many other occasions. I had travelled extensively in Australia and New Zealand, and had visited places as diverse as South Africa, Japan, Malaysia and Fiji. In the Mediterranean I had experienced the magic that the Romans and the Phoenicians had experienced before me, and also had had a glimpse of Egypt. All this was very different to other eras during which men had sailed the seas. Before the war, unemployment had been rife and the Merchant Service had been a hard, poorly paid profession. By contrast, a few years after I left the sea, the British Merchant Navy was all but decimated, to be replaced by fleets of ships sailing under Flags of Convenience that belonged to countries such as Liberia and Panama that paid low wages and had no tradition or real interest in the sea. At the same time, Britain, the nation that had been the world's greatest industrial and naval power was reduced to a nation in which service industries, such as tourism and catering, were the main sources of national product. If I had stayed at sea I might well eventually have been made redundant. As it was, I had enjoyed a life of Riley, but now it was over. In a week's time I was due to become a medical student at St Mary's Hospital Medical School in Paddington in London, and a new phase of my life was about to begin. I was about to be a man of very different prospects.

12

Postscript

I became a doctor and am pleased to say that medicine was kind to me. If you have the right temperament for it, medicine is exciting as it allows you to apply academic learning and science to the service of society and helping people in an individual way. It is concerned with human nature and the very processes of life, and what can be more interesting than that? It is demanding and stretches the mind. You are never on top of it. It is always advancing, and no matter how clever or learned you think you are, there are always new things to learn. As a consequence it is a never-ending source of stimulation and interest, and for all those reasons is one of the most interesting careers a man or a woman can pursue.

After almost forty years of attending to people as a medical student and a doctor, and ten years living in the close proximity of men at sea, I think I have finally gained a little wisdom. In no particular order of priority, among the things I have learned are that to be happy most people need a partner they love and who loves them. I am lucky in that respect, as my wife and I love one another and are each other's best friends. Other important things for a happy life include a need to be healthy, or at least healthy enough to do the things that you wish to do. Without health, enjoying life is difficult. We only have one health and it is important to preserve it if at all possible. Most of us also need to be happy at work and to have a sufficiency of money to lead a reasonably comfortable life. In addition, we also need a few good friends who we love and with whom we feel comfortable. My old friends Colin Paterson, the third mate from my days on the *Carnatic*, the naval historian Peter Padfield, and Michael Rhodes, the man who went to Oxford, along with a few others, fulfil that role for me. Finally, I have learned that I am just one of many millions of people and am no more special than anyone of them, and that therefore I should treat other people as I wish to be treated if I want to be treated well by them.

We carry the scars of our childhood with us, but the world changes and my scars are now almost healed, partly I suspect because in all the years I was a student and doctor I experienced only one half-hearted episode of anti-Semitism.

I am retired now, but I like young people and still teach medical students. Contact with the young is good for the elderly. The young are the future, and there is a great tradition in medicine of passing on the torch of learning to the next generation, and I am pleased to have been able to participate in it.

Before I retired, an elderly patient, a slightly breathless old man sitting propped-up on four pillows in a hospital bed, gave me four simple rules that he said helped him achieve a happy retirement. "Doctor, they may seem simple, but I can assure you they make a great difference. The first rule is get up by 8 a.m. every morning. The second is to shave and get dressed every day, or put-on your make-up and get dressed if you are a woman. The third is to go out every day, even if it is only for a few minutes, and the fourth is no booze before 6 p.m."

I manage the first three without any problems, but I have a weakness. I like a can of beer at lunchtime, as well as a glass of wine in the evening, and so I cannot lay claim to keep the fourth rule.

Despite numerous similar interactions with patients and the happiness I have derived from medicine and the fact that for years I have thought like a doctor, in many respects I still think of myself as a seaman. I am prouder of my Master's Certificate than I am of the various medical degrees I have accumulated, and if I had to choose between being identified as a doctor or a seaman, I would probably lean towards being a seaman. To my mind the term *Master of a Foreign Going Steamship* has a far more romantic ring to it than *Fellow of the Royal College of Physicians*. To me, the term still conjures up pictures of sailing ships, tropical islands and far away exotic lands that I should still like to visit. I suppose this is because the sea and its ways were ingrained into me when I was very young and impressionable. In my opinion, the experience I had at sea was probably a better educator for life than the experience I had at university.

Six years after leaving the sea I finally ran out of money during my last year as a medical student, and went back to sea for a few days in order to earn enough to see me through until the arrival of the next instalment of my grant. Fortunately I had kept my second mate's uniform. My old company Shaw Savill were unable to employ me for less than six months, so I phoned Blue Star, another large shipping company, and was sent a rail pass by special delivery and was told to report the following morning for a ten day voyage from Liverpool to Bremen in the north of Germany on one of their ships. It was one of the most powerful experiences of my life.

As I boarded the ship the last of the cargo destined for Liverpool was being unloaded and the crew were preparing the vessel for sea. Men were covering the hatches with thick watertight sheets of canvas. Down in the engine room the engineers were preparing the engines for Stand-by. As soon as I had dumped my bag in the second mate's cabin and had changed into my uniform I was thrust into the work of the ship, going up and down holds, checking that the cargo remaining on board had been secured with wooden supports to prevent it from moving during the coming voyage; getting out the charts and pencilling on them the courses we were to take; starting the gyro compass and making sure that it was working satisfactorily. It was as if I had never left the sea. Within minutes the world of medicine I had known for almost six years had ceased to exist and was completely obliterated from my mind. The only reality was that I was a seaman. Everything other than the ship and the sea were no longer real. The years I had spent as a medical student and the fact that I was married were erased from my mind, or at most, were memories of a past seen dimly through a clouded glass partition.

The feeling that the past was the present, the only reality I knew, was reinforced a few hours later as I stood on the bridge as the ship pounded through a rainy night on its way down the Irish Sea to the tip of Cornwall, and then up the English Channel and across the North Sea. I was a seaman and was experiencing the only life I knew. My home was the bridge of a ship with the lights dimmed and the bow pointing in a direction I knew that I had to go.

The voyage had its lighter moments. Because of my medical knowledge I was asked to run the ship's daily sickbay. The crew soon got to know that the second mate was a medical student, and as we were steaming up the English Channel one of the seamen, a small wizened man with a face lined by years of smoking, came to see me in the sickbay – a ordinary cabin that had been converted into a small surgery, complete with an examination couch and, screwed to the bulkhead, a locked cabinet in which proscribed drugs such as morphine were kept.

"I hear you're something of a doctor, second mate," the sailor said in a thick Liverpudlian accent. "What would you do about this, doc?"

With that he unbuttoned his trousers and laid his huge drongo across the palm of his hand. On the shank of it was a sore.

I was taken aback by the speed with which he had exposed himself. There was something almost comical about it and on the spur of the moment I reacted in a reflex manner that was highly inappropriate, just as I had done more than eight years previously when I had laughed inappropriately, and couldn't stop laughing at the Smiling Bastard during the rainstorm on the bridge of the *Ceramic*, as the ship made its way across the Pacific Ocean.

Without hesitating, in a deadpan voice, I snapped at the seaman, 'Chop it off, man!'

I suspected that I had gone too far and that he might hit me. But instead he merely gave a low growl and said, "I see you're something of a joker then, second mate."

At a more serious level, the way the sea still influences me almost sixty years after I ceased to be a seaman is reflected in the way that every time I venture out from my home in Westminster in the centre of London I look up instinctively at the sky and note the weather, the position of the sun, the height and type of the clouds, and the direction of the wind. At night I look upon the moon as my friend. If I see rain falling in the distance I instinctively know the way it is moving and whether it is coming my way simply by noting the direction in which the clouds are drifting.

Because I was a navigating officer I have an innate sense of direction and how to find my way about. A few years ago a friend and I motored across Paris at midday in just twenty-five minutes despite not having a map. Instead, knowing that the sun was in the south at that time of day, we simply kept it behind us and in no time at all were on the road heading north to the port of Calais and home. The man I was with was Colin Paterson, my old ginger haired friend, the third mate with whom I had sailed on the *Carnatic* all those years before.

I am proud to say we had both been seamen.

Printed in Poland
by Amazon Fulfillment
Poland Sp. z o.o., Wrocław